THE DEATH OF BRITAIN?

The Death of Britain?

The UK's Constitutional Crisis

John Redwood

First published in Great Britain 1999 by
MACMILLAN PRESS LTD
Houndmills, Basingstoke, Hampshire RG21 6XS and London
Companies and representatives throughout the world

A catalogue record for this book is available from the British Library.

ISBN 0–333–74438–1 hardcover
ISBN 0–333–74439–X paperback

First published in the United States of America 1999 by
ST. MARTIN'S PRESS, INC.,
Scholarly and Reference Division,
175 Fifth Avenue, New York, N.Y. 10010

ISBN 0–312–22193–2 (cloth)

Library of Congress Cataloging-in-Publication Data
Redwood, John.
The death of Britain? : the UK's constitutional crisis / John
Redwood.
p.   cm.
Includes bibliographical references and index.
ISBN 0–312–22193–2 (cloth)
1. Great Britain—Politics and government—1997–   2. Great
Britain—Economic policy—1997–   3. European Union—Great Britain.
I. Title.
JN231.R39   1999
320.941'09'049—dc21   99–12709
                                                                CIP

This book is printed on paper suitable for recycling and made from fully managed and
sustained forest sources.

10   9   8   7   6   5   4   3   2
08   07   06   05   04   03   02   01   00   99

Printed and bound in Great Britain by
Antony Rowe Ltd, Chippenham, Wiltshire

For Gail

Contents

Preface

The United Kingdom is in the grip of a constitutional revolution. The cumulative effect of the treaties of Rome, Maastricht and Amsterdam would pose problems enough to tried and tested British ways. These are now made more radical by the quickening pace of European integration on the continent. Treaty clauses which lay dormant or meant little suddenly become significant. The European Court of Justice is making more and more advances, taking vague words in a treaty and giving them specific revolutionary significance. The Court now overturns acts of Parliament, or warns Parliament away from certain types of legislation.

The Labour Government, elected in 1997, has adopted much of the European agenda as its own. Where previous Conservative governments were reluctant to accept that Europe was or should be much more than a set of trade and commercial relationships under the umbrella of a single market, Labour willingly advance the cause of more European government. They have adopted the Social Chapter, opening the way to much of our social and employment legislation being made in Brussels rather than settled in London. They have signed us up to the European Charter of Human Rights, limiting our legislature in judicial and criminal matters. This was a curious decision, constraining Parliament, the fount of our liberties, on the grounds that it might otherwise make unfair laws. They have said that in principle they would like to abolish the pound, and accept a common economic and monetary policy from Frankfurt, where it would be determined by unelected officials.

Much of Labour's constitutional radicalism represents a bowing to the European model. They seem to be saying that they do not think they can fight all this, that an integrated European state is inevitable, so they may as well pave the way to it by pretending that they want these things anyway. Labour's plans to split the kingdom into regions are often urged to ensure we have regional governments that can act as supplicants for European funding. It is part of the mighty Europe of the Regions agenda. Their plans for Regional Development Agencies are designed to fit in with patterns of Euro financing.

Even their plans for proportional representation are part of a scheme to bring us into line with the continent. Most continental countries use systems of PR or alternative voting. The British Government has decided to introduce these for elections to regional parliaments and to the European Parliament, and is considering a referendum on the same issue for Westminster.

Whilst it is true that Left-wing dislike of hereditary peers and the monarchy predate Britain's involvement with Europe, the Blairite enthusiasm for the abolition of the one and erosion of the other is in part related to the difficulty of fitting a monarch as constitutional head of the United Kingdom into the framework of a European state.

Labour's policy is said to be Third Way. As one commentator, Matthew d'Ancona, has so aptly said, Labour are less motivated by the Third Way, more by the quest for a second term. The idea of the Third Way was to find a style of politics which was neither Right nor Left. It was to be consensual. It rapidly degenerated into slavishly following the emotional shifts of public opinion as measured by polls and distorted through focus groups. It was allied to a hatred of Parliament, which remained stubbornly confrontational and argumentative.

The problem for Labour lay in their very electoral success. So many MPs were without a proper job in Parliament. Only a small fraction could be given ministerial jobs. Under the new regime MPs were required not to cross-examine the executive, lobby the government or try to hold the government to account. New Labour decided the best thing to do was to give them time off from Parliament on a regular basis, to script lines for them when they are in Parliament, and to tell them that their main task is to explain government wisdom and policy to the electors. The old task of explaining the electors' grievances to the administration was actively discouraged.

Ensuring Parliament met as infrequently as possible, arranging set-piece meetings on subjects like Northern Ireland more likely to produce cross-party agreement, and scaling back Prime Ministerial appearances at the despatch box from two a week to one a week were all part of the plan to try to prevent parliamentary argument disrupting Third Way consensus. A Parliament elected by a different means that did not produce a majority government would be the ultimate conclusion of this course of action. In the meantime we are given the Prime Minister as actor, appearing to act out the nation's grief or shock or love or enthusiasm whenever occasion warrants.

This book sets out the full scale of the European revolution, and the way that the Labour administration in Britain is furthering it. It shows how the treaties bringing together the member states set out a blueprint for a new country called the European Union. It examines different constitutional arrangements in federal states, and explains the difficulties that lie in the way of creating a successful federal state in Europe.

It shows how the monarchy is being undermined and the House of Lords changed into a compliant government quango. It chronicles the debates over reform of the Commons, and exposes the new style of management of the lower House, to try to tame its wilder freedoms. It examines how proportional representation would weaken British government and shift power from electors to politicians. It argues that devolution Labour-style will devolve more power not to people, but to politicians and administrators. Far from cementing the United Kingdom, it will pull it apart as advocates of a Europe of the Regions intend. The book explains the significance of the single currency to the united Europe plan and how British business fits into the global market place. The danger of the European corporatist agenda is that it will cut British business off from the liveliest and most competitive areas of the world. Britain needs strong transatlantic as well as European links.

Many on the Left are as dismayed by the search for the Third Way as are Conservatives. The phenomenal success of Mr Clinton for six years in the United States of America has now ended in predictable crisis and humiliation. On further examination people are seeing that Mr Clinton did not develop a distinctive Third Way agenda. He did little to interfere with the successful conduct of economic policy by the Federal Reserve Board during his period in office. Early attempts at Left-wing reforms of health were defeated and the President was left without a reform agenda.

In the United Kingdom, Left-wing MPs led by Tony Benn dislike the gradual destruction of UK democracy. They would like the Government to be more openly interventionist in the economy and to spend even more on health and welfare. Conservatives are unhappy with the same constitutional damage, and blame the Government for boosting welfare bills, putting up taxes too far, and damaging British business by its anti-business policies. The consensus in the middle has proved difficult to define and establish.

The book argues that all of this amounts to the biggest constitutional revolution these islands have seen. The Government seems to want us to sleep-walk into it. It is unprepared to make a powerful case for more European integration, yet all its policy roads lead to Brussels and Frankfurt. As it dithers between saying we must be positive about Europe and then being sceptical about particular policies, the relentless drive to a European state continues. It is time to ask the question, will this government break the United Kingdom apart? How far do they wish to go in transferring government from London to Brussels and regional centres?

PART I

A Country Being Torn Up By Its Roots

1 Can There Be a British Revolution?

The British people are not very keen on revolutions. Many agreed with Burke's conservative criticisms of the French Revolution. Even those who flocked to buy Thomas Paine's *The Rights of Man*, which was more sympathetic to the French cause, did not follow it up by seizing the Fleet prison or taking over the British government. It has made us as a people curiously unprepared for the European revolution now unfolding. Indeed it has made many reluctant to believe it is happening.

Yet on the evening of Thursday, 26 February 1998, beacons were lit the length and breadth of Great Britain. As the flames spread through the great piles of oak and pine, a living tradition caught fire. Beacons have been lit over the centuries in times of trouble and at times of national rejoicing. Royal Jubilees and glorious victories have been celebrated by burning stacks of timber. The hilltops have been set alight to warn of impending invasion, to tell of united resistance to a threat. In February 1998, it was as if the British people were releasing their anger at the many assaults upon their way of life. The countryside was to march to the town. The rural idyll felt disrupted by the urban law. It was not prompted by the presence of the federalist scheme, but it showed that people are worried about too many changes to their traditional way of life.

The British people are slow to awaken to provocation. Six hundred years separated two sets of poll tax riots. Most changes in Britain have been achieved peaceably through parliamentary argument and trenchant expressions of opinion in newspapers, pamphlets and broadsheets, and more recently on television and radio. In 1998, the countryside protest summed up the feelings of many that our decent, understated, self-deprecating way of doing things was being tested to destruction, pushed beyond its normal limits.

The Countryside March began as a protest in support of fox-hunting. The country gentleman through the ages has been caricatured for preferring the hunt to other more cultured pursuits. Many in country areas see hunting as a continuity in their lives, providing exercise for dog, horse and man together on the hunting field, providing employment for dog keeper, groom and stable lad. English painting is rich with hunting scenes, and the books of English poems and songs are full of light-hearted hunting ditties. Hunting brings together the different elements of rural society, the squire from the manor and the groom from the cottage.

The countryside movement soon became much bigger than a protest movement in favour of fox-hunting. Some people who joined in shared the view of urban legislators who felt that fox-hunting was cruel and becoming outdated. If asked they would have said they would prefer the country traditions to continue in pursuit of something other than a living fox. They went on the march because they sensed the symbolism and understood that more was at stake than the future of a national sport.

Many were upset by the growing encroachments of the suburbs into the shires. Many were rattled by the continuing pressure against the local butcher, the village post office, the village pharmacy and the other small business services in the countryside. Many had a more general, less clear foreboding that somehow England was in danger, that Britain was threatened, that our whole way of life was on the cusp.

In the past Britain has coped well with periods of explosive technical change. The agrarian and industrial revolutions of the eighteenth and nineteenth centuries brought mighty changes in the landscape and life styles of Britain. There was a mass movement then from country into town. There was an explosive growth of population in the new urban areas. Smallholdings were engrossed into larger farms, hedges around small fields were ripped up, whilst new boundaries and fences were placed around larger enclosures. There were sporadic acts of rebellion or riot against the enclosure movement and against the coming of the machine age which changed the relationship between employer and employee. In Britain alone, of the leading countries of Western Europe, the protests refused to become revolutionary. English evolution ruled: gradually the new world was assimilated by the old.

After the frenzy of the industrial and agricultural revolutions, much remained constant between the world of seventeenth-century Britain and the world of twentieth-century Britain. People still like to make their money and buy themselves a place in the country. The rural village still revolves around the pub and church, post office and village hall. Where once the blacksmith stood, the garage took over. The pub may well now stage great events on television to accompany the drinking and companionship, and the church may find competing for the attention of the village as difficult if not more difficult than ever. Old industrial buildings like the mill house and the smithy have been adapted to new residential use, and old farm barns have been converted to houses. People come and go into and out of village life but the rhythms of harvest time and the main church festivals still punctuate the daily round.

There has been considerable institutional continuity. People complain about their Members of Parliament as they always did and take an occasional interest in the noisy goings-on at Westminster. The Justices of the Peace keep their commission and provide swift justice in most local cases. Local councils may have replaced the Poor Law boards but the people involved in their government remain very similar.

An Englishman rejoices in his liberties. Scotsmen used to tolerate the union, with many coming to London to seek their fortune. The Celtic countries provided a little bitter-sweet anger and romance to leaven the more sedate, less easily aroused English breed. The British remain sceptical of those in authority, anticlerical in their distrust of expertise, suspicious of overwrought constitutions, unhappy with avaricious lawyers having too much power, confident that their islands will remain forever free.

As the twentieth century draws to a close, an even more rapid technical revolution is being hurled against Dover's cliffs. The coming of the electronic age gives unheard-of power to large corporations spanning the continents of the world and to national and international governments wishing to control and regulate daily life.

It is possible for the country idyll to adapt to the new world. In some ways the new technology will be kinder to it than the old. Large-scale factory organisation of the mid-twentieth century required new roads, new settlements, new industrial parks and new factories. The rhythms of rural life were more difficult to keep going against the demands of twenty-four-hour-a-day, seven-day-a-week factory working to maximise the use of the machinery. The new technology allows the return of homeworking. Many more telecottagers will spring up capable of undertaking much of their work from anywhere in the country. Instead of clocking on with the time-clock and the card at the factory door, they will log on through their computer and the worldwide web.

The remorseless rise of the superstore will be matched by the advent of shopping from home. It will soon be possible to type in your weekly grocery list through your computer and your home television. The local shop will take the order and deliver it in a cardboard box just as the old local convenience store or village shop did several decades ago. As the manufacturers of Asia become super-competitive in the wake of massive devaluations, so the emphasis of business and commercial life will move ever more towards design, marketing, flare, service: all things that can be supplied from the old bakery in the village as well as from a glass and steel office block in the City of London.

In other ways the new technologies seem a threat to traditional life styles. Culture, information and images are becoming global. A trend set in New York today can be transmitted at a press of a computer button instantaneously around the world. People can discover how the other half lives through their television and down their telephone line. As the market becomes truly global, so many are thrown back more and more onto the local and the particular. A nation which yearns for the latest French fashions or the best of Broadway's musicals is also one which yearns to return to the traditional feasts and festivals of our native land.

The present Labour Government of Britain feels that these problems can be tackled through and by the media itself. They think it is merely a problem of modernising and rebranding. They have launched the idea of Cool Britannia to replace the images, metaphors and ideals of what they think is a bygone age. There is a stream of republicanism in Labour thinking that feels the monarchy and the hereditary principle should now be confined to the history books. There is a strand of thinking which thinks that supranationalism must triumph over our sense of Britishness, that to Europeanise is more modern than to have a belief in country or a love of Britain. Such people see British nationalism as a threat but European nationalism as an opportunity. They wish to turn their backs on Savile Row as if they were themselves defending its dated rival Carnaby Street. In the name of the people, they wish to obliterate images, tunes, feelings which have stood us in good stead for many centuries.

Surveys at the time that Cool Britannia was launched showed that the British people, including the young, were more traditional than the Labour Government suspected. Tourists coming from abroad are still more interested in the continuity of British life than in its modernity. Whilst Docklands is a fine tribute to modern architectural design, most tourists would rather visit Westminster Abbey and the Tower of London than to continue their pilgrimage to Canary Wharf or Mudchute. There is an irony in Tony Blair anointing Canary Wharf as a mecca of his new world, when Labour were so hostile to the free enterprise which pioneered it a decade earlier.

There is nothing wrong with revering the past. It may be politically correct now to bemoan those who do as fuddy-duddy or old-fashioned, yet that sense of continuity in British life is our greatest strength. I remember taking a Russian visitor around the House of Commons shortly after democratic revolution in his own country. As I showed him the symbols of British history on the walls of the Palace of Westminster, he was visibly moved. He remarked that the strength of Britain lay in being at peace with its past. There on the same walls at the Palace of Westminster jostled the insiders and the outsiders, the governors and the opposition, men of the establishment and the rebels. Parliament can both celebrate the monarchy and place a statue to Oliver Cromwell who overturned it. Parliament commemorates the lying-in-state of some of our great monarchs and some of our statesmen who were impeached. We are at peace with our past. We understand the battles that were fought. Most of us would not be able to say which side we would have taken in the Civil War. Both royalists and parliamentarians have come to an understanding that a limited monarchy is a blessing which emerged from the conflict.

This country now faces one of its most difficult choices in its longstanding, important and sometimes troublesome relationship with the continent of Europe. The continental traditions have developed in many respects in very different ways. The continent has always favoured written law codes where Britain has favoured common law. The continent has preferred rigorous and more logical approaches often set in statutes of parchment or stone where Britain prefers things to evolve day by day, case by case, decision by decision. The continent has given more law-making powers to judges, the United Kingdom to a sovereign parliament. The continent has always held officialdom in greater respect and been more tolerant of its prowess than Britain. The British have usually been a more unruly, seafaring, adventurous, enterprising people. The continentals have been better drilled and have accepted rather more government.

The traditional role of the United Kingdom has been to keep the balance of power on the continent. Britain has always felt her interests lay in keeping an open trading system and in being allies with all those who supported free trade and freedom. The United Kingdom has been reluctant to intervene in continental squabbles but has done so if at any time one dominant power seemed likely to emerge on the continent. Slow to anger, the UK has in the end been prepared to resist the emerging dominant government. Sea power has been used to full effect. Military entanglements on the continent have usually followed. The United Kingdom slowly builds an alliance with the aggrieved, the oppressed, the small, the excluded, and from its base on the periphery advances on the centre.

A long period of Spanish and Catholic domination resulted in many battles and conflicts. England supported the sixteenth-century revolt of the Netherlands only to face Spanish invasion and the arrival of the Armada. The challenge from revolutionary France led by Napoleon took twenty years to halt. A well trained British army had to be created to fight its way from the Portuguese coast to Paris. In the twentieth century, the United Kingdom has had to stand alone and with others against German militarism.

Today the challenge is very different. Western Europe is blessed with a series of peace-loving democracies. The European project is not designed to advance at the point of a gun or on the prow of a tank. The European project unfolds through lawyers, through discussions behind closed doors between officials and politicians. It advances by the growing interconnections between businesses spanning European borders. Britain is there in some ways welcoming the changes.

The United Kingdom has been a keen advocate of more trade and friendship between the countries of Western Europe. Most of us have seen ourselves as Europeans keen to live in a prosperous and free continent. We do see more free trade, more exchange of ideas, more travel, more mutual understanding as beneficial in ensuring that the powers of Western Europe do not again take up the cudgels one against the other. German militarism is a thing of the past. France still has brilliance but is not in pursuit of glory of the traditional kind. There is no need for an Englishman to rest uneasy in his bed worrying about the build-up of armaments on the continent.

The fears today are different. Many worry that the continental system of government will come to London; that we will lose our birthright of freedom and democracy of the traditional kind. The fear is that the officialdom of Brussels will not know the limits of British tolerance and will go beyond the point of acceptability for their deeds. As the United Kingdom will have to adopt more continental ways, there could come a point where people are no longer prepared to obey the Brussels law or might take to the streets to protest when it doesn't suit. That tolerance, that understanding, that evolutionary approach, that pragmatism towards problems, that unwillingness to get involved in the didactic of too much political debate could be overturned by the growing incursions of European government.

In a way that is what the countryside protest of early 1998 was saying. Part of that protest was a dislike of the ban of beef on the bone. The ban had come about through the interaction of the London and the Brussels government over the unfolding beef crisis. In a way the protest was against the whole subsidised, controlled system of farming which had disrupted the countryside and then recently plunged farmers into financial difficulties. The protesters were complaining that there were too many laws and regulations beginning to change their way of life.

A few days before the Countryside March on London there was something similar in Paris. The issue at the heart of the Parisian protest was the wish of European law-makers to change the French approach to shooting. A shooting season defined over many decades was to be changed at the stroke of a legislative pen in Brussels. The French country interests felt that this was a step too far and came in their thousands to the streets of Paris.

There is nostalgia and fear in the air as there was on the eve of the First World War. Edward Thomas captured it well with his small rural voice at the turn of the twentieth century. In 'As the teams head-brass', he wrote how he 'watched the plough narrowing a yellow square of charlock'. 'I watched the clods crumble and topple over after the plough share and the stumbling team.' The poem describes the way in which the old rural order of the field and the horse-drawn plough was under threat and attack as men went to war and lost their lives, machinery took over on the farms and destroyed many lives on the Somme.

Today the threat to our way of life comes not from machine guns and artillery bombardments. It comes from a different kind of technology as surely as it did to the Edwardian settlement at the beginning of our century. As the new century dawns, it is to technology that we look for more advances in our living standards and changes in our way of life, but we also look ahead with some sense of foreboding. The twentieth century has seen a whirlwind of technical change. When the century opened, the horse was the main means of transport in the developed world. There were practically no motor cars and no aeroplanes. As the twentieth century draws to its close, man has ridden a rocket to the moon and regularly travels at speeds of 550mph through the air from continent to continent. Most families in the developed West regard a car as a necessity rather than a luxury.

When the twentieth century dawned, people kept accounts in ledgers, entering the figures by hand and adding them in their head or with a simple abacus. Most things were written and copied in longhand or sent to the printer for setting in moveable type. As the twenty-first century dawns, most accounts and sums are done on computers at lightning speed, whilst the advent of the word processor, desk-top publishing and home and business computing has transformed writing and communicating.

In 1900, if you wanted to get a message from one continent to another you wrote a letter and sent it by post. A physical letter travelled by coach and ship to its destination. In the year 2000, most messages will be carried instantaneously. Digital television and telephones using satellite cable and radio links are taking over from the nineteenth-century post.

The world has shrunk. People can see images of each other at opposite ends of the world simultaneously. News can be transmitted thousands of miles as quickly as the words can be written and said. Images sweep the world. The first stirrings of world public opinion can be seen in the response of those in the world in front of televisions to a common image of the suffering of war, of greed, of bloodshed, as it is transmitted from country to country.

It is the paradox of modern life that as the world comes closer together, as technology makes so many more things possible, people crave more and more particularity, familiarity and individualism. The twentieth century was the age of mass production and the mass factory. It was the twentieth century which marshalled armies of workers to perform repetitive tasks that can now be better carried out by machines. It was a century which expected of its peoples a wide-ranging discipline of factory work and factory behaviour in order to marshal production. The many aspired to the material privileges of the few from former ages. The twenty-first century offers something different. It offers the many the chance to be better educated, better informed, better amused and more individual. It gives to the individual home and desk the power to communicate, to sell, to market, to project right around the globe. Many find this new power terrifying. They understandably turn inward, seeking comfort in family, in street, in village, in small communities. They seek the comfort of the well known and the much loved as the thundering herd of change rushes past the window. Many want the excitement of the new but many also need the comfort of the familiar.

There is in every culture a battle raging between modernisers and traditionalists. There is in every generation, but in this generation it is most pronounced. The modernisers have at their finger tips such enormous power to release new energies and ideas. The speed of technical change is accelerating. What took years or decades in the early twentieth century to develop to the mass market can be achieved in months as the century draws to a close. The power of computing is transforming industry and services at a completely new pace.

The modernisers wish to reflect these massive technological changes in a whole series of institutional and social changes as well. They point to past periods of technological brilliance which have often been mirrored or balanced by reforms of the body politic. To them the coming of the industrial revolution in Britain in the early nineteenth century ushered in the enfranchisement of many more working men and the reform of Parliament. Twentieth-century technical revolutions bringing the motor car, electrical domestic appliances and the new suburbs were allied to granting a vote to all women and the eclipsing of the House of Lords by the House of Commons. To them the twenty-first century ushered in on a wave of internets and computer wizardry requires a similar constitutional change.

The traditionalists argue that the long march of democracy has resulted in one man, one woman, one vote, and in a series of effective traditions which it would be foolish to disrupt. To them further change at this juncture in our affairs would destabilise even more people. They reason that people are worried for their jobs, for their livelihoods, for their family security at a time of unprecedented alteration in the way things are done. The business community is adjusting to a rapidly developing worldwide market at the same time as it adjusts to successive waves of computer evolution. The social world is adjusting to the emancipation of women and the assumption of many responsibilities of family life by the State. Is this the right time, argue the traditionalists, to superimpose constitutional turmoil on everything else? The truth lies somewhere between the two cases. There is no necessity to throw the constitution up into the air because industry and society are undergoing metamorphosis in other directions. Nor is it reasonable to assume that all of the technical and social changes will leave the constitutional settlement untroubled. Some things are going to change whether the traditionalists like it or not. Others can and should stay the same however much the modernisers might like to give everything a new coat of paint or a new structure and appearance. The issue we should be debating is how we harness the inevitable changes to a direction that we find worth while. The industrial revolution which hit in the early nineteenth century did not merely affect Britain. Countries like Germany and Italy also underwent it but did not at the same time develop Westminster-style democracies based upon the universal franchise in the way Britain did. In the twentieth century we have seen the industrialisation of large parts of Asia without all of them adopting a Western liberal model for their constitutional evolution. There is no necessary link between a particular style of constitutional change and a particular pace and direction of technical and industrial development.

Of course, any system of government is going to be affected by the advent of so much more computer power. Governments are going to be able to keep much more extensive records and handle much more information than they could in the age of the quill pen and the written ledger. Politics is going to be affected. Politicians are discovering that where their forebears got their messages out by printing handbills or by holding public meetings which could be attended by large numbers of the electors, today they are more likely to communicate through television, through radio, on the internet and through other multimedia forms of communication. Politicians also have to respond to the advent of a global market. As people begin to see business problems on a worldwide scale, they naturally ask questions about the environment, or transport, or foreign policy, that are universal in their application. It would look old-fashioned for a politician in the age of global capitalism to say he has no interest in wider world environmental issues, merely in local matters back home.

All of those of us engaged in this large constitutional debate must ask ourselves what changes are inevitable through technology and social change and how do we wish to channel those changes in a direction we find convivial? To date the running has been made in the United Kingdom constitutional argument by modernisers who have adopted the Charter 88 agenda. They are suggesting that the new technology of the computer and the internet points naturally in the direction of more government. They are arguing that as the electorate becomes more sophisticated and has at its power more modern devices for passing and receiving information so it will expect more government and more communication from government. These modernisers propose an agenda of devolved assemblies as an additional layer of government. They propose freedom of information so that much more government material can be made available more quickly to those who might wish to read it. They propose codification, wishing more of the British constitution to be written down in a single document, making it less flexible but they think more robust.

This agenda is not particularly modern and it is certainly not inevitable. In a way it is a backward-looking agenda. The era of big government fitted rather well with the era of big factories and big industry. Governments treated people in an impersonal way, as a national insurance number or as someone to be regulated and channelled, just as factory organisation gave people a works number and expected them to behave according to a strict code of discipline. The wish to have everything cut and dried and carefully recorded in the constitution might slow it down, making it less easy to adjust to the rapid dynamism around it. Forcing through amendments to a written constitution is a much more difficult and time-consuming process than merely allowing constitutional practice to evolve through dozens of small, almost imperceptible changes over a period of months or years.

We should take the following basic propositions as given in this debate. Firstly, the technological revolution is going to accelerate not slow down. More and more things will be fed into computers, controlled by computers, displayed on computers and transmitted between computers. Government must understand the power of this technology and use it for benign purposes. Secondly, the electorate is going to become better educated, more flexible and better informed. Many more people will have university degrees or similar qualificiations in the twenty-first century than enjoyed them in the twentieth. Many more people will obtain work by showing flexibility and adaptability using their own mental agility to provide a service or improve a good. Such people will be expecting government to treat them in a more adult way than twentieth-century voters anticipated. Thirdly, the market place is going to be global. Every country that wishes to get ahead and to become more prosperous will have to be plugged into it. Success will depend on keeping the demands of government down and keeping them sensible. The countries that overlegislate, overregulate and overtax will find business leaving their shores. Fourthly, people will want something to cling onto in this tossing sea of ceaseless change. It may be a country sport they have loved in their youth, it may be the view over the green fields from their local village centre, it may be some tradition of their country, county or town. Whatever it may be, they will look for some elements in their life to remain stable, to provide some fixed point around which the rest can revolve.

Applying these principles to constitutional change clarifies the position no little. Changes to our constitution should be ones which give the individual more responsibility and more control over his and his family's future, rather than less. Changes should be in the direction of less big and expensive government rather than more. Changes should enable people to see more clearly the principal issues, to see who is making the decisions and whether those decisions are well made or not. The new power of technology should be unleashed to ensure that the individual can be well informed about the things that matter to him whilst unencumbered by the many things that do not. Above all, the family and the individual should receive greater choice and greater freedom as the fruit of participating in the remorseless change of the global market.

This means modifying, overturning, modernising the agenda of the so-called modernisers. Far from creating more layers of government we should, if anything, be reducing the number we already have. Far from broadening the scope which quangos, regional governments, national governments and European government have over our lives we should be looking for areas where we can reduce the scope or remove the hand of government altogether. In those areas where we do want government action we should make sure that it is global as well as national and local, that it is up to the magnitude of the task and that people consent. It is much easier to do this in an age of instant focus groups and opinion polls, in an age where it is possible to have an intelligent conversation between the governors and the governed and where information can be passed down quickly and intelligibly if government wishes to do so.

The big area of concern to many is the area of the environment. We have seen how part of the countryside movement was an expression of anger about the swallowing of green fields under further development. This is something we can all understand and where we think that between ourselves, our local communities and our local and national politicians, we should be able to do something about it. People are also concerned about the bigger global issues. Many people are worried that we are making the planet too dirty, that we are depleting its scarce finite resources of minerals too quickly, that we are in danger of distorting the atmospheric balance to the point where climate change becomes difficult to handle. The problem with all of these things is how does an individual government, let alone an individual or a small community, have any impact? Politicians in countries the size of Luxemburg or Belgium or Holland can fulminate and legislate all they like but no one can seriously believe that even with perfect environmental policies in those countries there is going to be any real difference to the world position. Even in a medium-sized country like the United Kingdom, following a perfectly virtuous environmental policy could be swamped by a couple of years' growth of the wrong kind in China.

In the area of the environment, as in others, politicians have to be realistic, set out the choices to people and show what can be achieved globally, nationally or locally. In the case of housebuilding it would be possible to devolve the power of decision to the local community. The local community would make its wishes clear and its local politicians would take the necessary action. At the other end of the spectrum is global warming: only worldwide decisions can have any impact on the scale of the problem. In between these two types of environmental issue are ones that can best be resolved at the national level. Clearly we are a long way off world government and so the global agreements have to be compiled by national authorities negotiating one with another to sign solemn treaties.

People do not usually like change forced on them by governments. Most of the correspondence I have received as a Member of Parliament living under either a Conservative or a Labour government takes the form of letters from people objecting to changes which the government of the day wishes to put through. People are particularly vocal if a government wishes to impose a new or additional tax that they were not paying before or if it wishes to remove a benefit or a subsidised charge which they have been enjoying. Businesses and individuals are often reluctant to see activity they have been carrying on without hindrance from the government brought under regulatory control. There are always very strong protests if the government proposes to ban certain courses of action, as we have seen with country sports. There are also objections if the government permits or does not prevent major changes in a local community being forced through by commercial interests, where people expect the government to be an agent for conservation rather than change.

Letters urging radical or evolutionary change by the mechanism of government are far fewer in number. They are usually related to a specific worry or grievance of an individual and often amount to no more than a person saying that they would like better treatment. They do not necessarily want a radical change in the law of the country benefiting everybody else if a way can be found for their own problem to be put right more simply. Exceptions to this rule lie in two areas, of lobbying for lower taxes generally or lobbying for higher benefits where the lobbyists themselves feel they fit fairly and squarely into the category of those who would be in receipt.

The public has adjusted to the twentieth-century State which operates like a great big fruit machine. They know that they have to pour a lot of money into the machine and they therefore intend to be suitably placed for any payments out. Many are aware that it is a negative sum game where overall people put more into the government machine than they get out. People are also aware that some are winners from the system, though few people believe themselves to be outright winners. These perceptions are interesting when much of the money taken in is disguised. Few people are aware of just how much of the price of a gallon of petrol goes in taxation – more than 90 per cent of the pump price. Few people realise how much VAT is charged on most goods that conceal VAT in the gross price. Nonetheless, people are aware that government is expensive and that they are more likely to lose than to win from the routeing of money around the system.

All this should make the modernisers beware. People aren't demanding a bigger say in government. They are demanding policies that are more conducive to their own interests. When people tell politicians that the politicians are not listening, they are usually saying in a polite way that the politician has proposed a policy which is trampling on the foot of the victim. The victim would naturally like the politician to remove his own feet from such a painful position. Politicians must listen more: that way they can avoid trampling on so many feet. The government often thinks it is sufficient to listen and to repeat the person's worries without solving the problem. This is not sufficient. When someone says the government is not listening, they mean they wish the government to change what it is doing.

A similar politeness or understatement occurs in political language when people say that the government is failing to get its message across. This usually means that the government is getting its message across all too clearly. In the case of the last Conservative government, people objected that the government was failing to get across the message of the economic recovery, yet opinion research showed that people were well aware that the economy was recovering. They had no intention of giving any credit to the government because they thought the recovery took place in spite of rather than because of the government's policies. This was not a failure of communication: it was a judgement of the people who disliked the experiences of the early 1990s when the Exchange Rate Mechanism did considerable damage to their house prices, their jobs and their businesses.

Modernisers in the Labour Government tend to take these words at face value. They think that the public want a government that listens more and explains more. Their answers are somewhat mechanical. They have government ministers attending more focus groups, commissioning more opinion research at the public expense and seeking to guide their words from the thoughts of people who are not primarily motivated by a wish to construct or conduct an effective public policy. Modernisers supplement this by the wish to produce a torrent of information through web sites, in printed form through the newspapers and on TV about the background to all the government's decisions.

This is to mistake the medium for the message and to confuse image and reality. People are much more worried about the reality than the image makers would lead us to believe. Whilst it is possible for slick governments to fool some of the people some of the time, it is not possible in a democracy with any kind of effective opposition for a government to present a completely different image of reality from the truth of people's everyday lives. If the government's message is that the economy is extremely buoyant and yet people in their daily lives see export orders being lost and manufacturers closing, they will not believe the government. They would rather believe their own direct experience.

It is a strange and dangerous idea of modern politics that public policy can be steered and guided by focus groups and inchoate public opinion. Public opinion is an important democratic force. Any democratic politician respects the wishes and the views of the electorate. But any person who has ridden the tides of electoral fortune for any length of time will know that raw public opinion is not a guiding device for settling policy. The public mood and the public ambition can help you define problems government needs to tackle. It should also act as a sanction against taking rash action which changes too much too quickly. It cannot inform the day-by-day decisions that ministers are called upon to make.

Let us take a relatively recent case from this Government. Public opinion generally wants there to be more jobs and higher incomes. At the same time it does not want a runaway price inflation which makes things too dear in the shops for many to buy. These ambitions should be obvious to any democratic politician and they show the innate common sense of the British people. The British people as a whole do not go to bed at night worrying about whether the Bank of England should be independent or not. Most people do not have a view on whether an independent central bank is more or less likely to create more or less jobs, or higher incomes, or lower inflation. They elect a government to do whatever a government can do to steer an economy in the direction of more jobs and greater prosperity. It is the government's job to decide whether that task is helped or hindered by making the bank independent. It is the government's job to explain the case for those who are interested. It is then for the public to judge over the cycle of a parliament whether that and other economic actions taken by the government have been broadly helpful or broadly unhelpful.

Going to focus groups before making the Bank of England independent is not likely to come to a well reasoned or conclusive answer on whether independence for the Bank of England is a good idea. Even going back to the focus groups after the action has been taken is likely to leave the Chancellor of the Exchequer bereft of clear argument or a decisive case. So it is with many other policies.

In areas more directly related to people's experiences, individual opinion should be and usually is based upon individual interest. If you ask a focus group what kind of reforms they would like to welfare, each individual in the group is very likely to favour reforms to welfare which point in the direction of him or her receiving more state money and neighbours that they don't like receiving less. For example, often in a focus group on welfare reform where working adults predominate you hear that there are too many scroungers taking advantage of the system. They should be dealt with. You also hear that the system does not do enough for decent hard-working people in the middle who have to pay a lot of tax but cannot rely on the system when they are in times of need. If the focus group is made up of the unemployed and single mothers, you will understandably hear that life is not much fun trying to live on current levels of income support and how the dignity of more cash might produce a better answer.

There should be nothing surprising to the seasoned politician in such findings from focus groups. Those who see themselves primarily as tax payers would like the welfare budget to be lower. Those who see themselves primarily as welfare recipients would like it to be higher. There are very few people who come to a conclusion on the right bounds between tax and welfare based on their own understanding of the size of the welfare budget, the signals it sends, the incentives it sends through the economy and what might be best in the national interest. In one of the focus groups I attended discussing welfare reform, only one of the people in the group claimed to have any idea what the welfare budget was. He confidently asserted that the total expenditure on welfare in Britain was £30 billion when the true figure is £100 billion. Everyone else in the group immediately accepted this figure as a reasonable guess and thought it was too large.

Public opinion is vital for a democracy. No democratic politician should be uninterested in it. Every democratic politician, if he is doing his job daily, has to balance public opinion against the needs of the country. A foolish politician is either one who ignores public opinion completely or one who accepts every twist and turn of it. The public may have one view of the problem today and a totally different view of the same problem in a few days' time. A political party, if it wishes to be statesman-like, has to offer greater consistency than the shifting sands of public opinion usually permit.

Constitutional change must capture all this. There should be less government. More government should be conducted closer to the people who really know about it and are affected by it. Government should not be conducted by politicians who seem to think that abnegating responsibility to focus groups and changing public opinion is the right answer. Nor should it be conducted by those who wish to delegate all the difficult decisions to independent quangos and bodies like the Bank of England when the politicians are themselves elected to make these hard choices.

This book will examine the unfolding crisis of the United Kingdom. It will show how the Labour modernisers' agenda is old-fashioned and dangerous. It will argue that the wrong kind of constitutional changes now can split the kingdom and destabilise our community life. We begin our story by examining the Treaty of European Union, a treaty which will give us two governments instead of one.

2 Treaty of European Union

At Maastricht on 7 February 1992, the member states signed the Treaty of European Union. Europe had come a long way from the original Treaty of Rome, when the first six members began the whole process in the 1950s. Twelve states sat down at the table at Maastricht. Three new members joined shortly after. The Treaty of Rome set out mainly to create a common market. The Treaty of Maastricht set out a comprehensive plan for economic and monetary union. The Treaty of Amsterdam, signed in 1997, advances the old EEC towards a common justice, defence and foreign policy. Taken together these treaties represent a blueprint for a new country called Europe.

As the architects of the European Union never fail to point out, many of those who had drawn up the original Rome Treaty had such a development in the forefront of their minds. Their general language, welcoming an ever closer union, only ripened into practical proposals and institutions in the Treaty of Maastricht and its extension, the Treaty of Amsterdam. Where in the Treaty of Rome many clauses had gone unremarked or unenforced, there was a clear quickening of pace at Maastricht. People will learn that the member states and especially the Commission were more serious this time. Maastricht brought home to the peoples of Western Europe the magnitude of the scheme unfolding before them and the intensification of effort being put in by the political and bureaucratic classes. They were out to transmute a common market into a single government.

The treaty was quite clear about the intentions. It begins by saying:

> This Treaty marks a new stage in the process of creating an ever closer union among the peoples of Europe, in which decisions are taken as closely as possible to the citizen. The Union shall be founded on the European Communities, supplemented by the policies and forms of co-operation established by this Treaty. Its task shall be to organise, in a manner demonstrating consistency and solidarity, relations between the member states and between their peoples.

The alchemy of the treaty is set out in a very wide range of objectives. The treaty aims to turn the base metal of common policy into the gold of a happy union. The new union is to promote economic and social progress. It is to abolish internal frontiers. It is to establish a single currency and a single social policy. The Union is to 'assert its identity on the international scene' 'working towards a common foreign and security policy', 'including the eventual framing of a common defence policy, which might in turn lead to a common defence'. The Union is to give each person in the member states citizenship of the larger whole. It is to work towards closer co-operation of justice and home affairs and is to consolidate all the governmental territorial gains the Community had already made.

Part one of the treaty sets out in more detail how wide-ranging the policy remit of the new Union is to be. It proposes a common commercial policy; an internal market; a common immigration policy; common agricultural and fishery policies; a common transport policy; an overarching European Union competition policy; approximation of the laws of the member states in the commercial field; the European social fund and stronger Community social policies; a Community policy for the environment; a research and techno-logical development policy; the establishment of trans-European networks; a policy for a high level of health protection; some involvement in education and training in member states; development co-operation; new policies to co-ordinate the work of the member states with their overseas countries and territories; and common policies in consumer protection, energy, civil protection and tourism. This list represents a programme for a comprehen-sive new government based in Brussels, Luxemburg and Strasburg. It consolidates many of the gains made in extending the territorial reach of the Brussels government over the preceding years. It makes quite explicit the method by which Community power has grown in the 1970s and 1980s.

The Community originally concentrated on persuading people that its prime purpose was the advancement of trade and prosperity. In order to create and complete a single market people were told that there did need to be some sacrifices of sovereignty by the member states. They were told that certain laws needed to be harmonised: the Community needed to intervene in aspects of regional, social, agricultural and economic policy. In practice, the single market was used as a method for the Community to gain government rights over many aspects of daily life throughout the member states.

Some of our partners in Western Europe had never been too enamoured with the idea of a free market without restriction or trade barrier. They felt that just allowing competition its head and removing tariffs could do damage to their businesses and to their social fabric. They always favoured a union which concentrated more on protection rather than a custom zone or free trade area. The British were unique in being told that the only purpose of the European Economic Community was the creation of a single market.

The Commission has always been keen on extending the reach of its power. It has shown phenomenal energy in drafting proposals for directives and regulations covering virtually every aspect of Community life. In the first instance the Community often produces a directive or regulation that has little impact on anybody. The purpose of the measure is not so much to change or improve the world as to establish the principle that the particular area is one in which the Community may interfere.

Once the principle has been established under Community law, the European Community then regards that area of life as one under its control. When the Community then wishes to make some real changes to the way that industry or group in the Community is regulated it is empowered to do so by European law itself. Should anyone challenge the right of the Community, the European Court will uphold the gain of EC power.

The doctrine of the Community acquis or authority has always been crucial. Once the member states have conceded any right to the Community to regulate or legislate in a given area, they have lost their right to sole control over that matter in perpetuity. The doctrine of the Community acquis is reaffirmed strongly at the front of the Maastricht Treaty.

The treaty goes on to set out the institutions of the Community that have the task of developing this pan-European government. The treaty confirms the role of the European Parliament, the Council, the Commission, the Court of Justice and the Court of Auditors. It establishes a committee of the regions and introduces the concept of the European system of central banks. It lays the foundation stones for the European Central Bank, which will be the progenitor and controller of the single currency. It also sets up a European investment bank.

The single market was introduced progressively over 12 years. The programme finally came to a technical conclusion on 31 December 1992. What was represented in Britain as a simple task of removing barriers to trade was transformed by Community action into a massive legislative endeavour spanning some 300 new laws. The programme was extremely detailed and its overall impact was more protectionist than liberating. Member states found it difficult to agree the necessary measures to open up areas like water, telecommunications and energy to full competition. They found it much easier to agree on limitations being placed on practically every business area concerning the type and range of products and services they could make or supply. To many interested in creating a strong European central government the whole programme was a triumph. It had kept wayward Britain on board by relating the extension of European government power to the British aim of a freer market, whilst giving the protectionists most of what they wanted measure by measure. The overall result was a greatly strengthened Brussels bureaucracy.

The central government of Brussels was always careful not to overextend. It concentrated on employing a relatively small number of very well paid and bright individuals who were interested in writing law codes. It did not specialise in employing the armies of individual administrators needed to administer each of the expensive and complicated programmes or to enforce them on the ground. Detailed administration of the Common Agricultural Policy, for example, was left to the domestic civil servants in each of the member states. Many times the number of people employed in Brussels on agriculture had to be employed in each Community country to work out on the ground how the overall policies, subsidies and programmes would be implemented place by place. Similarly, when it came to enforcing the nigh-on unenforceable common fisheries policy, the difficult work of arresting wayward trawlers and ordering people to return their catches to the ocean fell to the coastguards and navies of the member states.

The Community was able to say that the central government in Brussels was neither big nor powerful. They were able to say truthfully that there were many more officials employed in member states' administrations than in Brussels and to point out that difficult or unpopular enforcement decisions were those taken at the level of the member state. The whole structure of European government gave Brussels the power it needed without the misfortune of having to enforce the measures they had propagated. The legal structure of the Community meant that, for example, the British government had to enforce the British Fisheries Policy in British waters even though the British government objected to elements of that policy and even though it was extremely unpopular with British fishermen. The United Kingdom, if it failed to enforce the policy, would be taken to the European Court and fined extensively for its failure to comply.

When the single market was introduced, the Cecchini Report argued that there would be a 3 per cent boost to Gross National Product around the Community. Had this taken place, it would have been well worth while and could have been a useful justification for the extra powers the European government had taken over business. Unfortunately, at the end of 1992, when the single market came of age, Western Europe was gripped by a very damaging recession. Far from growing, the Western European economies either slumped or slowed right down. No one could find any evidence that the single market programme itself had made the recession less severe. It was difficult to see any extra business coming from the complicated measures which represented the single market programme.

The treaties now go a long way in the direction of creating common citizenship. Every citizen of the Union has the right to move and reside freely within the territory of the member states and the right to stand for election or to vote at the municipal level and the European parliamentary level. A Spaniard living in London has the right to run for the European Parliament for a London constituency and the right to vote or run in a London borough election. A reciprocal right is granted by the treaty to a Londoner in Madrid.

The original Treaty of Rome gave the power to the European Community to establish a common customs tariff. It permitted the free passage of goods throughout the European Community. Once an article had been imported into the Community and had paid the Community duties, people were free to route it around the Community without further hindrance. Right from the beginning of the EEC, some articles were enforced and some ignored. Article 37 said that member states could not run monopolies which discriminated in their relations with nationals of other member states. This clause was never enforced when it came to many of the giant public monopolies in operation on the continent.

The original Treaty of Rome itself exempted the common market in agricultural products from the competitive regime they set out for other industries. They decided on a Common Agricultural Policy right from the beginning. This had five separate aims including the stabilisation of markets and assuring the availability of supplies. They felt these aims required grants and subsidies on a grand scale and would not permit a proper competitive market being established. The fifth aim of the Common Agricultural Policy, 'To ensure the supplies reach consumers at reasonable prices', has never been properly implemented. In recent years common agricultural prices have been much higher than prices on the open world market. The consumer has paid a substantial additional tax for the privilege of belonging to the Common Agricultural Policy. The treaty itself was never that wedded to the idea of the consumer, as many more words and clauses were devoted to setting minimum prices for agricultural produce than to urging sensible prices.

The treaties give to every person living legally in a member state the right to move to another member state. This has caused considerable tension as some member states are much more lenient in their admissions policy than others. If the full freedom of movement was enforced, it would mean that any illegal immigrant entering a country like Italy or Greece and persuading the authorities there to give them the necessary paperwork could come on to a country like Britain. Fully enforced this would create endless rows in the Community. Individuals also have the right to set up a business wherever they wish or to go to another member state in order to obtain a job there. The treaty prevents any company or individual discriminating against potential employees on the grounds that they come from another member state. The free movement of capital is another cornerstone of the concept which has recently been brought into practice.

The Treaty of Amsterdam sets out elaborate procedures trying to bring the common immigration and asylum policy into effect. Article 61 outlines the need for a common visa policy. The Community itself will decide which nationals of which countries can enter the European Union without restraint and which need visas. The Union will set out procedures and conditions for issuing visas by each member state and a uniform format for visas. Similarly, the European Union will lay down minimum standards on how to receive asylum seekers into member states and standards over the qualifications of nationals of third countries as refugees. A five-year time horizon was imposed for the completion of all these necessary measures. The United Kingdom and Ireland have some exemption by one protocol and Denmark by another.

Article 70 establishes a common transport policy. The Union designs common rules applicable to international transport to and from the territory of Member states, laying out conditions under which non-resident carriers may operate transport services within another member state. The Community proposes measures for improved transport safety and there is a catch-all for 'any other appropriate provisions'. The Commission has the power under the treaty to ban grant aid or protection of any kind. It also has the power to permit subsidy or other favoured treatment on the grounds that it represents a sensible regional policy or tackles the problem of an underdeveloped area.

Articles 81 and 82 are the old Articles 85 and 86 of the Treaty of Rome. They establish a strong competition policy. They prohibit anti-competitive behaviour both through collusion between companies and from abuse of a dominant position. The Commission has the power to investigate cases of suspected infringement and has the power to propose measures to end such an infringement. Articles 87 to 89 give the Commission a similar wide-ranging power to investigate grants and state aids and to ban them if it sees fit. There are a number of permitted areas in which grant aid may be deemed to be acceptable. These are fairly loosely worded leaving considerable latitude to the Commission to make up its mind on whether it likes the particular form of grant or not.

Articles 90 to 93 prohibit any member state imposing indirect taxes on imports from other member states that are different from indirect taxes charged on its own domestic products in its own market. The Council is also encouraged to bring forward legislation to harmonise turnover taxes, excise duties and other forms of indirect taxation. Articles 94 to 97 are the original underpinnings of the single market legislative programme, encouraging the approximation of laws throughout the member states in the name of promoting a common market.

Economic and monetary policy co-ordination was central to the Treaty of Maastricht. Article 99 of the united treaty states clearly, 'The Member States shall regard their economic policies as a matter of common concern and should co-ordinate them within the Council.' The Commission is given power to keep the economies of the member states under review. The main purpose is to see whether they are pursuing policies that lead to 'the proper functioning of economic and monetary union'. Where the Commission is unhappy with the economic policies being pursued by a member state, it makes a recommendation to the Council. The Council, on a qualified majority, may confirm the recommendation and make it public.

One of the most draconian powers introduced in the Maastricht Treaty was the power to fine countries that pursue economic policies outside those laid down in the treaty. Article 104 demands that member states should avoid excessive government deficits. If the member state fails to come to heel, the Commission can send an opinion to the Council. Acting on a qualified majority the Council can decide that a member state is running an excessive deficit. It can then demand that action be taken to bring the deficit into line. If the member state fails to comply with the decision, the Council then has a range of measures which it can impose: it can demand that the member state publish additional information; it can limit or stop lending by the European Investment Bank to the member state; it can require the member state to make a non-interest-bearing deposit of money with the Community; and/or it can impose fines 'of an appropriate size'. The Council can do any of these things on a majority of two-thirds of the votes of the members weighted in accordance with the usual voting procedures excluding the votes of the member state in the dock.

Article 105 sets up a common monetary policy with the primary objective of 'maintaining price stability'. The European Central Bank and its branch banks, the former national central banks, hold and manage the official reserves of the member states, promote the smooth operation of payment systems, define and implement monetary policy throughout the Community and conduct any foreign exchange operations they think necessary. It is made quite clear that the European Central Bank is the controlling body. The treaty also permits the European Central Bank to pursue a policy of influencing or affecting the exchange rates of the ECU against foreign currencies.

The employment title sets out similarly grand aims in its chosen field. It states that the aim is 'a co-ordinated strategy for employment and particularly for promoting a skilled, trained and adaptable work force and labour markets responsive to economic change'. Each member state has to provide the Council and the Commission with an annual report on the principal measures taken in its employment policy. The European Union issues guidelines setting out what type of policies the countries should be following. The treaty sets out a common commercial policy. It aims at establishing a customs union 'to contribute in the common interest, to the harmonious development of world trade, progressive abolition of restrictions on international trade and the lowering of customs barriers'. It is to be based on 'uniformed principles, particularly in regard to changes in tariff rates, the conclusion of tariff and trade agreements, the achievement of uniformity in measures of liberalisation, export policy and measures to protect trade such as those to be taken in the event of dumping or subsidies'. This is reinforced by a perfunctory title encouraging customs co-operation.

Title 11 sets out a social policy and the Community's attitude towards education, vocational training and youth. Again the aims are wide-ranging and high flown. They include 'improved living and working conditions, so as to make possible their harmonisation while the improvement is being maintained, proper social protection, dialogue between management and labour, development of human resources with a view to lasting high employment and the combating of exclusion'. The treaty envisages the development of Community-wide industrial relations and gives the Commission power to consult both management and labour at Community level and to decide whether a Community-wide solution is desirable. Article 140 explicitly encourages common action in the fields of 'employment; labour law and working conditions', 'training; social security; prevention of occupational accidents and diseases; occupational hygiene; and the right of association and collective bargaining between employers and workers'. The principle of equal pay for male and female workers for equal work or work of equal value is set out in Article 141.

In the fields of education and vocational training, the Community is aware of national sensibilities. Nonetheless, the Community is keen to gain a presence. Article 149 gives the Community the power to develop a European dimension in education, to encourage the mobility of students and teachers, to promote co-operation between educational establishments, to develop exchanges of information and experience between member states, to encourage youth exchanges and to encourage the development of distance education. Article 151 encourages the Community to '[bring] the common cultural heritage to the fore'. The Community is empowered to improve the knowledge and dissemination of the cultural history of the European peoples.

Article 152 enables the Community to make a move towards control of health policy. We are told, 'Community action, which will complement national policies, shall be directed towards improving public health, preventing human illness and diseases and obviating sources of danger to human health.' Finally in this wide-ranging field, Article 153 sets out broad aims for consumer protection.

Title 15 encourages the Commission to develop trans-European networks to link member states together more successfully. Title 16 gives the Community powers to encourage industrial change and Title 17 to develop and promote 'economic and social cohesion'. The Community sets out to reduce disparities in development between the various regions. Both the social fund and the European regional development fund are geared to promoting employment and faster development respectively in the regions of the Community lagging behind the others.

Title 18 sets out a common research and technology policy. The aim is to strengthen the scientific and technological basis of Community industry. The Commission is given the power to run grant programmes to encourage certain types of technology, to stimulate training and mobility of researchers, to ensure research findings are published throughout the Community and to promote co-operation between the Community, companies and institutes. A framework programme is set out on a regular basis establishing scientific and technological objectives for the Community and the member states.

Title 19 establishes the green credentials of the European Union. The Community environment policy is designed to protect and improve the quality of the environment and to promote measures at an international level to deal with worldwide environmental problems. The Council has wide-ranging powers to choose action to promote environmental objectives. Unanimity is required to impose environmental taxes, to intervene in town and country planning and land use and to lay down rules concerning the member states' choice between different energy sources.

Title 20 gives the Community a role in development co-operation, pledging its support in the campaign against poverty in developing countries. The Treaty of Amsterdam also sets out an association of the overseas countries and territories. Article 182 states, 'The Member States agreed to associate with the Community the non-European countries and territories which have special relations with Denmark, France, the Netherlands and the United Kingdom.'

The treaty lays out the basis on which the principal European institutions have been established. The European Parliament draws its legitimacy from treaty Articles 189 to 201. These include an encouragement to form European political parties in order to form 'a European awareness and to express the political will of the citizens of the Union'.

The European Parliament has 626 members. Ninety-nine come from Germany; 87 each from France, Italy and the United Kingdom; 64 from Spain; 31 from the Netherlands; 25 from Belgium, Greece and Portugal; 22 from Sweden; 21 from Austria; 16 from Denmark and Finland; 15 from Ireland; and 6 from Luxemburg. The Parliament has to have an annual session at which it considers an annual report from the Commission. Its principal power has never been used. It is allowed by a two-thirds majority, as long as that comprises a majority of all the members of the European Parliament, to dismiss the complete Commission. Otherwise its powers are distinctly limited.

The more powerful body is the Council set up under Articles 202 to 210 of the enlarged treaty. The Council consists of a representative of each member state at ministerial level. In the Council, Germany, France, Italy and the United Kingdom each have ten votes; Spain has eight votes; Belgium, Greece, the Netherlands and Portugal have five votes: Austria and Sweden have four votes, Denmark, Ireland and Finland have three votes; and Luxemburg has two votes. If 63 votes are cast in favour of a proposal, that is a qualifying majority usually sufficient to transact the business. In other words it takes 26 votes to block a measure. This means at least three countries, if they are larger countries, need to oppose a proposition, or six or seven countries if they are smaller countries.

Articles 211 to 219 establish the Commission. The Commission consists of 20 members who have to be nationals of the member states. Each member state is entitled to at least one commissioner but no member state is entitled to more than two. The commissioners are chosen by the governments of the member states and are appointed for a five-year period which may be renewed.

Articles 220 to 245 establish the Court of Justice. It comprises fifteen judges assisted by nine advocate generals. The judges are appointed for a six-year term which can be renewed. The European Court of Justice can decide that a member state has failed to fulfil an obligation under the treaty. The member state then has to comply. It is under pain of fines should it fail to do so expeditiously. The European Court is given the power to define the meaning of the treaty. This is the crucial power which makes the European Court of Justice the supreme body unless member states are in session rene-gotiating the treaty on which the court is based. The rules of procedure of the court do require the unanimous approval of the Council.

Articles 246 to 248 establish the European Court of Auditors. Fifteen people of independent mind are charged with the job of auditing the expenditure of moneys by the Community institutions. The Court of Auditors draws up an annual report after the close of each financial year. This published report is usually a fund of embarrassing stories of moneys improperly spent. Little action is usually taken as a result.

Article 257 establishes an economic and social committee with repre-sentatives from each member state, and Article 263 a committee of the regions with similar geographical representation with membership taken from regional or local government. The European Investment Bank established under Articles 266 and 267 is designed to make grants and loans and offer guarantees on a non-profit-making basis to encourage the development of the less developed areas of the Community or to encourage projects that are too large for individual member states. Article 302 gives the Commission the power to develop and maintain relationships with the United Nations and other international bodies as part of the design to expand the European Union's legal personality into that of an international power.

Anyone reading this treaty for the first time would conclude that the intention is none other than the establishment of a new country called Europe. In every area where Whitehall has a ministry, the Treaty of Amsterdam has a title, chapter or clause giving the European Union wide-ranging competence. In some areas, transition from national to international government is more or less complete. The European Union has got furthest in establishing its control over customs duties, single-market laws, agriculture, fisheries and competition policy. In other areas, like health and education, it has made modest beginnings from a position a few years ago where member states agreed that the Community should have nothing whatsoever to do with these matters. Big advances made by Maastricht and Amsterdam are in the creation of a single economic and monetary policy in the first treaty and a common foreign and security policy in the second. The Community is busily trying to establish itself as a new country in the eyes of the world.

A Brussels Commissioner works away with the United States of America to show that he and not any individual member state is the responsible person when dealing with international trade policy. He will be followed in this by the new foreign policy spokesman and co-ordinator speaking for Europe as a whole on international matters. The Federal Reserve Board and the Bank of Japan will soon discover that they need to discuss matters with the European Central Bank and not with the individual member states. The countries trying to follow distinctive economic policies will soon be reprimanded and have to step back into line under the strict requirements of the Maastricht Treaty.

It is strange how misled people in Britain have been by the conduct of the debate. The relentless argument has been that Europe is good for our prosperity and if we do not plunge into each federal move we will lose trade, exports and influence. The 1972 government took us into a common market protesting that it was a trading arrangement. The subsequent government in 1975 put the matter to a vote. In the referendum campaign the three principal political parties and many business leaders came together to argue strongly in favour. No one then mentioned that we were on course for the creation of a new European state. People glossed over the fact that the European Community had a flag, an anthem, common institutions and a common destiny. The Treaty of Rome talked of ever closer union. The Single European Act, followed by the Treaty of Maastricht, closely followed by the Treaty of Amsterdam, all but completed that original vague ambition.

Some would say that none of this matters. Whilst it was true that many people in the early 1970s thought that we were primarily joining a trading arrangement, it has evolved and developed over the years. They would say that there is nothing wrong with this. The fact that other member states of the original Common Market were in favour of more centralised government than we were at the beginning does not make us wrong. The fact that we have been persuaded, albeit reluctantly, to go along with it implies that it is in Britain's interest to be one of the founder members of this new country.

The problems this book examines revolve around this central question. Is it possible to create a new country by peaceful means and sleight of hand? Is it possible to govern all the peoples of Western Europe as one? Is it possible for a country to emerge where people speak 11 different languages and where there are at least 15 different national ways of doing things? Is it possible for the once war-like powers of Western Europe to live in friendship, submitting to the power of Brussels?

There is no parallel in history for a successful union of as many countries on a permanent basis. Usually empires are held together by a single language as well as a single law code and a single currency. Many were only created and maintained by standing armies. Usually they owe loyalty and allegiance to a single figurehead. Europe has not yet tackled the problem of how to create a popular elected monarch or president. The issue of the presidency has been ambiguously handled. The president of the Commission is usually better known than the elected president for the time being, the prime minister or president of the member state who currently holds the chairmanship of the Council. To British eyes the president of the Commission is a rather grand senior official. In the eyes of some of the smaller countries of Western Europe he is an immensely powerful man who has more of the characteristics of a leading politician. Nonetheless, he is ultimately answerable to the Council and its chairman for the time being. Very rarely has a president of the Council asserted himself and projected himself as a European as opposed to a national leader.

The cleverness of the Community so far has been its development of creeping competence. The Commission has been masterful in the way that it has extended its powers without attracting too much jealousy or opposition from individual member states or groups of states. Each renegotiation of the treaty has proceeded with the Commission deliberately underselling its proposals. The treaty's style is to combine very high-flown and wide-ranging articles of principle with more modest and detailed articles specifying individual examples. The combination of the Commission and the Court has been adept, whilst firstly reassuring the member states that the general articles will not be used in a clumsy or wide-ranging way and then gradually extending the freedom of action of the European institutions drawing on the wide-ranging drafting of the original articles.

Patrick Neil, in a telling article, has set out how the European Court itself has extended its powers. The crucial development came when the Court moved from determining cases under the law to a more active role in determining the law itself. Just as the Supreme Court of the United States of America was the driving force in extending federal power at the expense of the states of the union, so the European Court in conjunction with the loose and general drafting of the Commission has proved talented at pushing forward the powers of the European federal system.

In the debates around these powers the Commission always stresses, in a low-key way, the need to have some border co-operation or co-ordination. This then becomes a platform for a more general Community policy. Much of it has been done in the name of promoting the single market, as the Commission has realised that the single market is the force most likely to unify relatively free-market United Kingdom and Germany with the more interventionist and government-friendly states of the South and West. Just as the German Customs Union was the way of creating a united Germany so the Commission state-makers see the European Customs Union as the driving force behind the creation of the European superstate. Not for them the loose political arrangements of the Hanseatic League or the European Free Trade Area. They prefer the extension of central government power to back up the free trade that has permeated the previous national borders.

One big problem the European state-makers face is consent. They would argue that they have proceeded democratically. It is true that all of the treaty articles have been negotiated on behalf of the peoples of Western Europe by democratically elected governments. It is true that every four years we can all join in the election of a group of European parliamentarians who are meant to hold the Commission to account and provide redress if we do not like what the Community is doing. It is true that there is a Community ombudsman to investigate complaints, a Court of Auditors to expose fraud and a vast amount of published work which the informed citizen can read if he wishes. But it is also true that the European parliamentarians have very little power. They cannot propose and enact legislation. They have no power to reduce or increase taxes. They have very limited power to call the

Commission to account, as they can only dismiss the whole Commission in one go, a power they have never dared to use.

It is also true that many member states' governments have not taken the matters of the treaties back to the people. It would have been much better for the future development of the European Union if the Union had clearly stated the true intention earlier in its development and if it had put the matter to referenda of the European peoples in each country. As it is, the Danes did understand the whole scheme and voted to keep their country out of large parts of it. As a result, Denmark is not part of the common immigration policy and is declining to enter the single currency. In France, where a referendum was held on the Maastricht element of the treaty, the result produced a tiny majority in favour. It revealed a big split in France between the outlying rural parts, which were against the treaty, and the Paris basin area, the richest part of France, which favoured it. The United Kingdom has had a referendum only on what people thought was the Common Market. Although Sweden held a referendum to approve her entry into the European Union, her government has decided that public opinion is now against the single currency and has engineered her exclusion from it. Norway voted against joining the enlarged European Union.

It would be more normal when creating a single country to establish strong democratic institutions at the beginning so that public opinion could be informed and channelled through a representative body. Debates in the European Parliament are rarely reported on radio or television or even in the newspapers in the United Kingdom. Attendance at European elections is lamentably low, reflecting most people's judgement that the Parliament has little power and will have little impact on their daily lives. People are realistic in their understanding of how the Community works, even though few could give you a detailed explanation of the different institutions, the forms of tenure of the principal actors and actresses and the voting methods used.

People do understand that considerable power resides in the Commission and in the Council of Ministers. They do understand that the way to try to influence the course of European development is either to travel to Brussels to talk to the Commission direct or to put pressure on a national government minister who may be able to have some impact on the negotiations before the measure is finally adopted. British businesses have largely determined in favour of the former method of proceeding. There has been a notable change of tack in recent years, with many more businesses deciding to represent their case direct in Brussels, where they can make more progress than through the intermediary of a British government minister who only deals with European matters from time to time.

Each of the treaties represented a major step on the way to a single country. Rome set out on a federal road, establishing the basic shape of the institutions of the proto-union and going a considerable way to creating a single government in agriculture, trade and commerce. The Single European Act took that one step further, establishing a common legal code for most commercial and industrial life and reducing the power of individual countries to veto proposals. The Treaty of Maastricht set out all the requirements for a single economic policy, a single budgetary policy and a single currency. The Treaty of Amsterdam finalised and formalised the single home affairs and justice policy, common frontiers, a common asylum policy and the common foreign and defence policy.

The unified treaty gives the Commission and the Council of Ministers most of the power they need to complete the job of creating the United States of Europe. If all goes according to plan under this treaty, in ten years' time there will be a single European country. It will have one flag, one anthem, one currency, one central bank, one set of law codes over much of public life, one set of presiding institutions, one supreme court interpreting and even changing the law, and one foreign policy – and it will be well on the way to having a common defence capability. We should expect the European Union to start arguing in favour of United States of Europe representation directly on the United Nations, the International Monetary Fund and other international bodies. We should expect to see pressure for an enlarged European Union budget, much bigger transfer payments around the Union, common taxation and many other federal policies. It is amazing how far the process has gone, and how few people have woken up to the intentions. It will become more difficult from here, as the ambitions of the Union start to outrun popular consent.

In Britain, Labour's Third Way will increasingly emerge as the European way. Europe has tried to overcome the traditional disputes between free marketeers and state interventionists, between socialists and conservatives, by offering some of each. Free marketeers are told that the idea of the single market is to open up a bigger market for all. They are told that there will be de-regulation of some state monopoly areas like telecommunications and post. Socialists are told that there will be a high level of social protection through social law codes across the union. So far both sides on the continent have accepted this strange compromise. Traditional political arguments have been frustrated through the lack of a proper debate over the policies being put forward.

One of the cleverest features of the Union, which has stifled any such debate, is the absence of any official opposition to anything the Commission proposes. No one is charged with the task of exposing the errors, dangers and mistakes of European legislation. There is no government which formally proposes and then an opposition which opposes. Each new law is put forward as a text to negotiate by the Commission. Countries only oppose or suggest amendments if it is clearly against their national interest. Many accept a new law, thinking it may have little effect in their country, even if they think it wrong.

In Labour's world this studied ambiguity and blurring of responsibility is ideal. They dislike the clear accountability of the House of Commons, and the clash of opposites offering people a choice. The consensual style transfers power to the politicians acting behind closed doors, and allows any one politician or party to deny responsibility if the policy or law miscarries. No journalist is allowed to watch the Council of Ministers at work, yet it is the most powerful legislature in Western Europe. No one seems to think it wrong that a group of politicians of differing political views, answering to different electorates, should pass law after law with no one formally opposing, and no one from outside watching. Yet that is what is happening, day by day.

3 The Federal Ideal – Experience from Abroad

The word 'federal' has caused many a problem in the British debate. To those wanting to keep an independent democracy in these islands it means the centralisation of power, followed by some devolution from the centre to the extent that the centre sees fit. It means the creation of a country called Europe. Enthusiasts for the idea say that the continental model is different, that the power remains in the individual states of the union and that we need fear nothing from such a development.

The German constitution is seen by many in the European Union as the model for a wider United States of Europe. Some claim it leaves the *Länder* very free to make their own decisions. Reading the text of the constitution, it does not seem like that. Those against a federal Europe think that Britain is different from the Rhineland or Brandenburg. The important thing about the German states is that they are all German and wish to belong to the greater whole. The United States of America sometimes supports the idea of a federal Europe, seeing similarities between the German federal constitution and its own. There is a strong push towards a European Union based upon the German system of individual states or *Länder*. They come together in the *Bundesrat* or Upper House of the German Parliament to exercise some restraint or control over the law-making powers of the federal centre.

The German constitution is founded upon a basic law (*Grundgesetz*) which was brought into being on 23 May 1949 by agreement between German representatives and the British, French and US armies of occupation in West Germany. It was self-consciously based upon previous federal constitutions including the constitution of 1848–9, Bismarck's constitution of 1871 and the Weimar constitution of 1919. It was seen as a provisional measure divided into 146 articles with a short preamble. It lasted until 1990.

On 3 October 1990, the basic law was extended to 182 articles divided into 14 sections and became the constitution of the newly enlarged German nation. The five re-established eastern *Länder* were re-unified with the west.

The opening articles of the constitution set out equal rights, banning prejudice because of sex, race, language, homeland or religion. No one shall be forced to fight for his country against his conscience, whilst freedom of speech and association are guaranteed.

The new Federal Republic of West Germany in 1949 adopted the black, red and gold colours of the Weimar Republic. Each *Land*, district and parish was to have a representative assembly elected by universal suffrage in secret elections. The victor powers wrote into the constitution a ban upon preparing for aggressive war and made unconstitutional any tendency to disturb the peaceful relations between nations.

The Federal Assembly or *Bundestag* was established based on universal suffrage of all those over 18 years of age. Its power is to some extent balanced by the *Bundesrat* or Upper House. The *Bundesrat* consists of members of the *Land* governments. The largest *Länder* have six votes scaling down to the smallest *Land* with three votes. The *Bundesrat* elects an annual president and takes its decisions by simple majority vote.

One of the important characteristics of the new constitution in 1949 was to limit the powers of the Federal President. Just as the victor powers did not wish to see a resumption of aggressive, war-like preparations by Germany, so too they did not wish to see a restoration of a strong leader. They therefore decided that the Federal President should be a kind of elected monarch reminiscent of a constitutional monarchy. The President may be elected for up to two terms of five years. He or she has to be over the age of 40. He is indirectly elected by a federal convention comprising members of the *Bundestag* and an equal number of members elected by the *Land* parliaments. The President's roles include representing the federation in international relations and accrediting and receiving ambassadors. The President has to appoint the man chosen by a majority of the *Bundestag* to be Chancellor. He must dissolve the *Bundestag* within 21 days if a Chancellor loses the vote of confidence and if no other Chancellor is elected within the 21-day period by the *Bundestag* itself.

The most powerful figure in the new German constitution is the Chancellor. It may have surprised the Allied countries to discover how quickly he became the leader, although it should not have been a great shock given the powers granted to him under the constitution. The Federal Government or *Bundesregierung* is led by the Federal Chancellor (*Bundeskanzler*) and a team of federal ministers (*Bundesministers*). The Chancellor chairs his ministerial team meetings to settle general policy and is usually the leader of the most popular political party.

Where the basic law sets out legislative powers for the federation, the right of legislation rests primarily with the *Bundestag*. Where no such power is expressly granted to the Federal Parliament, the power of legislation rests with the *Länder*. Exclusive areas like foreign affairs, citizenship, immigration, monetary matters, copyrights, customs, railways, post and telecommunications are Federal Reserve matters. In some cases *Bundestag* legislation requires the consent of the *Bundesrat*. In other cases the *Bundesrat* may express its displeasure but may be overruled by the *Bundestag*. The Federal Government has reserved powers in a number of areas including the ability to place the police forces in various *Länder* under its own instructions. Judicial authority is vested independently in judges and exercised by the Federal Constitutional Court, by the Supreme Federal Court and the courts of the *Länder*. The Federal Constitutional Court decides on the interpretation of the basic law where it is disputed between the *Land* governments and the Federal Government. It has quite frequently decided in favour of an interpretation which helps the *Länder*, as with the famous case on broadcasting. It can also settle disputes between individuals and the constitutional authorities. For example, Professor Nölling's case, arguing that abolition of the DM was illegal, was tested in the Constitutional Court. On that occasion the Court held for the government's view against the professor.

The federation has the exclusive right to legislate on customs, excise duties and VAT. Other taxes including those on income are controlled by a concurrent power between the Federal Government and the *Länder*. There is a mechanism for burden-sharing, transferring money from the richer and more successful *Länder* to the poorer and less successful.

Tax revenue is divided between the federation and the states. Most is shared on a pooled basis. The basic law prescribes quotas of income tax and corporation tax for the federation and the states but there are no fixed quotas for VAT. Local authority expenditure is paid for from their share of income tax, local taxes and state grants.

The constitution provides for the establishment of a central bank. However, the only mention of the central bank is in Article 88 and it merely asserts, 'There shall be a national bank on the federal level.' The myth has grown up that one of the unique features of the German constitution, which is wholly admirable, is its provision for an independent central bank which controls economic and monetary policy. As this quote from the constitution makes quite clear, there is no such requirement under the constitution.

In practice the German central bank is under a duty to support the economic policy of the government of the day. There have been occasions in the past when there have been arguments and rows between the central bank and the government over whether it is doing enough to support the government's economic policy. No one has ever suggested that it should do otherwise. Any German government can use its parliamentary majority to change the status of the Bundesbank by a simple revision of the law. It is not a constitutional matter, as it is not recorded in the German constitution. Such a change in the law would not even require the agreement of the *Länder*, for the basic law does make clear that responsibility for the national bank resides wholly at the federal level. In 1992 the Federal Government decided not to give every post-unification new *Land* its own central bank. Instead it reduced the number of central banks from eleven to nine. Wein and Plattiner threatened to seek an absolute veto for the *Länder* over this matter but on taking legal advice saw that they were unlikely to succeed.

The German central bank is not responsible for economic policy. It has an advisory role where the Federal Government can ignore its advice if it wishes. The Bundesbank has no right to be consulted. Its only proper responsibility is for the stability of the German mark.

For most of the post-war period the Bundesbank has made a reasonable job of controlling inflation in Germany. It has been monetarist, targeting the growth in the money supply. It has put up interest rates whenever it thought money was growing too quickly and has lowered them when it thought it was not growing quickly enough. For most of the post-war period this worked very well. It gave the impression of an independent central bank because none of the main democratic parties wished to challenge what it was trying to do. Every democratic party in Germany knew that controlling inflation was most important to the electorate. No one wished to return to the hyperinflation of the Weimar Republic.

The independence of the bank only emerged as a sham when real conflicts arose between the government and the bank. The first occurred over German reunification. Chancellor Kohl had to accept the social democrat Karl Otto Pohl as President of the Bank, reselecting him in 1988 as he was well thought of in the international community. However, when Chancellor Kohl wished to reunify the two Germanys and cement the union with the merger of the Ostmark and the Deutschmark, the central bank panicked. It rightly saw that under Herr Kohl's scheme far too much money was going to be printed. The terms offered to East German savers were too generous. The central bank proved quite unable to do anything about the government's intentions. Relations deteriorated and the head of the central bank resigned.

It was a very instructive incident in German history. It should have warned any observer that there is no such thing as an independent central bank in a democracy. It should certainly have emphasised the weaknesses of the German constitution in this respect which allows the democratic politicians to override the central bank even when the stability of the Deutschmark is in question. The Bundesbank turned out to be right. The German money supply ballooned and German inflation duly followed upwards. The failure of the head of the central bank to resist this, and his own departure, demonstrated the problems.

The second clear occasion when Bundesbank independence turned out to be a chimera was over the evolution of the single currency for Western

Europe. No self-respecting member of the Bundesbank council could support the surrender of the Deutschmark. The whole point of the Bundesbank was to preserve a strong independent German currency. Yet Chancellor Kohl's determination to drive through the abolition of the Deutschmark and its replacement by the Euro triumphed against rather feeble central bank resistance. There could be no more telling exposé of the myth of central bank independence than the abolition of the currency which the central bank is charged to uphold and maintain.

Nonetheless, in politics the myths often matter more than the reality. In the short term they can predominate, in the longer term reality comes through. The German myths have been most influential in the evolution of a constitution for Western Europe. It is the German view that we need an independent central bank free from political interference, which has held sway in many of the debates. It is the German view that the nations of Western Europe should become like the German *Länder*, that has predominated. Even the idea of subsidiarity, much vaunted as a British proposal for limiting the damage Britain sees from a federal central power, is more inclined to the concept of the German constitution allowing freedom to the *Länder* in all areas where the federal state does not have its own express powers, than to any recognisable concept in the United Kingdom.

One of the German myths is that the *Länder* are more powerful than they really are. Whilst Germany claims that the *Länder* are their own free agents capable of legislating, taxing and making their own decisions, in practice a great deal of power rests with the centre. The only well known German politician is, and will remain, the Chancellor. The Chancellor often has a decisive influence over the direction of German policy both nationally and internationally. What the German Chancellor wishes to see happen usually does happen. His will can help shape policy in all those *Länder* under the control of his own party and even in those *Länder* under the control of rival parties, given the strength of federal law-making powers and the impact the federal decisions have upon the *Länder*.

The 1949 constitution was a provisional one. It has stood the test of time remarkably well. There is an irony in the present situation that many now think Western Europe needs a constitution which the Allies visited upon Germany to prevent Germany doing again what she had done in the 1920s and the 1930s. Many modern Germans do not seem to realise that this is the origin of their constitution, as they merrily go about their task of persuading the French, the Italians, the Spaniards and the British that a similar constitution would work for all of us.

If we wish to see a more successful and longer-lasting federal constitution, we should turn to that of Switzerland. The presently stable Swiss

Confederation emerged from centuries of political, linguistic, religious and cultural rows. Successful Swiss Confederations in the past have emerged through the threat of larger powers on their borders. The Swiss have discovered that they can band together in their mountain fortress and survive against threats from far bigger countries to the west, east, north or south. In 1648, the Swiss Confederation acquired full independence from the German Empire. This lasted until the French revolution, when a central government of the Helvetian Republic was imposed by a foreign army. In 1803, Napoleon had to accept that the Swiss could only be governed through a federal devolved system. Once Napoleon fell, the old confederations re-established in 1813 with some new cantons.

Fighting between the Catholic- and Protestant-dominated elements in the Swiss state continued in the Sonderbund War of 1847. The 1848 constitution resulted and the modern federal state emerged. More recently there have still been rows and conflicts of a non-violent kind. In 1978, the French-speaking minority in the German-speaking Bern canton succeeded in creating their own new canton, called Jura, so that they could be self-governing to a greater extent. There are currently 26 full and half cantons divided between Protestant and Catholic, speaking four different languages.

There is no head of state in Switzerland. The Federal Council or *Bundesrat* serves as the chief executive authority in the country. Seven members are elected every four years in a joint session of both chambers of Parliament to serve on the Council. Each member has to come from a different canton and there has to be representation of the different major parties. There are seven administrative departments to the Republic presided over by an individual member of the Federal Council acting as a minister.

The Federal Assembly has two chambers. The Council of the States (*Ständerat*) has 46 members. Two come from each of the 20 full cantons and one each from the 6 half cantons. The second chamber or National Council (*Nationalrat*) comprises 200 councillors each serving a four-year term. Laws have to be passed by both chambers of the National Assembly. Fifty thousand citizens or 8 cantons can demand a referendum on any given law. Constitutional amendments and decisions to join international organisations require the consent of the people in a referendum. Referenda are a regular feature of the Swiss system.

Each canton has its own executive council. It also has a *kantonsrat* acting as a parliament. Five of the cantons preserve the traditional open-air assembly of all voters, or *Landsgemeinde*. Cantons have substantial powers to levy taxes including income tax. The Swiss constitution prohibits the national government from maintaining a standing army whilst the cantons may have very limited permanent troops.

Switzerland, like many other countries around the world, has shown it is quite difficult for a strong central government to govern a country with very different languages, cultures, religions and backgrounds. Seventeen of the 26 cantons are German-speaking, four French and one Italian. There are three bilingual ones speaking both German and French and there is one trilingual speaking German, Italian and Romansh. In some respects Switzerland has been slow to move with the times. It was not until 1971 that women gained the vote in federal elections and as late as October 1984 that a woman was first elected to the Federal Council. On 30 April 1989, after five failed attempts, the mainly Protestant half canton of Appenzell Ausser Rhoden accepted the right of women to take part and vote in the *Landsgemeinde*.

When thinking of a new constitution for a federal Europe it would be better to look to the Swiss model than to the German model. The Swiss model has after all lasted for longer and was designed to deal with exactly the kind of problems that a European state would encounter. The German constitution was designed between the Germans and the Allied victors after the war, to provide some limitation on the power of an otherwise overstrong central state serving one people with one language and one dominant religion. In contrast, the Swiss constitution is designed to keep together in a loose federation peoples with very different languages, cultures, religions and outlooks.

Arguably, the Swiss constitution can only work in a very small country. Frequent use of referenda, some use of open-air meetings in the smaller cantons allowing all the voters to express their views and a perception of a common threat to their particular mountain way of life would not be easily duplicated in a state of 300 million or more people. Despite the perception of common threats and some common interest given the similarity of the ways of life, there have at times in Switzerland's past been severe conflicts and dis-agreements between the different cantons, religions and linguistic groupings.

The German constitution has in one sense been successful in achieving the ends laid down for it by the victor powers. Germany has not become an aggressive nation building up huge armed forces and threatening its neighbours again. This to some of us never seemed likely, as Germany has become a peace-loving democracy. To the victor powers of 1945 this was not so obvious and their main concern was to provide checks and balances over the build-up of military strength and central authority.

They were successful in preventing the President obtaining great power to lead the nation and to become too much of an individual focus of nation aspiration. In his stead the Chancellor has assumed a lot of the powers and is the clear centre of German politics. This is not as different from the prewar position as perhaps the framers of the constitution imagined. Hitler had to sweep aside an ineffectual president in order to gain supreme power.

The Germans for their part were obviously delighted that their constitution enabled Germany to achieve low inflation throughout most of the post-war period. They were naturally extremely keen not to see a resumption of the terrors of hyperinflation. Post-war German consensus has ensured that monetary policy has kept inflation within check save when the politicians have overruled and followed wider political objectives. The German constitution, with modest adaptation, was able to encompass unity with the five East German *Länder* quite easily. The *Länder* had to be restored, replacing the administrative districts set up under the communists. This was a relatively easy task as the old loyalties and allegiances were still very much in evidence.

It is difficult to see how this model, suitable for one people speaking one language with one culture, could be readily applied to a diverse group of nations with so many different cultures, languages and outlooks. There are not sufficient checks and balances to allow for the tensions likely to occur between peoples with such different views. The German constitution works well because there has been a broad consensus of outlook amongst most of the major political players in Germany over most of the post-war period. You would need something along the lines of the Swiss constitution to allow much more breathing space for the different races, languages and cultures of Europe. Even then it is difficult to believe that you could scale up the Swiss constitution from a country of six million people to one fifty or sixty times that number.

The Canadian constitution has shown that any central power can be resented by a concerted minority within an individual state or *Land* that disagrees with the outlook of the majority. The whole purpose of the establishment of different nations was to allow group organisation by those who felt they had more in common with each other than they did with those across their borders. The erosion of those self-same borders creates much greater difficulties of public order and democratic agreement by enlarging the boundaries for disagreement too greatly. The *Québeçois* have run a consistent campaign in recent years to establish a wider range of powers for self-government in Quebec. They have a different language and a different religion: they feel this makes them different. They have always kept extensive diplomatic representation in a city like London in recent years, seeking recognition from countries like the United Kingdom for their separate status. We will see similar tensions as the European Union develops its chain of embassies around the world, putting forward the common European policy which may at times be different from the nuances or ambitions of the individual member states who are still maintaining their own national embassies.

The other possible model for a federal constitution is that of the United States of America. The United States constitution is based upon a clear separation of powers. The legislature comprises the Senate, and the Congress. The executive is under the control of an elected President. Ultimate legal decisions and interpretation of the constitution itself falls to the province of the Supreme Court. The conduct of monetary policy, subject to some degree of political intervention, is carried out by the central bank.

The Confederal Congress developed between 1781 and 1789. In the process of throwing off the powers of the British Parliament, the thirteen states of the American Union were very reluctant to grant similar powers to a new federal body that they had so recently removed from the British Crown and Parliament. Each individual state had strong powers of self-government. The first unicameral legislature could neither regulate commerce between states nor levy taxes. The weakness of the Articles of Confederation soon led to alarm abroad. Seven states issued different paper money and individual states imposed taxes on trade with other states. In May 1787, the states decided to meet in Philadelphia to strengthen the centre and deal with some of the problems.

By 1789, the constitution that emerged from Philadelphia still contained restraint on the central power and created strict separation of executive, legislature and judiciary in a federal system. A bicameral legislature was established. Members of the House of Representatives returned to Congress had to be properly elected by white males, subject until the 1930s to a property qualification in some states. Members of the Senate were selected by each state's legislature. In 1920, the seventeenth amendment to the constitution translated this into popular election. Every state has two senators. The apportionment of congressmen between the states now varies between 1 and 52 depending on the size of the state's population. The Congress has the power alone to raise taxes and to spend money but in other ways is much more restricted than the British Parliament.

The constitution granted power over foreign affairs and defence, monetary policy and the regulation of commerce between the states to the federal authorities. The remainder is left to the states and to local government. There are also strict rules preventing overlap of personnel between the three different branches of the constitution. The President and the cabinet secretaries may not be members of the Senate or the Congress and must not be judges. Congress is entirely separate and politically independent from the Presidency. The President requires the goodwill of the Congress to secure the kind of budget he wishes to see. In return for this limitation on his power he is not subject to the approval of Congress to maintain his office.

All this is set out in the constitution first adopted on 4 March 1789. Its magnificent language has been an inspiration for democrats around the world. Section 3 of Article 1 makes explicit the power of the Senate to impeach high officials including the President. Senators and Congressmen, as with Members of Parliament, have immunity from arrest during their attendance at the session of the respective Houses and what they say in debate is protected by privilege from libel laws. The Congress and Senate have the right to initiate new laws. The President is asked to sign their proposals: if he does not do so it requires a two-thirds majority of both Houses to pass the law anyway.

The Congress was given the express powers amongst others to borrow money on the credit of the United States, to regulate commerce, to coin money and regulate its value, to declare war, to raise and support armies and to establish a uniform rule of naturalisation. The President is Commander-in-Chief of the army and navy. He has the power with the consent of the Senate to make treaties and to appoint ambassadors. Amendments to the constitution began as early as 1791. The first amendment establishes freedom to profess a religion, freedom of the press and the right to assemble and petition the government. The second amendment upholds the right of a free people to keep their arms. The fifth amendment gives people charged with serious crimes freedom from double jeopardy and freedom from having to bear witness against themselves. The tenth amendment reserves to the state those powers that are not specifically granted to the federal authorities by the rest of the constitution.

The thirteenth amendment, ratified after the Civil War battles, banished slavery. In 1870, the fifteenth amendment prevented discrimination on grounds of race, colour or previous condition of servitude against citizens of the United States. The notorious eighteenth amendment prohibited alcoholic drinks. This was subsequently repealed by the twenty-first amendment. In 1920, the nineteenth amendment gave women the rights of citizens.

In the twentieth century, most of the worries about the erosion of states' powers have gone away. The dreadful battles of the American Civil War are now well behind the American nation. Voters have agreed to or acquiesced in a process of transferring more and more power to Washington. Congress and Senate have been keen to see growing expenditures at the federal level. More and more things have fallen under the remit of federal programmes. States and local government have often co-operated in this process, turning to try to influence the quantity of money and activity flowing their way from Washington rather than trying to stop Washington getting the power in the first place.

Although the United States keeps its reputation as being the world's greatest free-market democracy, the twentieth century has seen a lot of damage done to this concept. The United States is now a highly regulated economy. There has been a massive build-up in law codes and regulatory activity in the twentieth century. Government programmes now represent an important share of national income. At the same time people have become more and more disenchanted with the American political process. Typically, only half the electors bother to vote in a presidential election to elect the most powerful man in the world. People have low expectations of their politicians. The party process in the United States has concentrated on raising ever bigger sums of money to maintain highly expensive commercial advertising campaigns, which seems to have distanced the politicians more and more from the reality of their electors and led to more distrust between the electorate and the elected.

The United States has shown that it is much easier keeping together a centralised state, or forging a more centralised country, where that country as a result can wield substantial influence in the world. The United States' success in the wars of the twentieth century and its ability to act as peace-keeper and policeman of the world's commerce have encouraged considerable loyalty to the United States and enthusiasm by new migrants to the country.

From its earliest days the United States was always based upon declarations of loyalty to itself. New arrivals in America were required to pledge to learn the English language, swear allegiance to the constitution and the flag and show a belief in American principles. It is much easier uniting a new country where people are volunteers than creating a new country out of a set of old ones where many people are reluctant.

It is difficult to sustain the argument, however, that the American federal system represented the best way of reconciling the wish to have local autonomy with the wish to have a sensible centre. The American Civil War is a great rift valley in American history. Before the Civil War, the accent was on preserving the powers and opportunities of the individual states. After the Civil War, there was a relentless but inevitable drive to more and more centralisation. The Civil War broke out over this very issue of whether the states should be self-governing or whether they had to come under common federal standards. The easygoing latitude of the first confederation had given way to a federal constitution which was continuously marching in the direction of more power for Washington. In a series of epoch-making Supreme Court judgments in the first half of the nineteenth century, the powers of the states were gradually eroded. It was merely a matter of time before the fundamental disagreements between the North and the South over how Americans should live would boil over into a conflagration. This would not be a good model for the new Europe, where the potential tension between states is considerable.

It is difficult to create stability between a federal power and fairly autonomous states beneath that federal power. With the exception of Switzerland, no country has succeeded in creating such a stability. In the case of the United States, centralising has been the trend in the twentieth century. Most of the passions have gone out of movements towards secession. In the nineteenth century, folk memories of the independent states were still strong and there were explosive issues that divided them until the Civil War completed the unification process. In the twentieth century, there have been many more things that have united the American people.

The only cloud on the horizon of a unified USA is the rapid development of a Spanish-speaking population in the states of Texas, New Mexico and Southern California. In the twenty-first century these fault lines may become important. The folk memory may go back to a time when these territories were acquired by war or purchase from Mexico. The Spanish speakers might feel that their separate culture and heritage have been overridden by the centre. For the time being, America is a centralised state where most are happy to swear allegiance to the flag and to accept government grudgingly from Washington.

Conversely, in countries introducing devolution to former centralised states there is a tendency for the pressure towards devolution to develop into something stronger. We see effective separatist movements in parts of Spain. Catalan nationalism looks back to a time when Catalonia was separately governed. It fosters a separate Catalonia and different Catalan attitudes. Once a country embarks upon a programme of devolution, it is difficult to stop sliding towards more independent states within states.

Language is a particularly divisive force in the life of countries. The failure to create a single common language is the most common cause of future disruption. The centralising tendencies of the United Kingdom were enforced through the English language replacing Welsh and Gaelic. The centralising tendencies of the Spanish monarchy were partially enforced through the adoption of Castilian as the main language of commerce and government. In the United States, unification was enforced through the adoption of English and the massacre of the indigenous peoples, the native Indians who spoke separate tribal languages. German and Italian unity has always been based upon linguistic groupings.

Religion too can be important. It was religion which pulled apart Pakistan from India; it is religion which separates North from South in Ireland and religion which split up the original Holy Roman Empire amongst the German peoples. It is easy to unite peoples where they speak the same language and worship the same gods. In modern terms they have a similar cultural inheritance. It is very difficult to unify a country with more than one language. It is quite difficult unifying a country with more than one religion and culture. It is proving almost impossible to unite peoples divided by both language and culture at the same time.

Architects of superstates should take a warning from history. They should understand the nature of federalism in Germany, in Switzerland, in the United States, in Spain and in the other countries that have adopted federal or devolved models. They should see that it is very rarely stable. It is either en route to proper unification under a central government or it is en route to a splitting of the kingdom through the powers of devolution becoming separatist in their inclination. Switzerland is the exception that proves the rule. Other federal systems are temporary resting places in a continuing struggle between smaller and larger units.

PART II

Labour's European Revolution

4 The Monarchy

The monarch has embodied Britishness and our constitutional position for many centuries. The Queen is both above politics and central to the conduct of Parliament. A typically British compromise has been arrived at. When other states turned to revolution and to republics, the United Kingdom remained a monarchy. We caricatured, savaged and pilloried the monarch, took away some of the monarch's wealth, limited the monarch's powers but decided that a monarch should remain as the figurehead of the country, as the ultimate arbitor if Parliament got into a mess. This robust constitutional settlement has been arrived at after many centuries of rows, arguments, parliamentary protests, the channelling of popular opinion, newspaper articles and even a civil war.

It is more difficult to see how a British constitutional monarch fits into a European superstate. Already our monarch has become a citizen of the European Union. At some point the EU will seek a ceremonial or a political head of state to whom our monarch will owe allegiance. The idea of monarchy in Britain will have been transformed into a kind of grand Lord Mayor in a much bigger country.

The monarch today carries out a number of important functions. The most important is to represent the United Kingdom abroad. It is the Queen and senior members of the royal family who travel and represent Britain without being associated with one particular view or another. The Queen is the figure of continuity. Prime ministers, governments and Members of Parliament will come or go but the monarch and her successors go on forever. It is the Queen who can act as hostess when important dignitaries from abroad come to visit. Foreign visitors are usually impressed by the monarchy and all its trappings. The state banquets at Buckingham Palace or Windsor Castle are important events: they are often treasured and remembered by our foreign visitors who talk about them when they return home.

The Queen has considerable experience and historical knowledge of the state of the world. She has built this up over many years as the result of regularly travelling and meeting a large number of foreign heads of state on their state visits. This expertise is made available to the government of the day. The monarch acts as the spokesperson for the country, putting forward the democratic view hammered out in Parliament and proposed by her government but being able to add to it the historical perspective that comes from the continuity she provides.

The second important function the monarch fulfils is to represent the country at home. There are a number of important ceremonies in the monarch's year. The Queen presides over Trooping the Colour and the Royal Maundy service, officially opens Parliament and reads the speech from the throne setting out the government's programme, lays a wreath at the Cenotaph to commemorate the war dead and is available for any other special events that punctuate the daily round. Any nation needs a focus and a figurehead. The Queen is a less contentious one to act on behalf of the whole nation than any democratic politician, however popular temporarily or however recently elected. People of all parties and of none can accept the monarch representing the nation on these solemn occasions.

The royal family in the twentieth century has also developed its public popular role within the United Kingdom. The royal family acts as the head of many charities and independent institutions. They highlight the work of good causes, of the public service and of successful companies. A whole series of royal visits puts people, families, institutions and companies in the news and rewards them for the service they offer or for the success they bring.

Recognition of success or service is strongly linked to the institution of the monarchy in Britain. A series of honours can be bestowed by the Queen or her representatives. Although many of these are done on the recommendation of the elected government of the day, they are all done in the name of the monarch and the more important ones are personally bestowed by the monarch.

The system of honours gains added lusture from the royal associations. Many people work long and hard in order to gain their right to an OBE, an MBE or a knighthood. The recent change of emphasis in the honours system towards rewarding those who have offered something more to the community than just doing their paid job well has given a further inducement to people to undertake charitable or public works for no financial reward. Part of the magic or the mystery of the system is founded on the long traditions of the monarchy and the monarchical trappings.

Why do people wish to receive such an honour? In part it is because they do want a good day out with their family at Buckingham Palace or some other royal palace. They wish to tell their friends and neighbours that they have been personally recognised by the monarch and have been entertained to the best in the land. The setting is important. The monarch speaks with the authority of hundreds of years of history behind her. She awards the honours to people in a historical setting which has seen many national and international dramas unfold. People have that sense of history, duty and tradition which is summed up in the personality and dignity of the monarchy.

The monarchy also has a judicious role to play in parliamentary constitutional government. Many commentators think it fortunate that for many years the monarch has not been called upon to exercise her ultimate power of deciding which leader of which minority party should be called to the Palace and asked to form a government. In most elections since the war a majority party has emerged in the House of Commons, leaving no choice to the monarch as to who should be asked to form an administration. Now that all major parties elect their leaders by a democratic ballot from within their own parties the monarch's choice is automatic.

In 1974, the February election produced a situation in Parliament where no party had the overall majority. The monarch's decision was taken for her by Parliament when the Conservative leader conceded defeat and announced the resignation of his party from government. The Queen then automatically invited the leader of the Labour Party to form an administration.

The position in that Parliament was quite evenly balanced, with 11,963,207 people having voted Conservative and only 11,654,726 having voted Labour. However, Labour had 301 seats whereas the Conservatives had only won 297 including the neutral Speaker. Given the Liberal Party's greater sympathies for Labour policies than for Conservative ones, given the fact that the Conservatives had clearly been defeated, losing seats in the general election, and given the decision of the leader of the Conservative Party, the monarch naturally turned to the Labour leader. She would have been placed in a more difficult position if Sir Edward Heath, the then Conservative prime minister, had refused to resign or if a challenge had emerged immediately within the Conservative Party which had produced a new leader who felt he might be able to carry the business of government forward. As it was, it showed that whilst the monarch has a reserve power to make a choice, ultimately the power rests with the parliamentarians, who are under some duty to sort out their own problems.

If at some future date a Parliament is elected where the position is less clear, then the monarch's residual power to invite someone to form an administration could be important. Any British monarch will understand that this is no longer a power enabling the monarch to choose his or her own preference of party where the electorate has produced a muddled result. The King or Queen has to act as a facilitator for the strongest person and the strongest grouping in Parliament to take the lead to form a coalition that can govern the country. Nor should anyone worry lest the monarch's power could be abused, were at any point in the future a monarch to emerge who wished to use this power to influence the direction of events. The power rests with Parliament to overturn any choice of the monarch's that is not to Parliament's liking. There is a strong constitutional convention which would always be observed that if a leader and a leading party loses a motion of no confidence in the House of Commons they automatically have to retire and allow someone else to take on the business of government or allow an election to take place to produce a Parliament with a clearer answer.

What then, people may ask, is the point of the monarch having this residual power at all? It is part of the nice balance of the British constitution. It is important that there is someone above politics to whom a prime minister can go to lay down the cares of office or to whom a victorious party leader can go to be visibly and ceremonially ensconced as prime minister and leader of the majority or the majority coalition in the House of Commons. In other countries such a role can be fulfilled by an elected president. Then of course the president can exercise considerably more power than an unelected monarch. In some countries, as in the new Russia, the elected president can make or break prime ministers according to his wishes for the conduct of his government. In Britain the head of state only makes or breaks governments when the British people have spoken or when Parliament has voted accordingly.

A little-seen and little-understood part of the monarch's role is to act as the sympathetic ear and the unseen councillor of prime ministers. This is particularly important where a monarch such as our present queen has long-standing experience of the business of state. The monarch does have access to state papers and is kept informed about the conduct of her government on a regular basis. The prime minister of the day traditionally has a weekly audience with the Queen to keep her up to date with matters of general importance. He can enlist her support and help in the conduct of foreign policy where the foreign policy needs the Queen to act as the mouthpiece of the whole nation and can sort out any issues relating to the conduct of the monarchy and the money needed to sustain it.

Prime ministers can have lonely lives. Whilst they never lack advisors and eager Members of Parliament wishing to serve in their administration, there must be times when a prime minister is grateful to be able to turn to someone above him and above politics who is there with a word of encouragement or caution and who will be completely discreet about anything he chooses to say.

There has recently been debate about whether it is any longer necessary for the Queen to drive to Parliament in a state coach and to read a speech from the throne at the start of every annual session setting out the government's programme. Everyone knows that the speech from the throne is written by the government. Everybody understands that the speech follows a convention, sketching the main state visits where the monarch has a role, making general comments about the conduct of foreign policy and then going on to list the important bills which are ready for introducion to either House of Parliament. People understand that the monarch has no power to vary what is going to be said in the speech from the throne and they know that the government of the day may choose to vary the programme in the Queen's speech as the year goes on.

Those against monarchy see an opportunity to reduce the presence of monarchy in a free Parliament. Many others see in the ceremony a way of bringing alive what would otherwise be a dry laundry list of measures of legislation that a government is proposing. It does mean that many more people turn on their televisions and watch what is happening because it is spectacle as well as high politics. It does mean that the government's legislative programme is heard in polite silence and comes across with authority. If a reforming government decided instead to announce the legislative programme in the form of a prime ministerial or leader of the House speech to the Commons, it would not carry the same weight and the opposition could not be guaranteed to observe a respectful silence. It would just be another day of combative politics in the House of Commons rather than an occasion when a whole nation hears what it has voted for and how the government intends to fulfil its pledges and promises.

The Queen is also the head of the Anglican Church. The masterful Elizabethan settlement of the second half of the sixteenth century has lasted to be graced by the second Elizabeth 400 years later. The terrible continental wars between Protestant and Catholic which characterised the sixteenth century were avoided and evaded by the Anglican settlement first developed under Henry VIII in the 1530s and then completed by his daughter Elizabeth I in the 1560s. The essence of the Anglican settlement was to leave a certain ambiguity about the most important doctrinal issue of the day, transubstantiation and the meaning of the communion rite, whilst endorsing Church and State working in tandem through the mechanism of the Queen in Parliament.

The Queen became the head of the Anglican Church. The leading bishops, episcopal princes in their own right, sat in the House of Lords to help debate the important matters, both temporal and spiritual, of the day. The monarch exerted influence through the patronage system, controlling the main appointments. The bishops exercised influence by being able to lead debate in the House of Lords and through the pulpits across the country. The arrangement worked remarkably well against the background of troubled times in continental Europe. There were Catholic plots, and the puritan element in the rebellion of the 1640s is an important part of the story behind the English Civil War. In comparison, however, with the continental Dutch and German wars, England got off very lightly as a result of the Henrician and Elizabethan settlement.

Many say that this is all now irrelevant some four hundred years later. There is absolutely no danger of a religious civil war in mainland Britain. The passion has gone out of the debates about how the Anglican litany should be organised and what role the Nonconformist and Catholic Churches should have in our society. Indeed, the problem now for the Anglican Church is keeping enough support from worshippers to maintain its position as the largest amongst many Churches rather than its former position as the only official and pre-eminent Church in the country.

Some within the Church and many without the Church say that keeping an Established Church is at best an irrelevance and at worst an abuse of a secular parliamentary democracy. Those of this view would like to see the bishops thrown out of the House of Lords, the Queen removed from her position as Head of the Church and the Anglican Church recreated as just another Church in England left to its own devices to recruit, support and raise money.

It is time to make out the case again for keeping the Anglican Church established. In some ways it is strange for a Conservative to do this. The Conservative governments between 1979 and 1997 faced a permanent opposition from many in the Anglican Church, including the bishops. The bishops were often active in the House of Lords leading the opposition to the detail or to their view of the general sentiment behind Conservative policy. The Anglican pulpit was often used by vicars and preachers to make out a case against what they thought were the uncaring personalities and policies being pursued by Conservative ministers. Many in the Conservative Party in their turn despaired of an Anglican Church which they felt no longer spoke to the many law-abiding Conservative voices in the country and was seeing its support dwindling much more rapidly than the Conservative cause itself.

Whilst I do not agree with many of the bishops' criticisms of Conservative policy in the 1980s I would defend their right to voice them. In a way it makes it easier for me as a Conservative to defend an established Church because I am not seen to be defending an organisation or institution which has been friendly towards my party's cause in recent years. As a democrat I welcome opposition. As a politician I reserve the right to deal with criticism and opposition strongly and to express my disagreement in debate.

The importance of keeping bishops in the House of Lords is that it acts as a signal and a reminder that there is a moral purpose to legislating and that legislation itself does have to be set in some kind of moral or religous framework. But, of course, heads of other Churches that can attract substantial support in the country have a case to make that they too should be represented in the House of Lords. It is easier to make the case for more religous representation in the House of Lords than to make the case for none at all.

The Prince of Wales has toyed with this problem. He has made it clear that he wishes to have strong links to the Jewish, Nonconformist and Catholic communities as well as to the Anglican. He has also been interested in non-Christian faiths that are represented in the United Kingdom. There is, however, a distinction to draw between welcoming pluralism and having a belief of one's own. British and English identity are still bound up with an Anglican Established Church as well as with toleration of other faiths. We do not wish to debar people from public office or contribution to the debate by reason of their faith. We can nonetheless be true to our ancestry by continuing the tradition of an established Church.

The monarch's special relationship with the Church of England is important in many civic and religious functions in the national calendar. The monarch is ceremonially crowned in a leading Anglican cathedral. The big events of national commemoration, remembrance, mourning and celebration take spiritual and televisual form through church services attended by the monarch as head of the Church and State. Parliament begins with prayers every day and in the Anglican service there is a special prayer to assist the work of the monarch, the royal family and all those in authority in the country.

This fabric of national and community life is important. Those who think Britannia needs to be cool can sneer at these inherited traditions. In so doing they quietly upset or disorient millions of people who have grown up with the Anglican liturgy, the supremacy of Parliament and the embodiment of national life in the office of the monarch.

One of the most poignant photographs in 1998 was the photograph of the Royal Yacht *Britannia*, stripped of the royal colours, being towed by a tug to her last place of mooring. The debate over the royal yacht personified much of the debate between modernisers and traditionalists. It was quite normal for the cost of the royal yacht to come up in annual discussions of public expenditure. The cost of maintaining and operating the royal yacht were borne by the defence department budget. The Royal Yacht *Britannia* was part of the Navy Royal. The crew were all navy personnel. With successive rounds of cuts forced upon reluctant defence secretaries, there was always the temptation to suggest that the Royal Yacht *Britannia* should be pensioned off to shift these expenditures from the defence budget. It was never quite clear how all the savings could be made, given that the ratings involved were likely to be redeployed to other duties rather than being made redundant. It was true that some modest savings were on offer from not running the royal yacht, not victualling her or fuelling her fairly thirsty engines.

The argument also became involved with the question of whether the yacht needed a refit or not. It was quite true that the yacht was an aging lady: a good case could be made for modernising some her facilities. Some feared that the yacht needed more fundamental treatment. It was commonly thought in the defence department that the yacht needed completely new engines that were more fuel efficient. Others who knew the yacht told me that her engines had been overengineered and were still working extremely well. They felt the engines could have kept going for another five years without problems.

Traditionalists wanted to see the yacht continue. Modernisers who believed in the monarchy wished to see a replacement yacht purchased. Republicans saw an opportunity to remove one of the trappings of the monarchy, to continue the process of gradually chipping away the magic. Although the republicans were not in a majority, it was a fitting tribute to British debate that they eventually won through the exhaustion of the combatants on the other two sides.

A 50-year-old royal yacht is certainly not part of Cool Britannia. Cool Britannia would either have no royal yacht or have an entirely new vessel suited to the modern age. It was interesting seeing the designs that came forward when people were debating what new symbol of monarchy would be appropriate to the modern era. Some designed floating gin-palaces that represented scaled-up models of the kind of yacht that any flashy businessman would buy as a symbol of his success. One design was for an imaginative large sailing vessel – with the necessary engines should time or tide require – which could also be used as a naval training ship when it was not on royal duty. There were discussions as to whether it would be possible to raise private finance. Images were conjured up of royal yachts sponsored by large British companies with the sponsorship decked out over the funnels or hull. Attempts were made to put together financial packages on a time-share basis, with suggestions that the Queen should pay for any royal family holiday time, that the nation should pay for any royal family-led trade missions and official entertaining and that the rest of the time the yacht could be leased to the commercial sector.

Despite all these imaginative attempts to define a new type of yacht and a new type of financing for a new type of era, the end result was a decision to pension off *Britannia* without reaching any agreement on what type of ship could replace it or how the money could be found. The new Government decided it was much better to spend over £700 million on a millennium dome than to spend a tenth of that on a new royal yacht that could trade for the nation and represent Britain abroad. The Conservatives discovered that proposing a publicly financed royal yacht was not an especially popular announcement.

So it was that in April 1998 the Royal Yacht *Britannia* was towed to what may be her last resting place. The press delighted in pointing out that it was a German tug that had been chartered to perform this historic mission. *Britannia* looked neglected, old and sad. The personal effects and trappings had been removed so that the public could only gaze on a hulk and a shell of the former glorious royal vessel.

The photograph of the *Britannia* being towed away was soon replaced in the public mind by a photograph for the new cool Blair era. The Queen was seen stepping into a taxi owned by the Duke of Edinburgh which had recently been converted to run on natural gas. Here was the transport of the future, here was the people's monarch stepping into the people's taxi and using a green and friendly fuel. It was a curious mixture of images. There was the liveried royal chauffeur, there was the old model taxi dressed up to look modern and there under the bonnet was the symbol of energy-conscious novelty. The monarch and the monarchy adapts subtly to the spirit of the age and accepts guidance from the elected government of the day.

At its height of popularity in the immediate post-war period the monarchy was still resplendent. Large crowds would always turn out to see the King and then the Queen who replaced him after his untimely death. There was a great sense of national mourning when the King died prematurely. The sense of loss was heightened by the way in which both King and Queen had stayed in London during the Blitz and had been prominent in visiting the damaged buildings and the suffering victims after major attacks. The new Queen came to the throne as an embodiment of hope and of a new spirit. The new royal yacht was a symbol of Britain's seafaring past and glittering global future. A new Elizabethan age was born. Could it rival the glories of Shakespeare, of Nicholas Hilliard the miniaturist, of the poetry of Spenser, the seafaring successes of the Elizabethan adventurers and the daring of the Elizabethan entrepreneurs?

A monarchy could be judged on how it travelled. Pride of place was given to voyages by sea and to entertaining foreign dignitaries on board HMS *Britannia*. At home there was the royal train and for state occasions the state coaches drawn by magnificently well groomed horses. The Queen was renowned for her love of horses and her skill in handling them. The Duke of Edinburgh took a personal delight in driving coaches and carts around the estates. For other occasions there are always the large black British-manufactured limousines.

So, at the turn of the second half of the twentieth century, the monarchy was established, assured and popular and travelled both by the very modern, the royal trains and yacht, and by the very ancient, the state coaches and landaus. By the end of the twentieth century there was a new hesitation about whether there should be this great distinction between the way the monarch travelled and the way everybody else travelled. Stories appeared in newspapers that the Queen was prepared to travel in Concorde with other passengers on the plane. Stories appeared of first-class rail carriage journeys without the full panoply of the royal train. Then there was the demonstration of the royal taxi.

It is difficult to tell how well meant much of the Blairite agenda for the monarchy is. It is undoubtedly the case that many in the Labour movement harbour long-standing republican ambitions or nurture long-standing egalitarian chips on their shoulders. Many of them were brought up on a politics of class antagonism. They see the royal household as the top of a social pyramid based upon inheritance, privilege and easy access to money. To them the trappings of monarchy are part of the problem rather than a symbol of national identity. Mr Blair and his colleagues protest their good intentions towards the monarchy. They claim that they want a modern monarchy rather than no monarchy. They are in danger of giving too much ground to their republican allies and seeing their own intentions, even if they are honourable, swept aside by unleashing emotions and forces they cannot control.

The conundrum for Mr Blair, as a 'touchy-feely' politician, is what to do about the undoubted emotions in national life that are personified and whipped up by members of the royal family. The Queen herself best embodies loyalty, duty, respectability, responsibility, but she can also capture the mood of the nation in sorrow or in joy. Her coronation captured the spirit of hope about the post-war period. It came at the same time as rationing was being abandoned and luxuries were re-emerging in shops, the bomb sites were being cleared and the new Britain was being constructed. When she spoke of her *annus horribilis*, she captured a darker moment in the nation's soul where many others had their own private reasons to feel upset, sorry or depressed. No discussion of the monarchy's emotional impact can begin or end without a glimpse at the extraordinary events that followed the death of Princess Diana.

The marriage of Prince Charles to Princess Diana had been billed as the fairytale romance. The public had believed in it, had wanted to believe in it and wished it well. There was a palpable sense of relief that the prince had chosen an attractive English girl from a good family with no known skeletons in her cupboard. The public witnessed the transformation of a nursery-school teacher who was a little camera-shy and unsure into a star of stage and screen. As the marriage hit rocky times and as stories were leaked from the two camps about who was to blame and what had gone wrong, the nation split sharply in its affections and sentiments. Whilst it is probable that many more sided with the princess than with the prince, the princess was someone who split opinions and encouraged people to come to a judgement by the brilliance of her continuous, relentless presence in the news media.

The press was beginning to write more hostile stories about her at the time when she died. They were beginning to detect a further unhappy twist to the story as the princess's affections took her elsewhere from the royal household. Her untimely death changed all that immediately. The media was quick to sense the importance of the event to the public mood and quick to sense the enormous public sympathy for the princess that her death in an underpass in a Mercedes in Paris was bound to create.

On the Sunday immediately following her death, all normal television was brought to a halt to provide endless coverage of the few short events leading up to her death, eyewitness accounts, accounts from people who would have like to have been eyewitnesses, experts commenting on the safety or otherwise of the Mercedes car, the likely condition of the driver's mind and health and the possible causes of the accident. The television had read the public mood right. People wanted to go over and over the events in their own minds and did want to talk endlessly about them. There was an immediate sense of national loss. Those who felt otherwise were well advised to keep their thoughts to themselves given the surge of public sentiment.

The Palace and the Government were soon swamped with demands from the public to do something to commemorate the life and mourn the death of the People's Princess. Long queues formed outside Harrods and outside every royal palace. Huge bundles of flowers were brought and left at railings or by the roadside. In every town and village an informal shrine was established where people could go and pay their last respects and leave their offerings. Bottles of champagne, teddy bears, hearts, cards and drawings by children were all piled up alongside the flowers with their overwhelmingly powerful scent. Commemoration books spawned long queues and irritation of people at the shortage of pages and books to sign. On the day of the funeral itself the whole nation was brought to a stop, as everyone had their private thoughts and paid their tribute in their own way.

The Government, through Mr Blair, understood that there was this very strong feeling. Whilst responding well at the time, it then went on to attempt to channel or use the feeling to say that it proved that people wanted a different kind of monarchy. The press pilloried the Queen and the royal family for regarding it as a matter of private grief. They then praised the Queen and the other members of the royal family when they went on television and appeared in public to try to say something about how they too felt about the loss. The Government implied that the princess showed how a modern monarchy should work. Her life was used as a kind of criticism of the life of others.

Traditional monarchists felt that this was unfair. Whilst many of them mourned the death of Diana and the loss of a mother to the two royal sons, they also felt that the important charity work and sporting work of the Princess Royal, the work of the Queen herself representing Britain at home and abroad and the work of the Prince of Wales through The Prince's Trust and the endless rounds of meetings and visits should not go unnoticed or be criticised by implication or contrast. What exactly was Mr Blair saying about the other members of the royal family through his insistence that the family had to learn from the death of the Princess? How exactly did he want the royal family to change? The Princess of Wales had learnt much of her skill of handling the media, representing charities and campaigning for causes from other members of the royal family and the royal household.

It was difficult to represent the reaction to the death of the Princess of Wales as evidence that the country wished to move in a republican direction. Lady Diana had only come to public prominence because of her marriage. She had only been able to do all the charitable work she did through the publicity and the platform which becoming a royal princess had afforded her. She had shown how these assets could be used for good purposes. She did not of herself represent a case against any kind of monarchy at all.

The monarchy is still big box office and is still important in the national debate. Some see it as a kind of grand, free soap opera presented for the nation on behalf of the nation. Some try to belittle the role of the monarch in politics or in public life. Yet so much of the nation remains fascinated by stories of and about the monarchy, a fascination which reached an intense height in the life and the death of the princess. If anyone is prepared to criticise or to comment on the institution or the personalities of the royal household they are guaranteed massive publicity.

In May 1998, a royal chaplain decided to present the case for an elected monarch or some other form of new monarchy. He made a speech explaining why he thought the hereditary principle was wrong and why it could produce unwelcome, unwanted or ineffective monarchs. Because he was a royal chaplain, and because of the great public interest in his subject, he was on chat shows, news programmes and in the newspapers. No one had heard of Canon Eric James before his speech of May 1998. His fame may fade as quickly as it arose. He has no history of being a constitutional expert, a royal commentator or a well known public figure. Because of the subject matter, because he was prepared to give voice to arguments and sentiments that the press wishes to see debated but the political establishment does not wish to debate, he was there prominently displayed in all of the media.

It is a sign that the monarchy still has a strong hold on the affections or on the traditions of the United Kingdom that no mainstream elected politician will give voice to a case for the abolition of the monarchy. Whilst we know that there are republicans on the Labour benches who from time to time betray their true sentiments by saying something negative or carping about a royal action or a royal personality, none of them are prepared to come out in the open and argue the case for doing away with the institution they secretly dislike. Some in the media think it would be good sport to have a proper public debate about whether the monarchy should continue in any form at all. A Queen's chaplain will be used if he is the best on offer.

The same power of the monarchy to arouse passions could be seen when a little-known academic wrote a book commenting on the public reactions to the death of the Princess of Wales. Because he was prepared to say after her death some of the negative things about her personality that the media were commonly describing before her death, he was immediately pilloried in the public press and on radio and television by fashionable chat show performers for being insensitive. He was accused of misunderstanding the love affair between the public and its dead princess.

Those who seek change or abolition do have to answer the question, what change is desirable or what should be put in place of the monarchy? We have to ask this question about each of the monarch's roles. If there were no monarch there would still need to be a head of state. There does need to be someone who can represent the country abroad and who can preside as the host or hostess over great state occasions when foreign dignitaries visit. Of course it would be possible to say the elected Prime Minister of the day should take on these duties. At the moment, the Prime Minister undertakes certain diplomatic tours abroad and the Queen other state visits. It would mean some shift in the balance of work between domestic and international matters and that the Prime Minister would have to give up more of his time for ceremonial and national functions and would have less time for executive matters.

We would lose something in our international diplomacy. We would lose the magic of monarchy and we would lose the continuity which we gain when a well established monarch is on the throne and has a carefully built-up series of friendships and relationships over several decades. There would certainly be difficulties reconciling some of the state occasions with the parliamentary timetable. In circumstances where a Prime Minister has a narrow majority in the House of Commons, he would have to come back and vote during the course of an evening even if there were a state banquet taking place. At the moment it is possible to finesse this with foreign visitors as the Queen and other members of the royal family are present as the principal hostess and hosts for the occasion. The Prime Minister can slip out to do his duty. It would be more difficult if he were the host.

There is then the question of who would represent the country at home. Who would be head of the honours system, who would perform the necessary functions? It would be possible for the Prime Minister to do these things for himself. He could open more new office buildings, more stations, more new bridges. He could undertake more regional tours within the United Kingdom. He could perform the knighthood ceremonies himself. But again it is another set of functions which would interrupt his attention to the detail of running the country and would create more potential conflict between the Prime Minister as the political leader and the Prime Minister as head of state. The buffer has gone. In the company world, the analogy is between the non-executive chairman and the chief executive. It is now thought to be good practice in larger British companies to split the roles. The chairman is there to handle the shareholders, to represent the company at home and abroad and to keep an eye on the chief executive's conduct. The chief executive is there to run the business day to day. The two roles can be combined but it does concentrate an awful lot of power into one pair of hands and it does make the life of that person particularly arduous and complex to arrange. Not everyone would want to receive an honour from a party leader.

Who would carry out the sovereign's role of convening a parliament and appointing a Prime Minister? This role could pass to the Speaker of the House of Commons. The Speaker is widely regarded as neutral and would be under a duty to make sure that the prime minister appointed was leader of the party that could control the majority. This important role would of course place particular tensions on the neutrality of the Speaker, as all Speakers have formerly been party politicians and were originally elected to Parliament as partisans.

The role as head of the Church could pass to the Archbishop of Canterbury in conjunction with the disestablishment of the Church. The role of the patron of various charities could be passed to other public figures, especially to life peers who could be appointed if they took on some such role.

Doing without a head of state, however, would not be easy. Substantial extra work would fall on the Prime Minister, making his or her task doubly difficult. It is more likely that abolitionists will campaign for a different type of head of state. A head of state could either be elected or selected. Some believe it would be possible to have an elected head of state who had little or no power and therefore made little difference to the current constitutional balance. It is difficult to envisage how this would happen. In most states where the president is elected he wields considerably more power than the prime minister. The elected president of France makes or breaks prime ministers and directs much public policy. The elected president of the United States of America controls the executive and is the head of the armed forces. The elected president of Russia is very much the most senior politician in the country as well as the head of state.

It would be quite tempting for any elected president in the United Kingdom to wish to influence or affect the conduct of political debate. If the president is elected at a different time from the government, it would be quite possible to have a president elected of a different political persuasion to that of the government of the day and for there to be inevitable conflicts and tensions. The presidential office could be used in subtle ways, even if it did not have direct political power, to undermine, criticise or expose the government. It would not have been easy for a Conservative government to serve under Neil Kinnock as elected head of state. I am not sure Mr Blair would enjoy serving under Margaret Thatcher as an elected head of state. Nor could such figures bring together the nation in the way the monarch can. Given that any likely candidate for presidential office would have had a long and distinguished career in politics before they were allowed to run, they would probably have created many enemies as well as friends.

Practically all senior politicians in Britain are strongly linked with a particular political party. In recent decades no political party has been able to speak for more than 50 per cent of the electorate in a popular election. This means that any elected president would be elected by only around half of the country and would come from a party which could not even command majority support. This would make it particularly difficult for the president to speak for the whole nation and to represent the whole nation at times of national crisis or celebration. People's attitudes towards the head of state would naturally be coloured by their attitudes towards the party from which that head of state had come and by any actions the head of state had carried out in a previous executive political capacity.

Some say that some system of selection should be designed. Who should be the selectorate or electoral college that would choose the successful person? If the power were vested in the government of the day at the time when there was a vacancy, then there would be ensuing difficulties if and when the complexion of the government changed. If a committee or gathering of specified great and good people were to make the selection, it is quite likely that the public mood would react strongly against their choice, as there would be resentment about the nature of the process and ultimately about the person who had been chosen.

Some in the media played around with who might win an election should we opt for the elected model. Curiously enough some existing members of the royal family command strong support in opinion polls when asked. There would be a chance that if a government went over to an elected monarch the Queen herself or her successor might secure her or his own election. Whilst this would bring into doubt the wisdom of putting the monarchy up for election in the first place, it also begs the question of why the existing monarchy should wish to go through such a process. The whole nature of this monarchy is to be above the political process, not to have to seek votes, not to have to set out party programmes and not to have to canvass actively in a way a party politician does. Much of this magic would be lost and the existing members of the royal family might well decide that they have no wish to enter such a lottery or contest when all that could happen was that some of their mystery could be shed and some of their ability to pull together the country could be dissipated, assuming the election was contested.

An elected monarch would clearly seek more power than the current monarchy wishes or enjoys. The present monarch is in some senses head of our armed services. Would an elected monarch wish to take this duty more seriously and be Commander-in-Chief rather than titular Colonel of various regiments? An elected president would have a far bigger popular mandate than any other politician in the country, including the newly elected Mayor of London. It would be very tempting for anyone who had been through the ordeal of securing such an election victory to wish to turn this popular mandate into something more than the right to appear at national ceremonies and to say things that bring the nation together from time to time. An elected monarch is far more likely to arouse the jealousy of an elected prime minister than a hereditary one.

As always with constitutional reform, it is easier for the critics of the present arrangements to find fault with what exists than to find a better way of doing things. Labour's wish to modernise the monarchy is in danger of belittling it. They are unleashing republican sentiments without thinking through what that means for Church and State, army and honours, the convening of Parliaments and the respresentation of Britain at home and abroad. Whilst for the time being, in some form or another, Mr Blair says the hereditary principle is safe for the head of state, he is busily undermining it in the House of Lords. It is to there that we must now turn. Can you keep a hereditary monarch if you abolish the hereditary peers and remove the Established Church? Labour's approach to modernising seems to be a series of salami cuts into our inherited ways.

5   House of Lords Reform

'No bishop, No King', thundered the defenders of the established order in the seventeenth-century constitutional struggle. Today some wonder if it's now a case of 'No peer, No Queen'. The peers of inheritance, the oldest powerful families of the land, are threatened with the loss of their parliamentary votes and rights. The Government is encouraging a feeling that the time has come for them to depart, to follow the path of their great homes and houses to become tourist attractions or to be put to new more democratic uses.

The present powers of the House of Lords were established in the 1911 Parliament Act. Lloyd George, a radical Liberal Chancellor of the Exchequer under Prime Minister Asquith, introduced a budget which included a graduated income tax and a tax on land values in 1909. The Lords rejected it. It precipitated the general elections of 1910 and a new settlement which prevented the House of Lords interfering with the wishes of the Commons on matters financial.

The House of Lords settlement was a typically British answer to a typically British crisis. Whether a constitution is largely unwritten, or where it is written down in a hotchpotch of acts of parliament and statements of precedent and practice, or where it is recorded in one formal document, it is always possible for one element in the constitutional balance to overreach itself. Their Lordships decided to take on a radical and reforming Liberal government when they had misjudged the mood of the public. For many years the elected chamber, the House of Commons, had been growing in stature and power. For many years there had been no real challenge to its ultimate authority. The crisis of 1909–11 required a Prime Minister to threaten the creation of enough new peers to see through the business. The passage of a Parliament Act codified in law a new balance of powers.

The remarkable thing about the 1911 settlement was its far-sighted solution to the problems in the first decade of the twentieth century. It ushered in a settlement in the House of Lords which survived for virtually the whole of the twentieth century. The 1911 Act rested on three principal corner-stones. Firstly, the House of Commons would be supreme in matters financial. It was accepted that elections were often about the issue of how much tax could be taken out of people's pockets and that only those directly responsive to the electorate should settle the taxation charges of businesses and individuals. The second principle was that the House of Lords should not seek to block in perpetuity a measure that was fundamental to the programme of the elected government of the day. This became refined in practice to giving the House of Lords a delaying power which they were unwilling to use over items clearly stated in the manifesto of a new government. The third element in the settlement was to confirm the prime ministerial right to appoint additional peers to influence or change the balance of the House of Lords in the event of difficulties. This reserve power has always been present through the Prime Minister's right to advise the monarch on the creation of new titles.

The House of Lords still contains hereditary peers and life peers created by the present or recent administrations. The system has only once fallen into great disrepute, under Lloyd George as Prime Minister. During his period of office between 1917 and 1921, four marquises, eight earldoms, 22 viscounts and 64 barons were created. There was a great fuss at the time about the sale of honours, as many thought that the Prime Minister had stumbled on an easy way of raising money for his party by offering the promise of ennoblement to those who were loosest with the cheque book. In 1923, after the Lloyd George era, there were 708 lay peers. Of these,198 had titles created in Queen Victoria's reign, 46 in Edward VII's reign and 176 under the then King George V.

In the second half of the twentieth century, life peers have been created, an important constitutional innovation. In recent years the idea of creating hereditary peerages has lapsed, but it has not technically been abolished. Today there are 1310 members of the House of Lords: 784 hereditary peers and 526 life peers.

The new Labour Government has decided that this well tried and tested settlement is no longer up to the challenges of the modern, media-driven, New Labour world. They have discovered that opposing the idea of hereditary peers sitting in the House of Lords is a popular cause in their party which combines the wishes of both the traditional Left-wing Labour MPs and the modernisers. The Left wing have always disliked the idea of inherited property and titles. They have always resented the thought that some power and influence in our society is wielded by those who have inherited position rather than striven for it themselves in the first instance.

The modernisers see in the hereditary peerage an easy target. They come to the problem from the position of wanting to create and develop an elected dictatorship controlled by a small handful of men at the top of the Labour Party machine. The House of Lords has the ability to inflict defeats upon the Labour Government's programme. It has the capacity for people to make speeches critical of the Labour Government's intentions. The House of Lords is a more reflective chamber than the House of Commons and often gives rise to speeches and debates which look forward to the future and are quizzical about the prevailing ethos or the trend of government policy. None of these sit comfortably with the Labour modernisers' belief that the Government is always right, that the important thing is to get its message out through all channels and outlets and that Parliament has to be part of that message-giving machine.

In Labour demonology it is now accepted that the defeats inflicted upon this Government in the House of Lords have emanated from the presence of hereditary peers, especially Conservative ones. The facts often defy this particular analysis. Firstly, in many cases the Labour Government has lost because its own recently ennobled supporters did not turn up to the divisions in order to back the Government. Indeed, there have been occasions when the opposition has been surprised to win the vote, expecting the Labour poll to be rather better than it has proved. Secondly, there have been occasions when Labour peers themselves have abstained deliberately because they disliked the Government's policy or even joined the opposition forces to vote against the Government. It was a cross-party coalition with cross-benchers in train that put through the so-called 'Murdoch amendment' to the Competition Bill at a time when the official Conservative opposition abstained on the measure. Thirdly, analysis of the division lobbies shows that it has rarely been the hereditary peers voting in large numbers who have swayed or determined the vote. The current balance of the House is such that more life peers vote normally than hereditary peers.

Labour spin doctors argue that the whole hereditary principle is now old-fashioned. Indeed, recently a Labour MP challenged me with the greeting 'not even you could make out a case in favour of hereditary principle'. Labour should beware lest their old and new-found belief in the importance of individual effort rather than inheritance extends too far. There has certainly been no attempt when modernising the Labour Party to change more policies against the inherited principle.

The official Labour line supports the principle of inheritance when it comes to the monarchy. Similarly, one assumes that they support the inheritance of the Duchy of Cornwall, the Princedom of Wales and the other royal titles. They do seem clear that the monarch would still be required to open Parliament and to read the speech from the Crown, although perhaps with less circumstance and pomp and on a less regular basis than we have been used to.

More fundamentally, Labour clearly support the hereditary principle when it comes to most of the rest of us. There are no statements in the Labour manifesto that the inheritance of property, shares, land, buildings or businesses is against the public interest or should be stopped. Labour went to considerable pains to disabuse the public of the notion that much more penal taxation might be introduced to prevent the passage of a farm or small business from generation to generation. It would not be an attractive political programme to put before the British people that the family home should have to be sold and the money given to the State or that the family business should await a similar fate.

Of course there have been arguments in the twentieth century over the level of property and the amount of cash that should be allowed to pass from generation to generation, and the extent to which the State should be able to take a proportion of it. Most Labour spokesmen have fallen short of demanding confiscation and this New Labour Government has been keen to establish the idea in people's minds that the inheritance of a small family business or farm is a perfectly reasonable way of proceeding. It is contradictory to seek a strong family policy, as the Government claims it does, if family property is to be subject to substantial government fiscal attack on the passage from one generation to the next.

If Labour wishes to establish the case for reform in the House of Lords, it has to do better than to say that titles are unsuitable for passage from generation to generation when they accept that many other forms of property should reasonably pass from generation to generation. When they say that it is old-fashioned and absurd for a title to pass, they are implying in their argument that choice of legislators or choice of those who can check the executive should be done on a basis other than genes and inheritance.

It is quite true that sometimes an inheriting son or daughter can lack the charm, wit, insight and judgement of the father or mother from whom the title or property has passed. It is quite true that nature can throw up difficulties. A family business might pass to a feckless generation, in which case the money will be wasted and the business collapse. It is theoretically possible for someone to inherit a peerage but not to be seriously interested in the business of legislating. It is difficult, however, to see how such an inheritance can wreck the House of Lords. The most likely outcome of a hereditary peer inheriting a title when he has no serious interest in legislating is that he will not exercise his right. He will attend the House of Lords infrequently, if at all, and will not vote on matters of public interest. If by any chance someone who inherited a title wished to disrupt the legislature by banalities, pranks or jokes of a kind unsuited to their Lordships' house, he or she would soon be dealt with. There is no evidence in history of one or more hereditary peers inheriting titles and then doing damage to the legislative process as a result of their position in the upper chamber.

What inheritance does do is change the balance of the House of Lords. Rarely are people given life peerages under the age of 40 and infrequently under the age of 50. It is an accepted convention on both sides that life peerages are drawn from those who have achieved things in the world of business, trade unions, the arts, culture, education and public service. Permanent Secretaries have to retire from their jobs before being eligible to join the House of Lords. Bishops have to achieve senior bishoprics before they become ex officio members of the House. Trade union leaders and senior businessmen are usually in their fifties or older. The House of Lords also forms an agreeable retirement club for some members of the lower House who have achieved high office whilst there. Most former Cabinet ministers can enter the House of Lords if they wish. Most of those tend to be in their late fifties or older.

It is, paradoxically, the hereditary principle that brings some younger members into the House of Lords through the lottery of life. Those younger members are often required to perform the more junior tasks. Former Cabinet ministers, trade union leaders and senior businessmen are not too keen to become junior whips or junior spokesmen for the opposition in the House of Lords. Some are even reluctant to become junior ministers and would not enjoy whipping on the Government side either. In order to get the job done, in order to ensure that the daily work of the House succeeds, it is necessary to have some people prepared to do these jobs.

Before trying to reform the House of Lords the Government should ask itself why it wishes to reform the House and what it is seeking to achieve. In 1911 the purpose of reforming the House was very clear. The will of the lower House had been thwarted on a most important issue. The verdict of the people had been given supporting the elected House. There was a climate for change and a clear purpose in the change to limit the power of the Lords to disrupt the government of the day. There is no such cause at the moment. Whilst the Government may lose one or two votes a week in the House of Lords through carelessness, failure to organise its own supporters or an insouciance over the arguments, none of the defeats are lethal to the Government's programme. The Lords can not defeat taxation and the central budget judgements and has avoided defeating the principles of the manifesto legislation. The second-order defeats inflicted on the Government lead either to a change of plan and better legislation or to a reassertion of the original idea when the legislation returns to the House of Commons. The Lords is carrying out its duty of questioning, revising and probing the detail but not getting in the way of the main thrust of the Government's strategy.

If the Government wishes to create a House of Lords which defeats it even less often than the present House it could do so quite easily. The neatest way of winning more votes would be to whip its own supporters more energetically, as it has already created a substantial number of peers who should be enough to carry most business most of the time. If the

Government is still unhappy with the balance of the House, it is in the power of the Prime Minister to recommend to the sovereign that more Labour peers be created. None of this of itself requires the removal of the vote from the hereditary peerage.

In order to justify this removal the Government has to establish in the public mind why it is better that the Lords' power should be exercised by favourites of the existing Prime Minister than by the sons and daughters of the favourites of previous Prime Ministers, Kings and Queens. There is greater opportunity for independence amongst those who inherit their title than amongst those to whom the title is given by the present incumbent at Downing Street.

The Conservative opposition has set out a series of principles which should be embodied in any reform which this or any future government might undertake of Parliament as a whole. You cannot reform the House of Lords without considering its impact upon the House of Commons. If the power of the Lords is reduced then clearly that of the Commons is increased or vice versa. The opposition does not believe that the Prime Minister's current powers of patronage should be increased. It is healthy to have some people in the House of Lords who are not beholden to the Prime Minister of the day for their position. If the make-up of the House of Lords is to be changed, it has to be different from that of the Commons to ensure that the Commons still has primacy. There should be an independent element in the House of Lords, in order to influence the House in the direction of providing some independent judgement concerning the government. The House of Lords should maintain membership from the whole of the United Kingdom despite the devolution of certain functions to a Scottish Parliament and a Welsh Assembly. It must continue to speak for the nation as a whole. Any reform plan must demonstrate that the reformed House will operate as a scrutinising and revising chamber better than the present one.

Many people with an independent mind as well of conservative disposition think these principles entirely sensible. There is a need, given the weight of legislation going through Parliament, for the House of Lords to provide some independent and detailed scrutiny of the measures. The Commons is not always willing or able to deal with all the detail. The Commons is best at the set-piece debates over the big manifesto pledges, over the clash of principles, and over the day-by-day scrutiny of the way in which the executive goes about its business. Whilst many Commons bills committees also do good work on the detailed legislation, this can be well backed up or sharpened by work on the floor of the House of Lords and in Lords committee, where some of the political pressures are less acute and where the informed official or backbench spokesmen may bring a special expertise to bear on the problems.

The current prime ministerial view is that the hereditary peers in the House of Lords should lose their vote and be replaced by nominated peers chosen by the Prime Minister. As a negotiating gambit, the Prime Minister has also suggested that for a transitional period some of the existing hereditary peers might be converted into life peers so that they could carry on their present active work in the House of Lords.

Such a plan would give considerably more power to Downing Street. It would remove an important independent element in the House of Lords. The House of Lords would come to replicate the party struggle in the Commons with no one willing to nominate or speak out for cross-benchers when every party was seeking to maximise its own voting strength in a more heavily politicised upper chamber. Such a chamber would have less power and influence than the present House of Lords. People would be more suspicious of a chamber where the majority lay always with the Prime Minister's men and women and where the independent element had been squeezed out. There would be much more emphasis on getting the business done and much less emphasis on scrutinising it in the interests of better legislation.

Some favour more ex officio members of the House of Lords to remove some of the powers of prime ministerial patronage inherent in the preferred scheme of reform. At the moment, senior bishops are ex officio members of the House of Lords, appointed when they gain their bishopric. This model could be used for other leading personalities from other walks of life. Whilst it is usually the case that a Cabinet secretary on retirement enters the House of Lords, it would be possible to nominate certain office-holders who hold public office for automatic membership to the House of Lords for a limited period. Whilst it is already the case that chairmen of the largest and most prestigious British companies stand a reasonable chance of getting into the House of Lords, it would be possible to have a formula which enabled them to do so automatically. The size of their companies could be determined by stock market valuations or level of profitability or number of employees, and a fixed term specified for their membership. Similarly, general secretaries or presidents of the leading trade unions could automatically qualify.

The big problem with such a scheme is that it is inviting people to be legislators in the upper chamber at exactly the point in their life when they are at their busiest and most successful. The President of the Chartered Accountants has an extremely busy term of office as the leading chartered accountant. He also usually has to keep his livelihood going in the practice from which he comes. It would be almost impossible for such a person to take a serious interest in proceedings in the House of Lords at the same time as heading his profession and keeping his job going. It would not be easy for the chairmen of the leading companies struggling to keep their share prices and profits up to spend enough time in the House of Lords to do the job justice.

If, instead, the Civil Service precedent were adopted of giving the House of Lords job to an immediate past president of a professional body or the immediate past chairman of an important business, then the obstacle of lack of time is in part overcome. However, part of the purpose then of the ex-officio nature of the post is lost. The person during his term in the Lords is no longer in the senior position which gained him the entitlement in the first place. In this respect it is unlike the bench of Bishops, who do have enough time both to run their diocese and to be in the House of Lords as legislators, should they choose to do so. They are not having to do a third job, as is the head of a professional institute, and are not under the same daily market pressures as is a senior businessman. The longer the person has been out of office, the less directly relevant experience he has to bring to bear on the task of legislating.

The ex officio post will also have the same drawback that is alleged against the hereditary peerage. Whilst some former chairmen of big companies may make ideal legislators and be very interested and privileged to enjoy such a role, others would have no interest at all. They might well enjoy being called Lord so-and-so but would rarely, if ever, turn up and would not wish to spend hours and days in debate scrutinising and revising legislation at a very detailed level.

This system would have attractions compared with the Government's idea. It would give the Prime Minister less direct power of patronage, it might bring to bear more relevant experience to improve reviewing and scrutinising, and it might produce at least some members of the House of Lords who turned out to be active, energetic and very useful. It would not guarantee a landslide in favour of one party and may produce some independent cross-benchers to replace or supplement those from the hereditary peerage.

It would be possible to build on the current appointment of life peerages but to include some limitation of the term or some performance element. There could certainly be an age of retirement from a life peerage, presumably higher than the normal age of retirement for full-time jobs but one which ensured most life peers had energy and enthusiasm for the task. It would be possible to say that in order to maintain a life peerage a life peer had to attend the House of Lords for a specified number of days in the year and/or participate in a specified number of divisions. The system of allowances could also be made more generous as an encouragement to life peers to be more active, with the allowance paid for specific duties carried out in committee and on the floor of the House.

This scheme would be an evolutionary development of the current practice. Prime Ministers do try to make up a list of working peers, as they are called. The intention is to ensure a pool of talent on both sides of the House of Lords capable of conducting their Lordships' business. It is not always successful, as some people who make promises to gain their working peerage then find that they are rather too busy once they have been given the title to fulfil the obligations. The aim of this reform would be to incorporate in a type of contract or statement of practice what those obligations entail, in return for the advantages of membership of the House of Lords.

It would also be possible to vary the current mix of the House of Lords by nomination based upon some other election. Just as the idea of ex officio members who were presidents of professional institutes is a scheme of indirect election, so it could be extended to politicians as well. People who had achieved a certain eminence in local government could ex officio sit in the House of Lords and bring their expertise of local administration to bear on the problems of the day. Certain mayors, leaders of councils or chairmen of the local authority bodies themselves could automatically be entitled to sit in the House of Lords for a fixed term or for the duration of their period of office. It would be possible to entitle some Members of the European Parliament to sit in the House of Lords to give Parliament the benefit of their advice from their European experience. Both these routes could bring in younger people than traditional life peerages, if the electorate had elected such people to their prime job. This again, like reforms to the appointment terms, could be an evolutionary way of improving the balance and the quality of debate in the House.

The disadvantage of this is that the people who are most senior in elected office in other bodies are also busy and very committed to those other bodies. They might not take the House of Lords as seriously as other parliamentarians might like and might not have enough time in their busy diaries to do the job well.

The two biggest possible reforms that some are discussing represent a more revolutionary approach to the problem. Either the second chamber could be directly elected itself or it could be abolished. Again, before making either such proposal the Government needs to think through what its purpose is in recommending reform of the upper chamber.

If the purpose of reform is to expedite Commons business, to ensure that the Commons majority does prevail and to avoid too many questions or cross-examinations of ministers in the upper House, the neatest solution from the Government's point of view is to abolish the upper chamber completely. This would be more honest than packing the House of Lords with enough placemen of the Prime Minister's choosing until the same point is reached. Why should the public have the cost of maintaining an upper chamber whose only purpose is to do the will of an elected Prime Minister? The will of the Prime Minister can be enforced and challenged in the Commons without having to go through the charade of putting all the proposals again to an upper chamber which has been carefully designed to offer no resistance.

The Queen could still come to open Parliament, the people could still be offered peerages as rewards for public service but there would no longer be an agenda and regular debates or any votes in the House of Lords. The Lords chamber could be used for great state occasions at the instigation of either sovereign or Prime Minister. The Conservative opposition would truly regret such a change, as we do believe there is a role for a revising second chamber capable of providing an additional check and balance over the elected majority in the Commons.

The alternative radical proposal is to have directly elected members of the upper chamber. This is the most common practice in other democratic legislatures around the world. Again, the Government has to decide whether it wishes to have more scrutiny or less scrutiny from its revised Lords chamber. If it wishes to have less scrutiny, it would be possible to do so by electing the upper chamber at the same time as the House of Commons. There would have to be some division of work different from the present one to make it worth while to stand for election to the upper chamber at all, but the conjunction of the two elections is likely to produce a similar party balance in both houses, meaning that on all occasions the Government has as much chance of pushing its measures through the Lords as through the Commons.

It would be difficult to see how government could easily handle a majority in both Houses from a popular election. It would certainly need to change the workload to give both Houses the feeling that their tasks were worth while. If nothing else changed apart from directly electing the House of Lords, the members of that House would be extremely frustrated at their lack of power for elected members. The Lords could rapidly come onto a collision course with the Commons not over the Government's programme, which both supported, but over their relative say and importance in proposing and developing that programme.

If the Government wished to impose a more effective check upon itself, the best way of doing so would be to have a directly elected second chamber where the elections took place at a different point in the electoral cycle from the elections to the Commons. In normal political times under most governments, this would be likely to produce a rather different balance of party forces in the upper chamber from that in the lower. In the United States of America it has been quite common, where the executive and the legislature are split, for the mid-term elections to the legislature to produce the opposite answer to the full-term elections to the presidency. The American electorate quite like the idea of a powerful president having to battle for his legislation with a Congress and Senate of a different political party. Even when the Republicans were thought to be very unpopular and doing badly under a very popular President Clinton, they nonetheless won and held the elections to the Congress, as the American people wanted a balance of power and of ideas.

In the United Kingdom, where the House of Commons has no fixed term, reform to work in this way might require a fixed term for the Commons as well as for the Lords. If a Prime Minister can influence the relative timing of Commons and Lords elections, then he can clearly overturn the theory that there should be a mid-term test of popularity where, if the electorate so decided, his government could then be subject to more scrutiny and control from a hostile second chamber. Any legislation would therefore need to specify fixed or minimum terms for both Commons and Lords to keep the timetable that a powerful Lords would require.

An elected Lords would change everything. A new Parliament Act would have to define the limitations of the powers of the two respective Houses of Parliament. A Lords under a different party control from the Commons under present practice could start to draft and debate its own bills. It could also vote down all of the government's bills. Without some restriction on the power of an elected Lords, or an elected Commons, elections at different times would produce legislative logjams of massive proportions. It is difficult to see why a newly elected Lords, with a different party balance to the Commons, would have less right to propose legislation or overturn legislation than a Commons elected two or three years earlier when the parties had very different popularity ratings. The most recently elected chamber would have the most reason to claim the popular mood and the popular mandate.

Similarly it would be difficult to see why an elected House of Lords should continue to restrain itself over money matters. People elected to the House of Lords would of course wish to have a view on the level and types of taxation and on State spending patterns. If they were not given this power expressly by the Act of Parliament creating a franchise for the Lords, they would soon be demanding it in rumbustious debates and arguments.

What functions should we expect our House of Lords in the twenty-first century to carry out assuming that this Government does continue with a second chamber of some description? In a way, the need for the House of Lords is greater rather than the less. As we enter the twenty-first century, a new constitutional settlement is being forced upon us by our signature on the European treaties and by the growing institutional changes coming from both above and below as Europe's and this Government's programmes unfold. There may well be the need for a kind of constitutional court or constitutional arbitrator in the United Kingdom as the number of democratic bodies and government quangos multiplies. The British Government is inventing a wholly new layer of government at regional level, including some elected assemblies and elected officials like the Mayor of London. European government has invented a European Parliament and a whole range of European quangos. The march of the British quango goes on apace with the development of powerful new agencies, half-European and half-British, to control areas like competition and food safety.

There will be many cases where there is a conflict of jurisdictions or where the system feels oppressed by the presence of so many executive and administrative agencies and arms of government. The House of Lords could develop a new competence as the senior constitutional arbiter in the United Kingdom, settling disputes in a quasi-judicial capacity between the competing powers of different branches of government both from Europe and at regional and local level in the United Kingdom. There is a growing feeling amongst many that we need a counterweight to the power of the European Court of Justice. The European Court presumes to interpret, clarify and codify the laws of Western Europe. The traditional role of the House of Lords as the High Court of Appeal could be metamorphosed into the supplementary role of the High Court of Appeal in the United Kingdom concerning the jurisdiction of courts both foreign and domestic and the interpretation of the law.

This would be building on something happening in British jurisdiction over recent years. Government is subject to legal challenge in many more areas. It is much more common now for companies and even rich individuals to consider challenging the jurisdiction of a department or a minister. This may be done through the domestic courts under the ultimate control of the House of Lords or through the European court system under the control of the European Court of Justice. It would be possible to fashion a new enhanced judicial role in the House of Lords which asserted the House of Lords' right to make the final decisions over our constitutional settlement, in the interpretation of the treaties in Britain and other matters and to offer redress to those who seek it.

There is also a need for more and more hours and energy to be given to scrutinising European negotiations and European legislation. Both the House of Commons and the House of Lords have scrutiny committees at the moment which attempt to go into the detail of the directives and regulations coming from Brussels. The present scrutiny process does, however, find it difficult to keep up with the volume of such measures and to be in good time to have any hope of influencing them. The House of Lords could carve out a niche for itself in organising regular debates and committees to discuss future negotiations that ministers will be attending on behalf of the United Kingdom, so that there is a real chance of influencing the minister who could hope to have an effect on the outcome of the Council of Ministers' discussion.

Government and the Commission could be required by the House of Lords to give as much information as possible in advance of Council of Ministers meetings about the agenda and the draft directives likely to be debated. The House of Lords could have the power to summons ministers before it to discuss in good time what course of action the British Government was recommending and to debate the tactics of how to influence other member states where Britain was unhappy with the draft proposal. The House of Lords could become a forum for setting out the best parts of the British case in a European context.

At its most superficial, modernising Britain seems to mean nothing more or less than changing the appearances of things, rather than the reality. Modernisers seem to object to the fancy-dress elements of British public life. The House of Lords is the personification of that alliance between authority and historic clothes that sums up so much of the continuity in British public life. Just as the Church has stuck to vestments that bear much in common with those of former ages, just as some councils have preserved seventeenth- or eighteenth-century dress to distinguish the councillors, just as regiments of the army have kept some of their old uniforms for ceremonial occasions, so the House of Lords has preserved the red carpets and the ermine that are in Britain the symbols of ultimate secular authority. It would be quite possible to sweep all this away without having any dramatic impact upon the reality of the British legislature. It would be less of a tourist attraction, less picturesque, maybe it would look more ordinary shorn of special clothes and special ceremonies. The modernisers, however, should be made to accept that if this is all they wished to do they would have achieved very little.

If at the heart of their objection to the House of Lords is merely an argument against the hereditary principle, then they had best beware in case radicals in their own movement take their opposition to the hereditary principle much further than they had originally envisaged. Take away the hereditary principle in its entirety and it is difficult to see how much of a family policy there is left. It is difficult to conclude that the objective of the Government is any more or less than making it easier for the Government to have its way. If this is the case, the simplest reform to undertake, albeit a contentious one, would be the abolition of the House of Lords as a legislature at all. It would be the most honest way of demonstrating to the public that this Government can brook no rival and cannot even bear a little scrutiny and revision from time to time.

If the real aim is to provide a serious check to the government, the best way of doing it is to have an elected second chamber. It could have a dramatic impact upon our constitution. It would require the separate election of the second chamber and the likelihood of the second chamber having a different political party in charge. It would have a more dramatic impact upon the process of government than in the United States. The presence of a different legislature from the President still leaves the President a great deal of executive action and quite a lot of charisma and political power to influence things in the direction he wishes. A split legislature with one chamber of the legislature in favour of the Prime Minister of the day and the other half not in favour could be a recipe for chaos. The second chamber would clearly want to gain an ever bigger foothold over the executive as well as trying to generate a completely different legislative programme from that which the executive has in mind.

The opposition is open to persuasion regarding evolutionary reforms which would make the workings of the House of Lords better. The House of Lords is not perfect. Some of its members have no serious interest in its work. Some of the life peers appointed to support the government or to oppose the government are notably absent for most of the time. To some it is a rather grand retirement club.

Yet when you look at its day-by-day work, at the detailed divisions which sometimes cause the government to think again, and the detailed amendments which sometimes lead to an improvement in legislation, it is clear that it does have a role. When you look at the explosion of quangos, new assemblies and European political power which is now being wielded, there is plenty more for the House of Lords to do. It could have an exciting future as a reinvigorated body putting to scrutiny and review the actions of a whole host of political and administrative actors and institutions.

The House of Lords is currently a way for senior businessmen or others of great experience in the outside world to get a fast route into ministerial office. Such promotions have not always been blessed with success, but there are many who believe that such a route is a necessary part of our governmental system. This Government thought that Sir David Simon, the then chairman of the British Petroleum Company and a leading advocate of European integration from the business community, would make an ideal minister. They promoted him to the House of Lords and gave him a minister of state job in the Department of Trade and Industry with some Treasury duties. His early introduction to political life was marred by his own confusions over whether he had to declare his shareholdings in BP and whether or not he should sell the shares. It served to remind the business community at large that the business of politics is rather different from the business of business and that different standards and considerations come into play when a businessman does become a public figure.

Nonetheless, many in the business community feel that government can be strengthened by allowing senior business people in rapidly to ministerial posts. If the House of Lords were to go, or if our constitutional settlement were to be changed in a radical way, this particular route of entry would be closed off. At the moment every major Department of State has a Lords minister as a two-way means of communication. It should keep the department in touch with its business in the House of Lords and it should keep the government in touch with the feelings in a second chamber more exposed to outside professional and business interests than the House of Commons. Whilst it is the duty of every member of the House of Commons to represent all of his constituents, to broker deals and to come to agreements across a wide range of opinion and life styles, there is no such duty incumbent on each Lord. It is permissible in the House of Lords for people to represent a sectional interest, as long as they have declared this. People are often best in the House of Lords because they speak up for a particular way of thinking or a particular group in the community. The House of Lords can embody the lobbying forces of the country just as the House of Commons has either to stand up to or to broker agreement between the lobbying groups that try to influence any particular problem.

In a south-eastern constituency in England, it would be unusual to find a Member of Parliament who wanted to voice the view of the housebuilding industry that more houses should be built in the south-east. The most enthusiastic free marketeer amongst Conservative MPs would immediately recognise the enormous strength of opinion in his constituency against any such policy, resulting in his giving a voice to the view of the constituency that there has to be some control. In the House of Lords, where opinion is not answerable in the same way to the public, it is more likely that someone can be found who can advocate the housebuilding industry's view that they can create jobs and provide homes if they were given more planning permissions in sensitive areas. This is a necessary part of the public debate. It is also important that the final decisions on the big issues are taken by those

Members who do have a duty to represent a wide range of interests including interests with which they personally disagree. The two different types of representation are prominently displayed in the two present chambers of Parliament.

In Britain an institution either adapts or dies. A company doesn't continue trading merely because it was set up several hundred years ago and was successful. It continues trading if its new generation of owners and managers are good at meeting the public need. They may be strengthened in this by the fact that their company has been in existence for hundreds of years. Their customers may find this reassuring. It may have given the company additional experience or expertise. It may mean that they have built up a big pattern book or have a big stock of machines or products out in the country which they can service to their profit. They still have day by day to prove that they are running a truly modern business building on the best of the past and drawing strength from their tradition. So it is with any part of our political constitution. Councils have waxed and waned in endless reforms of local government. My own Wokingham Town Council, which once administered the town, is now a mere Parish Council, where the important decisions have been taken upwards to the new Wokingham Unitary. Berkshire County Council, which flourished for a little over 100 years, from the late Victorian period, is no more. The County itself survives, represented by cricket and hockey teams and by county signs, but there is no longer a seat of government.

The House of Lords will survive and flourish if the present generation of peers in conjunction with the Commons of the day defines and strengthens an important role in our constitutional settlement. There are roles there for the taking. There are things which the Lords already does well which need doing. Those who wish to change or abolish it have to make out a case why they believe these roles can better be performed elsewhere or by others. They have to deny that opportunities lie ahead for a vigorous and interesting second chamber.

In an age of multiplying government, it is a paradox that there is even more need for a second or revising chamber. Someone needs to carry out the role of an ultimate Court of Appeal. Someone needs to carry out the role of constitutional court for the United Kingdom. Somewhere in the Palace of Westminster more time and attention needs to be given to scrutiny of European matters. All of these things lie in the future for the twenty-first century of the House of Lords. It is up to modern parliamentarians to show the relevance of the two-chamber system, a system which has been inherited and adapted in the four corners of the world.

It would be a great pity if the House of Lords were brought into ridicule or disrespect by a Prime Minister whose one intention seems to be to put as many of his friends in it as possible and to remove the most obviously independent element. It is difficult to establish the case for more of the Prime Minister's friends and placemen appearing in the second chamber of our legislature. It may well be better to be the great-great-great-grandson of a former favourite of a king than to be the present favourite of a Prime Minister who does not seem to brook rivals or criticism with any great enthusiasm.

I anticipate that the Government will go ahead and abolish the hereditary vote, only to discover there is no easy alternative. The administration will be angry every time it is defeated in the Lords, and will find it difficult to marshal all its life peers for unpopular causes. New Prime Ministers will have to follow the precedent of Mr Blair and ennoble their friends to change the balance of the House. The growing use of prime ministerial patronage will not enhance the Lords, but doubtless it will muddle through, as it has before. Every time it defeats a government in a popular cause it will show we still have need of it.The more it is undermined by the executive, the more it will contribute to the break-up of the constitution of the kingdom.

6   The Commons – Marginalised or Modernised?

Tony Blair's Government has given the impression of being tired of the House of Commons. New Labour sees Parliament as a problem, not as part of the solution. They have gone out of their way to undermine the institution. They seek to avoid proper parliamentary debate, choosing other means to put across their messages and make announcements to the country. They are out to break many British traditions.

In constitutional theory and for many years in constitutional practice parliamentary sovereignty was respected and reflected in the conduct of government business. There were many unwritten rules. A minister could not tell anyone, outside the government network, a new policy or a new government intention, until he had told Parliament first. Decisions were set out in statements to Parliament, allowing the minister to be cross-examined by members of all political persuasions. The Prime Minister was subject to twice weekly cross-examination on any matter affecting the government. Each departmental secretary of state and supporting ministerial team was answerable for the actions of that department once a month in departmental questions.

Government backbench MPs, whilst well aware of the opportunities of Parliamentary debate and questions afforded to make political points in support of the government, also regularly used the opportunity to cross-examine the government to help hold them to account and to see how government action would affect their own constituents. The Speaker has always been scrupulously careful to balance those called to ask questions or to make speeches in debates. With the help of the clerks the Speaker ensures that there is balance between the parties and between the different parts of the country, and that priority is afforded to those who have a strong constituency interest or a special knowledge of the subject under discussion. The Speaker also has an eye for what is topical or important to the nation outside, both in deciding on whether emergency questions should be allowed and in deciding which speakers to call on any particular issue.

The new Labour Government decided that this got in the way of a sensible media strategy. The media itself had been making incursions into the style of parliamentary behaviour. Backbenchers over the years had to come to learn that they might have more impact on the government by giving a short interview or asking a pointed question to a camera perched on College Green outside the House of Commons than by going to the trouble of asking the point in the chamber itself. Government ministers in previous governments had been known to give a general indication or a hint on an off-the-record basis of what new policy might be coming up, what Cabinet discussions had been underway, how the agenda might move on. However, previous Conservative governments did attempt to live by the rule that where a major news statement was to be made it should be made first to the House of Commons.

The spin-doctors of New Labour clearly decided that the media agenda was more important than the parliamentary. They find it irksome that an important anchor news programme like the *Today* programme, going out on BBC radio every morning, will only run a government announcement fully if they get it before it is made in the House of Commons later that day. Very often the requirements of the media are for a press conference prior to the time of parliamentary statements. The parliamentary statement cannot be made until 3.30 p.m. and may be later. The minister may not be out of the chamber before 5.00 p.m., leaving all too little time to steer the newspapers before their deadlines for the first editions. There has been a growing tendency to announce more things by way of leak or formal press conference before Parliament is informed.

It is not just the demands of the media that have pushed New Labour dramatically further in the direction of marginalising Parliament and breaking its conventions about announcements. There is a deep fear of Parliament itself. The new politics is meant to be based on consensus. The old politics of Westminster is based upon proposition and counter-proposition, on government proposal and opposition resistance, of dividing the House, on seeing that there are always two sides to an issue and that you can vote yes or no. Labour fear that Conservatives will gradually get the better of them in the House of Commons. They know that there everyone is equal and only as good as the last speech they have made. Labour ministers find it extremely difficult to adjust to the intense scrutiny and cross-examination. After 18 years of making all the difficult points and asking all the unpleasant questions, they are finding it problematic when the boot is on the other foot.

The symbol of how much New Labour wishes to change and marginalise Parliament is their decision to reduce Prime Minister's Question Time from twice a week to once a week. Whilst it is true that the Prime Minister now faces questions for half an hour on Wednesday instead of for 15 minutes on both Tuesday and Thursday, the change is undoubtedly to the Government's benefit and to Parliament's loss. Under the old system, the opposition had two opportunities a week to highlight any major issue it wished. The media always follow Prime Minister's Questions. After every session there will be newspaper comment and usually something is run on both television and radio. It gave the opposition two days out of the five-day working week when it could have a real chance of influencing the parliamentary and the national news agenda. Now there is only one opportunity.

Defenders of the changes point out that the leader of the opposition, who could regularly ask three questions on Tuesday and three questions on Thursday, now has the chance to ask up to six questions on Wednesday. It is also true that it is possible for the leader of the opposition to choose two different subjects on Wednesday to highlight two important issues. It is not, however, the same as being able to highlight the main news item on two separate days of the week. However strong the stories, it is unlikely that the national news media will give prominence to both of the main issues that the leader of the opposition raises on Wednesday. It was a racing certainty that they gave prominence to the two main issues previous leaders of the opposition raised when they did one on Tuesday and one on Thursday.

The Prime Minister has also helped to close down the interest of Prime Minister's Questions by his style of answering. Whilst under previous governments collusion between backbench government MPs and the Prime Minister's office was not unknown, it has become obligatory under New Labour. Very rarely does the Prime Minister experience a question from the Labour side that is unfriendly or that he does not know about in advance. It means that for half of the half-hour, Question Time is not a question time but a series of good news statements by the Prime Minister, engineered by his office whilst masquerading as questions from his own side. It enables the Prime Minister to come over as positive, friendly and helpful, because most of it has been stage managed.

For the other half of the time the Prime Minister does have to face questions from opposition MPs. Sometimes the questions from the Liberal benches are deliberately helpful, as the Liberals and Labour go about their task of coalition building with the view to changing the voting system. Only the Conservative questions can be relied upon to be unknown to the Prime Minister and designed to challenge him and the executive he leads.

The Prime Minister's style in answering opposition questions is usually to avoid answering the question at all. He has a repartee of alleged past Conservative failures which he uses with abandon, whatever the question the Conservatives may be asking. Whilst it is fair for a prime minister to appear at the dispatch box in his role as leader of a party seeking party advantage for part of the time, it does pall. It defeats the object of Prime Minister's Question Time completely if he never steps outside this mode to perform the duty for which he is paid, to answer questions on behalf of the government as a whole about his conduct and his future intentions.

A similar routine often emerges in monthly departmental questions. Whilst they are not as brilliantly organised by the Government's side as Prime Minister's Questions, the intention is similar. Every month, at the Trade and Industry questions, the Parliamentary Private Secretary to ministers in the department prominently gives out the approved DTI briefing, which tells Labour members which questions they should ask and gives them information of a positive nature to weave in to their supplementary questions. When responding to opposition questions, ministers have a tendency not to answer the question posed but to go into spasms of anger about alleged Conservative misdeeds from the past.

The whole Government apparatus gives the appearance of being in opposition with a majority. It proceeds by means of a quote of the day, a sound bite of the week, a promise of the Parliament, whatever the circumstances, however divorced from reality the words may have become. The Government still seems to think that a sound bite in time will allow any problem to vanish. The Government appears to believe the problems are entirely or mainly ones of media presentation rather than being real problems requiring attention.

The contempt for Parliament is reflected in the wish to take decisions without debate in the House, and to find more and more areas of life where responsibility can be assumed by people outside government who are not accountable in the normal way to Parliament. This was most visibly displayed in the breathtaking decision to make the Monetary Committee of the Bank of England responsible for fixing interest rates. Elections in the United Kingdom in the post-war period have usually been about the state of the economy. The level of mortgage rates, the ability of a company to borrow from the bank, the rate of money growth and therefore of price increases have all been crucial issues in general election campaigns.

In the run-up to the 1997 general election, Labour did not clearly indicate their intention to give responsibility for these matters to people meeting at the Bank of England. Shortly after the election, the Chancellor of the Exchequer announced this policy through the media. He did not make a statement in the House of Commons to explain his intentions. The row which the opposition generated about the absence of a statement did lead the Government to say it would make more statements in Parliament in the future. It was also one of the things behind the Speaker's insistence that ministers should behave in the customary way when making important policy announcements.

The decision to hollow out government responsibilities is also reflected in legislation. The Department of Trade and Industry had two important pieces of legislation in the 1997–8 session. The first was a bill to introduce a national minimum wage to the United Kingdom. This was a clear manifesto commitment of the Labour Party in opposition. In the run-up to the general election, they had avoided commenting on the level at which the minimum wage would be set. They were well aware that the opposition to this measure is centred around the proposition that if the minimum wage is set too high it will destroy a lot of jobs and if it is set too low it does not mean very much. The rate of a national minimum wage was clearly crucial to the whole scheme. Socialists and Conservatives alike could unite in seeing that the rate was central. A socialist who believes that you can raise wages by Act of Parliament without many or any damaging consequences for employment, would wish to see as high a rate fixed as possible. A Conservative, worried that interference in the market would destroy the opportunities of the young, the unskilled and the disabled, would be more and more concerned the higher the rate went.

When this measure came to the House of Commons, the Bill was remarkable for two things that were omitted. Firstly, the Bill specified no starting rate for the minimum wage. Secondly, it did not even clarify exactly who would and who would not be affected by this proposal. The Bill went through all its House of Commons debates and committee stages with the Government adamantly refusing to clarify these two central issues. The Bill gave massive powers to the President of the Board of Trade and to a newly appointed quango to settle these things which were of great interest to Parliament.

Of course, the Government could point out that there was a gap of a couple of years between the Commons' debates on the minimum wage legislation and the coming into force of the minimum wage itself. They could say that any rate they told the House of Commons in 1997 or 1998 would have to be increased by 1999 or 2000. This, however, was not a convincing argument. It was quite possible for the Government to tell the House of Commons what the minimum wage was going to be as a percentage of average earnings. This was the way Labour had put it forward in its 1992 manifesto. It would also be quite possible to state a rate in money of the day and tell the House that it would be updated in line with either wages or prices when it was implemented.

The Government's reluctance to name the rate was part of their wish to close down parliamentary debate on things that mattered. It was also part of the wish on the part of the ministers to avoid responsibility for important decisions. They set up a Low Pay Commission. This quango was charged with the task of examining the evidence and recommending to the Government a level or rate for the minimum wage. The Government was not even prepared to say whether it would regard itself as bound by the advice of the Low Pay Commission or not. Whilst ministers did not want the responsibility which came from saying that they would definitely make their own decision in the light of the Low Pay Commission's advice, they were also unprepared to accept whatever the Low Pay Commission might come up with. They were left tongue-tied in their ambiguity.

A similar hesitation or indecision attended their actions on who would be covered by the minimum wage. Opposition to the proposal centred on the fact that in countries which had the minimum wage a large number of exemptions had been put through to avoid the minimum wage doing damage to those least able to compete in the market place. The Government in the committee stages was unprepared to say whether disabled people, young people and others would be included in its scope or not. Again this was something where it said it needed the advice of the Low Pay Commission. If you accept that there is something in the advice of an independent quango on matters like these, ministers should have decided to await that advice before putting the legislation in front of Parliament.

A similar set of hesitations and failures to answer attended the passage of the Competition Bill. The newly elected Government decided to pick up an idea which the previous Conservative administration had been examining over an eight-year period. Conservative ministers had declined to put new competition legislation to the House of Commons because of the difficulties in thinking through all of the consequences that would follow. While some Conservatives welcome the idea of basing British competition law more firmly upon European Treaty Law, Articles 85 and 86 of the old Treaty of Rome in particular, it proved to be an extremely hazardous task. Conservatives deferred legislating because it was so difficult getting the detail right. The New Labour Government decided it was just the thing to pick up and run with. It would show that they were more European-oriented than the outgoing government; it looked radical and dramatic whilst they assumed it would be a relatively easy task to do it.

The legislation they presented to the House of Commons was long and complex but did not tackle any of the detailed problems that had defeated their Conservative predecessors and led to the delays. Existing business practice in a complex market place like the United Kingdom has been built up over many years. Many companies and industries proceed by recommended prices, discount structures, vertical agreements, franchise arrangements, partnerships and co-operative activities in a complex web of business relationships. Any one of these contracts, agreements or practices could be deemed to be anti-competitive. All of them over the years have been tried and tested by the existing competition authorities in the United Kingdom. In some cases the practices have been overturned or modified. In other cases they have been found to be in the public interest.

A radical and general new piece of legislation threatened to throw all of these business practices up into the air and leave people unclear as to whether any or all of them had to be modified or stopped to comply with the new law. The position was made more difficult by the Government because the new law prohibits practices and fines companies retrospectively for carrying them out. The law it replaced allowed businesses to do as they wished subject to independent investigation and a requirement to desist in future should the practice be found unsatisfactory.

In the Commons stages of the Competition Bill, ministers persistently refused to answer any of the legitimate questions posed on behalf of business about the likely consequences of the new legislation. They were asked if newspapers could continue to recommend cover prices and continue to distribute through powerful wholesalers under special contracts. Ministers could not answer. They were asked if it meant the end of resale price maintenance in over-the-counter medicines: a practice which all agreed, including ministers, sustained more community pharmacists than would be possible if it were abolished. Again ministers were reluctant to give a clear answer. They were asked if the existing arrangements between brewers and pubs were anti-competitive or not. There was no answer. In a whole host of business cases ministers replied that they could not tell the House of Commons what the impact of the legislation would be. They went further and said they did not wish to and did not think they had to. All of these problems were to be passed to a new super-quango, the Competition Authority, which would in due course come to its own conclusions on all of these matters.

This practice of hollowed-out legislation, of ministers legislating on the hoof and refusing to tell Parliament what the consequences of their legislation will be, is something entirely new. The previous Conservative administration looked at the possibility of an Enabling Act to give it the necessary parliamentary protection to privatise any industry in government ownership. The idea was strongly rejected within the Conservative admin-istration on the grounds that it would not afford Parliament sufficient scrutiny of each individual privatisation. As the result, each individual privatisation required at least one and often two pieces of primary legislation so that all the aspects of the privatisation could be discussed on the floor of the House of Commons.

The contrast between this and the development of Labour's social programme is very stark. Not only has Labour been refusing to answer questions on areas which do require primary legislation, like the national minimal wage, but they have also decided to bring in much of their social employment and trade union reform by the back door, through signing the Social Chapter and adopting other social policy measures from Brussels. This permits them to legislate for these things by secondary legislation under the European Communities Act. There is a lot of difference in the way Parliament handles secondary legislation and primary legislation. Each piece of primary legislation, each new parliamentary enactment, has to go through a series of complex stages in both the Commons and the Lords. There is a full-scale second reading debate on the principles of the legislation in each House, a lengthy committee stage examining the detail, a report stage from the committee to look at the most important amendments and a third reading on the principles of the legislation.

Secondary legislation either does not get debated at all or gets one and a half hours of cursory debate. It cannot be amended and nearly always goes through on the back of Government votes in the way the Government first intended. It is a much less democratic and satisfactory process. It was a perfectly reasonable process all the time secondary legislation was, as the name implies, of secondary importance governed by primary legislation. Now that primary legislation is becoming so vague and so general and is often fixed in Brussels, secondary legislation is taking on more of the characteristics that primary legislation had a decade or so ago. Parliamentary scrutiny has not been changed or improved to recognise this important change of practice.

Cabinet government is not faring a lot better than Parliament under this new regime. Stories abound that major decisions are being taken by a small group of media advisors and courtiers. The inner circle of Peter Mandelson, Secretary of State for Trade and Industry, Mr Campbell, press advisor to the Prime Minister, the Prime Minister himself, and a fluctuating group that may include Geoffrey Robinson, the Paymaster General, Stephen Byers, Chief Secretary to the Treasury, Jack Cunningham, Cabinet Office supremo, or others depending on the issue, often make important decisions. More often than not the important decisions are taken in response to media stories. The Government has a clear media strategy but often lacks any clear government strategy.

The curious case of the coal industry illustrates the pressures and the problems of this approach. The coal industry is very clearly the responsibility of the Energy Minister reporting to the President of the Board of Trade (renamed Secretary of State for Trade and Industry in July 1998) within the DTI. The coal industry does raise cross-departmental problems. There will be occasions when it raises issues that need the Chancellor of the Exchequer's involvement over subjects like energy taxation and even energy prices. It will clearly involve the attention of the Environment Minister and his boss, the Secretary of State for the Environment, Transport and Regions, as decisions on how much coal is burnt will have an important impact upon green policy. The traditional way of tackling these problems is to bring them to the Cabinet Committee with the lead minister, in this case the Energy Minister, opening up the discussion and making recommendations.

Under New Labour, things have been handled rather differently. The Prime Minister attended an international conference on green issues. He decided he wished to make a press splash by going further than the other countries present in his offers on behalf of the United Kingdom to help clean up the planet. He pledged that the United Kingdom would cut its carbon dioxide emissions by 20 per cent. It does not appear that there was any proper inter-departmental staff work before this statement was made, to spell out to the Prime Minister the consequences this would have on the coal industry. When the opposition pointed out that this and other Government commitments would entail the closure of a large number of pits and this appeared in the press, the Government panicked. Instead of convening the proper Cabinet committee and hammering out whether the Government wished to be more green or whether it wished to favour the coal industry more than its predecessor, the Prime Minister sent in Geoffrey Robinson, the Paymaster General at the Treasury, to negotiate a short-term fix with the principal coal company and the electricity generators. The Energy Minister and the President of the Board of Trade were sidelined.

The Prime Minister used Prime Minister's Questions to announce the coming fix to the House of Commons, even managing to announce it before the Paymaster General had been able to negotiate it. The Paymaster General eventually returned triumphant with the news that some coal due to be supplied to the generators in the third quarter of 1998 would be purchased by them in the second quarter. He did not secure the burning of any more coal by the electricity generators. His action just meant that the decline in coal needed in the third quarter would be even more severe than if he had left the pattern of supply undisrupted.

Because the press rumblings about the closure of pits and the unhappy outlook for Britain's leading coal company continued, the Prime Minister then dispatched Mr Peter Mandelson to massage the media. He decided to visit a coal mine and attract attention to his visit. He believed that the problem could be solved by creating an impression that Labour loved mines and the miners because he, Mr Peter Mandelson as chief spin-doctor, was seen visiting a pit.

Meanwhile, back at the DTI a large number of applications rested on the President of the Board of Trade's desk to build new gas power stations. Each one of these gas-powered power stations would mean further pits closing if the stations were approved, once they were up and running. The President of the Broad of Trade dithered over what she was meant to do. As the pressure mounted through the press for some answers on the subject of these gas-powered power stations, she decided to impose a moratorium on the grant of any new gas station licences. Again there was a failure of collective government to come to a decision. The industry did not wish to know that they would have to wait six months or more for an answer. They wanted to be told what the Government's view was.

None of this was properly announced in Parliament. It was debated in Parliament when the opposition engineered opportunities to get it discussed. It showed the failure of collective government at the highest levels. The Prime Minister's decision to override responsible ministers meant that the people handling the issue did not have a proper grasp of its complexity and were not backed up by all of the official advice that they needed. The failure of the Cabinet Committee System to sit the Environment interests, the Treasury interests and the Energy Industry interests down around the same table and make them come to a decision has already cost the Government dear and will cost it more political losses as the tragedy unfolds. A Prime Minister who is famed for saying he knows government is about making hard choices has on this, as on many other occasions, spent his time running away from making just such a hard choice. If you wish to have a much cleaner country, you have to close down a lot of coal-burning power station plants and the pits that go with them. If you wish to help the miners, you have to enable them to gain access to a bigger power-generation market by the decisions the Government has to take on how electricity generation and pricing operate.

One of the most disturbing characteristics of the new Government is the growing divorce between the sound bite and reality in so many areas. We are told that the Government is good for the coal industry and the miners in a way that the Conservatives were not, yet the closures continue and the Government is unable to make up its mind in favour of coal. We are told that the Government intends to stick and has stuck to Conservative spending plans for the first two years of the administration. The Government's own financial statement and budget report for the March 1998 budget makes clear that this is not true. The Labour Government's spending plans for the year 1998–9, its second year in office, showed total spending running £5300 million higher than the outgoing Conservative plan for the same year. More strikingly, the biggest changes compared with Conservative plans lie in the area of increased welfare spending and the absence of privatisation receipts.

This is surprising given the rhetoric used in the run-up to the general election and since, over how Labour would keep to Conservative spending plans whilst doing a better job on health and education. The constantly repeated mantra was that Labour would spend less on economic failure. They would cut the welfare bills by promoting employment and opportunity for all. In their first two years, all they have succeeded in doing is boosting overall welfare spending by more than the outgoing Conservative Government had planned, with consequent pressures upon other areas of expenditure.

Before the election, Labour made it clear that the loss of privatisation receipts would not make a hole in their accounts. They even suggested that they would carry on privatising so that they would still have the privatisation monies coming in. In their second year in office their own figures show that they will be £1500 million short compared with the Conservatives, owing to the cancellation of privatisation plans.

There are many areas where the gap between the sound bite and the reality has become large. There are many areas where they are already deep into broken-promise territory. One of Labour's most effective and favourite sound bites was that in office they would keep their promises whereas the Conservatives had broken theirs. The first promise above all was the promise that they would cut health waiting lists by 100,000. It is quite true that they did not put a specific time period on this although they said it was an early pledge. Given the insistence of Labour that unlike the Conservatives they would make health a real priority and get the waiting lists down, no one was expecting that after one year in office health waiting lists would already be 140,000 higher than they inherited. It was against the spirit of the promise that they first put them up, even if they subsequently do find enough money, people and hospital space to bring them down again.

It is not only the language and the role of the government that has changed in its approach to Parliament, but also the role and the language of back-bench members on the governing side. The Member of Parliament has traditionally had several roles to fulfil. Unless a government minister or whip, all Members of Parliament are elected to hold the government of the day to account. As a government backbencher, I never thought it my duty to say supportive words about everything the government did regardless of whether I and my constituents thought it right or not. The backbench member on the government's side is expected to exercise his conscience and to be a voice for his constituency where the government does things, or fails to do things, against the interests of his constituents. The MP also has a duty to speak out for the public good if he believes the government is wasting money or making the wrong decision.

The MP is there both to represent the constituency to the government and, in the case of a government-supporting MP, to represent the government to the constituency. New Labour has decided that only half of this function should be carried out. Whilst the powers that be are very keen that the MP should represent the Government's policies to the constituency and relay sound bites of the day and week on a regular basis, it is far from enthusiastic about the other part of the role, representing the constituency to the Government.

The Government has systematically gone about its task of trying to ensure as little back-bench trouble or intervention from their own side as possible. MPs are encouraged to be away from the House of Commons in their constituencies when Parliament is in session. A typical Labour backbencher may get one week off in four to spend time in the constituency. This is a surprising development. Parliament does not conduct any business on some Fridays so that MPs can spend those in their constituency. Parliament has long holiday breaks at Christmas, Easter, Whitsun and in the summer to allow MPs to spend time listening to their constituents and catching up on constituency problems. On Fridays when there is parliamentary business, it often takes the form of private members business of no especial interest to that particular MP or constituency. Very often Members of Parliament are not required to be present in the House of Commons until 10.00 p.m. on a Monday. They are certainly never required to be present in Parliament on a Monday morning.

Any MP can look after his constituency well using Monday mornings, some Fridays, the long holidays when he is not himself on holiday, and parts of the weekend when many constituents do wish to see an MP taking part in local activities. The decision to make or to encourage MPs to spend additional working days away from Parliament seems to be more motivated by the wish to prevent them being there to cross-examine the executive than anything else.

Allied to the constituency breaks has been a passion for even longer holidays. The idea of Parliament not meeting for quite long periods did begin to develop under John Major as Prime Minister. It was then, however, allied to a relatively light legislative programme requiring Parliament to be in session less often. Under the new Government, everybody agrees that there is a very voluminous complex legislative programme, yet the Government tends to hasten things through the House of Commons and insists there is little time, partly because it chooses to have long holidays. The first summer recess of the new Government was the longest in living memory. A relatively long Easter break was followed just a few weeks later by another ten-day break for Whitsun.

There is little point in Labour backbench MPs knowing the views of their constituents well unless they express them forcibly in the House of Commons and in the media, so that the Government understands the difficulties. Labour silence on the scandal of the increase in waiting lists has been palpable. It has been left to a few brave Labour backbenchers, like Dennis Skinner on the coal industry, Diane Abbott on the Independent Monetary Committee of the Bank of England and Anne Clwyd on the so-called Ethical Foreign Policy, to voice the criticisms that many Labour supporters are voicing out in the country. Many traditional Labour supporters feel cheated that the health service does not receive more money to cut waiting lists. They dislike the way the arms trade continues under the Labour Government when they thought it would be restricted much more severely. They dislike the closure of many pits and the closure of so many factories.

As the backbench member is actively discouraged from undertaking debate on the conduct of Government policy, so the role of the MP changes further in the direction of the MP mixing the duties of minor royalty in the locality with that of a social worker. There is nothing wrong with an MP being a well known local figure who is prepared to open a fête or attend a carnival. It is a traditional part of the job. Nor is there anything wrong with good MPs, as they do, holding constituency surgeries and taking up local matters with the council. This should be a supplementary part of the service rather than the whole purpose of the occupation.

Most commentators of the political scene would agree that the most colossal issues that confront our nation are those related to our membership of the European Union. From the Labour benches there is a stunning silence. There is a refusal to engage in proper debate about whether the single currency will be a good or bad thing. There is a bland assertion from the Government that the constitutional changes it entails are not important, without any attempt to explain why or to engage in serious discussion on the issue. It is difficult to see how anyone can be a proper member of this Parliament without giving voice to constituents' views and fears on this most important British relationship with the continent. Yet Labour MPs when asked for their personal views and the views of their constituency on the single currency, the common foreign policy, the possibility of the common army, the drift towards government by treaty in European Court of Justice, shrug their shoulders and say that that is a Conservative issue and not one which they are troubled about. They are part-time MPs reluctant to undertake the main task of an MP, which is to be a national voice for their constituents on the big constitutional issues of the day.

The Labour Party in power has decided to cloak some of its changes to the role of Parliament in the guise of modernisation. Some Labour MPs arrived with a burning passion to overturn many of the symbols and traditions of the institution they had just joined. They did not like the formal language, the use of the third person when referring to another member, the order of debate, the ability of one MP to cross-examine another during the course of his speech, the need to be present at unpredictable times of the day or night to vote on measures before the House and a number of minor points in the dress and procedural code. As the modernisation committee got down to work, the newer more radical members soon discovered that there were good reasons behind many of the existing practices and that they were more deeply entrenched even in their own party than they thought.

One of the battles has been over voting. The ability to choose the time and the number of votes is one important power which rests very often with the opposition. When a bill is before a committee of the House or being debated on report on the floor of the House itself, it is the opposition that largely determines which items will be voted on and when they will be voted on. Labour members and some members of the Government find this inconvenient. It offers the opposition the weapon of time to hold up or to annoy the Government with a view to trying to get concessions, improvements and changes in the legislation. Some on the Labour side would like to sweep away what remains of the time weapon from the opposition.

Some believe that voting in person in the House of Commons should be abolished and replaced by electronic voting from a distance. Others accept that one way of making sure that MPs do come to the House of Commons and have the opportunity to talk to each other and lobby government ministers is to require them to be present on a regular basis to vote. It is likely that there will be a compromise, with some mixture of electronic methods still requiring the Member of Parliament to be present in person to carry out the vote. Meanwhile, the Government is itself making increasing use of what are called timetable or guillotine motions. All governments have in the past used guillotine motions in certain circumstances. When an important piece of legislation is being deliberately held up by a dogged and determined opposition, the government can table a motion saying that the amount of time for consideration of the bill will be limited. Assuming this motion passes, then the time available for discussion of that bill is limited by the terms of the motion, and anything the opposition wishes to say on the bill has to be put into that new timetable. The Conservative opposition has always accepted that this is reasonable conduct in extreme circumstances where a bill has made little progress after many hours of debate.

The new Government has taken this practice further and has started timetabling important bills right from the beginning without any knowledge of whether the opposition will or will not try to use time as a weapon to delay the measure. Some in the Labour Party wish to timetable all bills so they know exactly where they are with their general legislative programme. This would be one further reduction in the powers of the opposition and a further assertion of power by the executive. What might start out as relatively well intentioned, with an allowance of reasonable time to debate important matters, could soon become a device in the hands of the Government to prevent debate at all on the things that were most sensitive and most embarrassing.

Parliament rarely comes to life with this media-friendly, soundbite-ridden Government. The media has sensed that the big events and the big stories are likely to take place outside the chamber rather than inside. They know that the Government has a contempt or a dislike for Parliament and whereever possible they will stage things outside the House of Commons. In a world of photo opportunities, a man in a suit standing at the dispatch box offers no effective competition with a photograph of the Prime Minister entertaining the First Lady of the United States or the Deputy Prime Minister attempting to drive an eco-friendly car. This Government tries to say it with pictures more often than it wants to say it with words in the House of Commons.

Day after day there is good-quality debate in the House of Commons with the opposition making a series of points on constitutional reform, on the state of the health service, on the collapse of the manufacturing industry or the twists or turns of an ethical foreign policy. Day after day the galleries are empty of reporters and the stories come from elsewhere. We live in a world where media control from Number Ten has reached new heights of success. Accredited lobby journalists believe the best and truest source of stories is the Number Ten press machine. They know it will be there day after day and they have learnt by bitter experience that if they do not take it seriously it may pass them by. The media has been changing too. A few years ago, the main broadsheet newspapers reported quite a bit of Parliament's daily debate. They did often retain a single sketch writer who would also write an amusing column commenting on the dress, the mannerisms, the lighter touches of parliamentary life. More recently, much of the serious reporting of Parliament has ceased and those that do remain as lobby journalists seem often to hanker after being sketch writers themselves. All the journalists are now much more interested in the personal stories, the mannerisms and the family backgrounds of the politicians, than they are in what the politicians are saying on the big issues. It is far easier to get a story into the newspapers about the Lord Chancellor's choice of wallpaper than it is to get a story in about the way in which Scottish devolution may lead to the break-up of the United Kingdom. We live in an age where everything a politician says and does is thought to be significant save the speeches he spends most time on and which matter most to him. These are often studiously ignored as being in some way unrepresentative or misleading of the politician's life and work.

We are fast approaching a time when the British people will have to decide whether they want an active Parliament with strong opposition or not. As Mr Blair continues to sidle up to Mr Ashdown, the leader of the Liberal Party, with a view to creating a new consensus politics, there is even discussion of reorganising the seating plan in the House of Commons to make it less confrontational. Those of us who believe that you are either for a proposal or against it are said to favour division and to be old-fashioned. The new idea is that groups of politicians should huddle together behind closed doors and try to find a form of words or fudge which will bridge the unbridgeable, paper over the cracks and prevent the need for dispute or debate. This way of thinking is inimical to the history, traditions and style of British democracy. At its best it has been argumentative, lively and noisy. Parliament would never have won any prizes for the daily conduct of its members, but it has won many prizes in the past for being one of the foremost representative and democratic institutions in the world, truly the Mother of Parliaments. It was outrageous behaviour by members that led to checks and balances on the power of the Crown. It was assertive power by parliamentarians that forced the executive to accept that Parliament should get some redress for people's grievances before voting taxation. It was noisy and strong campaigns outside and within Parliament which led to the breakthrough of votes for all and the recognition of the role of minorities in our society. It was Parliament which gave voice to the need to resist Nazi tyranny in the 1930s and 1940s and it was Parliament that gave liberties to the former colonies of the United Kingdom.

Many abroad would be amazed if we threw away this great institution which has been a beacon of light and enlightenment, a source of hope for many. When the Eastern European countries threw off the tyranny of communism, it was to the Mother of all Parliaments and to the American Senate and Congress that they turned for their inspiration. When the European Parliament thought that it should provide a little more bite and control over the European executive, it turned to the British Question Time to see how it could be done. If you listen to the arguments in the pub or on the football terraces, people are either for things or against things and they act out exactly the type of arguments that we have on a good day in Parliament.

The New Labour politics of consensus, with absentee members of Parliament and an unwritten rule that if you are on the Government's side you cannot cross-examine it in a hostile way, are destructive of our very liberties. All those of us who believe in freedom and democracy now have to assert our right to a noisy, to a disputatious, to a long-winded, to a vexatious, to an exciting, to a dynamic, to a divided Parliament. That is the embodiment of our liberties. It is a living tradition. If we lose it we will have lost much that is special in British life.

There were times in the first year of the New Labour Government that Parliament has broken through despite the odds. It has revealed the follies of the ethical foreign policy and the cravenness of our agricultural policy, and has worked closely with the countryside movement to explain the needs and desires of our rural communities. It has exposed the profligacy of Labour's spending plans, the dangers of its relations with lobby companies and some of the tensions between the main ministerial figures. It will be much needed in the future whoever is in power. Modern government is so complicated, so powerful, so expensive it needs strong and powerful voices in a free Parliament to hold it to account and expose its follies. It is especially good at revealing the tensions and contradictions in a government. It can hold up a mirror to broken promises. It can provide an antidote when power goes to their heads. It expresses the nation's anger when government gets it wrong. It can be the nation's cockpit, fighting with words and votes the causes that could otherwise erupt in violence on the streets. It is not time to roll it up or dismiss it, as some in the new Labour project would prefer. If anything, it is time to strengthen it, to ensure the nation's voice is heard before constitutional change from afar washes much of our liberty away.

7 Proportional Representation

There are two enduring characteristics of the British electoral system that are readily understood by the British electors. The first is the relationship between an individual Member of Parliament and his constituency. Everyone either knows or can find out easily who is his Member of Parliament and each Member of Parliament knows who are his constituents. The second is the fact that the person with the most votes in the election wins the seat. Sometimes a winning candidate has more than half the votes. On other occasions a winning candidate may win with 40 per cent of the votes, with the other 60 per cent split between two, three or more challengers.

This system has been generally described as the first-past-the-post system. The election is often seen as a horse race where the horse that gets to the finishing post first wins. No one suggests at the end of a horse race that there should be a series of complicated calculations to discover whether more people would have liked the second- or third-placed horse at the finishing post to be adjudged the winner. Many people have regarded the electoral system as entirely fair because it always delivers the result that the person in that individual contest with the most votes gets the job.

There are now advocates for two different types of change to this system. Some people believe that we should move away from the idea of one person representing one group of electors. They believe it might be better to have teams of representatives for a larger region or even for the whole country. Some wish to change the way in which the votes are counted and the seats awarded to individual candidates. There are two different families of proposals on offer. There are truly proportional systems where reformers wish to see the number of parliamentary seats awarded being directly pro-portionate to the total number of votes cast for the parties, taken across a much bigger region or area than the traditional one-member constituency. There are others who wish to see people who vote for less popular parties or candidates given the chance to exercise a second preference or a second vote to influence the choice between the two most popular candidates or parties.

These two systems are rather different. The truly proportionate one is based on the wish to be fairer to the majority as well as to the minorities. Proportionate systems in a pure form do exactly as they describe, awarding seats in strict proportion to the votes cast. Alternative-voting or second-preference systems are designed to be particularly helpful to minorities. Their prime motivation is to give to those who vote for unpopular candidates or parties the opportunity to have another go, denying a similar opportunity in most cases to those who voted for the two most popular candidates or parties.

Britain is on the threshold of massive change in her electoral practices. New electoral systems and devices have been brought in by the present Labour Government both for elections to the European Parliament and for the elections to the new Scottish Parliament and Welsh Assembly. A commission is sitting on the whole question of whether the voting system for Westminster should also be altered. Modernisers want to 'bring us into line with Europe', copying one or more of the different electoral systems in use on the continent.

The Liberal Party has long been an advocate for what it calls 'fair votes'. By this it usually means any system which is likely to give Liberals more parliamentary seats than it has held during most of the twentieth century. The Labour Party, having been an exponent of the traditional first-past-the-post system, has become the party of experimentation with different electoral systems. There is no one overriding principle behind the piecemeal reforms introduced so far. It is believed that the Prime Minister and senior Cabinet members favour a different system for Westminster elections from that which they have chosen for either Europe or the regional assemblies or parliaments. Some in Labour say that they want a more proportional system, yet some claim that they are attracted to the alternative-vote system. This system if applied in the May 1997 election would have given more seats to Labour, even though Labour's performance in seats was far more successful than its voting strength. All who come to the business of recommending change in the electoral system have to defend themselves against the charge that they are seeking to gerrymander a successful system in the interests of more seats for their own party.

The single-member constituency has created a most important bond in British political life which has been central to twentieth-century Parliamentary activity. The single-member constituency encourages a two way conversation between the member and his constituents. It should be a mutual source of strength. The MP should know exactly how government policy and parliamentary law-making are affecting his constituents. Enjoying a close relationship with them, he can consult them widely on what he wishes to know. They can also lobby and explain to him their views on what is working and what is not working as government policy and executive actions unfold.

The current size of constituencies, with around 67,000 electors in each, is thoroughly manageable. A Member of Parliament has a case load, handling the problems of constituents on their behalf. He normally holds what is called by medical analogy a surgery, inviting constituents to come to see him to talk him through the difficulties they would like him to take up. The post bag can be voluminous but not unmanageable. Where there is an important local or national issue, people will write in considerable numbers to their Members of Parliament to explain what is wrong or what needs doing. Most Members of Parliament, equipped with a reasonable office cost allowance and secretarial back-up, answer these letters sympathetically and in detail.

A successful MP is one who can interpret the shifting sands of public opinion in his constituency and who can bring to bear his constituents' views on the process of government. It is also his job, whether on the Government benches or on the opposition benches, to explain government policy and opposition challenges to government policy to his constituents. If he is elected on the government's side many of his constituents will expect him to support the government on most issues. They will also expect him to stand up for their specific interests if they differ with the government and would expect him to campaign for things that mattered to the constituency whether the government begins from a sympathetic position or not.

Similarly, a Member of Parliament elected to the official opposition would normally be expected by his constituents to oppose the central parts of the government party's programme with which his party disagrees. But his constituents would also expect him to be able to negotiate with and do deals with the government on their behalf. They would expect him to co-operate with the government where it is in the interests of the constituency to do so. All constituents will expect the MP to be sufficient of a diplomat to resolve some of the tensions within the community or to find common ground which could be said to represent the constituency's view. On other occasions the MP will be expected to show leadership for the community, resolving disputes in favour of one side rather than the other. A sensible MP sets out in his manifesto for election his principal statements of policy and belief, so that constituents know in advance where he is likely to come down on some of the most vexatious issues of the day.

This should not be thrown away lightly. Any move from a single-member constituency pattern to regional or national lists breaks this relationship in a fundamental way. Whilst it is possible to understand the broad opinions and concerns of 67,000 people in a single-member constituency, it is far more difficult understanding all the strands of opinion within a region of several million people and even more complicated in a country of 57 million people. Where it is possible to find a common view in a town or a cluster of villages in a particular place, it is much more difficult finding that common view or expression of unified opinion in a region or a whole country.

The normal pattern of an MP's life would be greatly changed for the worse. The typical MP will spend days in the constituency on a regular basis visiting local schools, hospitals, businesses, shops, charities and other institutions. By this means he will build up a very accurate picture in considerable detail of how a given law, tax or government decision has an impact at the grass roots. A regional Member of Parliament will not have the same close working relationship with particular schools, colleges, hospitals or companies. The better known regional MPs or national MPs will still be invited to visit particular schools or companies. Other MPs less well known or not known at all will have to engineer invitations if they wish to stay informed.

Members of the public will similarly be impoverished in trying to get their view represented. A member of the public has a hold over his existing Member of Parliament unless that Member of Parliament has decided to retire or resign. No MP, however big his majority, can afford to be continuously unhelpful or rude to individuals or groups of constituents. If he tries to shirk his responsibilities, refusing to take up cases, write letters or campaign on behalf of strongly held views in his constituency, he will lose votes at a subsequent election and he will make the task of his opponents in that election much easier. In a regional list system no such pressures will apply. An individual Member of Parliament could always claim that it was not his speciality or not the part of the region with which he felt the most affinity, fobbing off the enquiry. Some MPs on regional list systems may choose not to answer any correspondence at all. If the press tried to get to the bottom of it there would be several ways in which a Member of Parliament could disclaim responsibility or claim there had been some mistake. Accountability would be gravely reduced in a regional or national list system.

Although in any constituency under the current single-member system you can find people who do not like their Member of Parliament or wish they had a different one, poll findings show that people have a much higher regard for their individual named MP in their constituency than they do for MPs and politicians in general. People have the opportunity to meet their Member of Parliament in the locality on a regular basis. Many Members of Parliament choose to live in their constituencies. They become well known local figures and can be respected across the political divide, even though many of their constituents at the next general election will vote against them for party rather than personal reasons. This too would be lost in a regional list system. That important tie which binds a fair-minded Member of

Parliament to a well informed constituency would be broken for ever. Constituents would no longer get the same speedy individual attention and redress. Members of Parliament would no longer be as well informed at the local level about all of the problems and difficulties.

The first-past-the-post system also has advantages at the national level. Whilst it is true that a party with less than half the votes can and often does form the government, it is also true that our system throughout the twentieth century has normally produced stable governments with decent majorities. This makes the national majority party more directly accountable for government than in a system which produced a balance of minority parties and shifting coalitions. Where a major party wins an election outright with a majority, everyone knows who is to praise and who is to blame. The public does expect the government to keep to its pre-election promises. It does treat the manifesto of the major party as a serious document and, whilst it has got used to parties not living up to all their manifesto commitments, it still sets as a standard the implementation of promises made. At the end of the four- or five-year term in Parliament the public can make a fair judgement about whether it has got what it asked for and whether the party in power lived up to the expectations it created when campaigning in the previous election.

If an electoral system is adopted which encourages strictly proportionate representation in relation to the votes cast, it is most unlikely that any party will get a majority in the House of Commons. Two or more parties will decide to coalesce to form an administration. They will have won their seats in the election on the basis of different manifesto commitments from each other. Indeed, in a proportionate system there is every reason for more parties to be established and for those parties to adopt more extreme positions in order to try to influence the resulting policies in the inevitable coalitions. As a result, the one thing you can guarantee about coalition government is that none of the parties in it will be able to implement in full their manifesto promises. None of the blocks of voters that voted for the minority parties forming the administration will be entirely satisfied, whilst of course, by definition, those who backed the parties that are not part of the coalition are sure that they too will not see their promises and dreams realised.

In a situation where two or more minority parties have to form a coalition after the election, there has to be bargaining usually behind closed doors to settle the agreed policies of the new government. These may be the lowest common denominator between the two or more manifestos of the parties concerned. It might be easier to form a completely new agenda for government largely unrelated to the separate manifesto, put forward by the competing parties that were successful in the general election. In this way the accountability of a government to the electorate is broken the day after the election result is declared. Whilst it is unavoidable that the politicians will have to break their promises even though they are forming the government, it does not get the new government off to a good start. It has to cobble together a different programme from that which the parties presented to the electors separately in the election.

The lack of accountability is amplified by the normal actions of the politicians in a coalition. When anything unpopular has to be done by the Government, the coalition partners are normally quick to point out privately if not publicly that they themselves were not in favour of these measures but they were forced upon them by their coalition partners or by circumstances. Sometimes coalition ministers break the normal premise of collective responsibility and give interviews or make speeches that go beyond the collective agreement. It is not always possible to remove these ministers from office, as they will claim that they are speaking out in favour of the line that they put to the electorate and that without their support the coalition would crumble. We have recently seen an example in the French coalition of a Eurosceptic minister speaking out strongly against the single-currency scheme which is the preferred main policy of the French Government of which he is a member. This would become a regular pattern of behaviour if we had coalition governments like that in the United Kingdom.

When things go wrong for a government, the first-past-the-post system gives the public an easy way of getting rid of it. There is no such easy way of getting rid of an unpopular coalition government in a proportional system. The tide of electoral fortune can conspire to ensure that minority parties that may have been part of the reason why the government failed turn up again with sufficient strength in the House of Commons in order to form the necessary part of the subsequent coalition. The free democrats in Germany, with a small proportion of the vote in each election, stayed within the government, whatever was happening to the bigger parties in Germany, as the result of the workings of their proportionate and coalition-based system. Many in Britain think it is better that if a group of politicians in a government have let the country down they should be removed from office in no uncertain terms by the electorate and a fresh group given a chance. This is only possible under a first-past-the-post system.

The Government, in its commission of enquiry into a new voting system, has set out four criteria for any new voting system: it says it seeks a broad proportionality; it seeks an extension of voter choice; it seeks a link between MPs and geographical constituencies and it sees the need for stable government. In each of these respects the first-past-the-post system is superior to any of the other options it considered. There is a broad proportionality to the results under the first-past-the-post system. This could be strengthened if all constituencies were of an equal size. That is the one kind of proportionality that makes a great deal of sense. One of the reasons why the number of seats varies from the number of votes cast is the presence of a large number of constituencies with well below or well above the average number of voters. Each Boundary Commission Review tries to do something about this, but even so it usually leaves in place a large number of anomalies. It also does not extrapolate past demographic trends.

Soon after the Boundary Commission has reported the whole process of population shifts creating unfairly sized constituencies begins again. An MP in a part of the world like my own, where many new houses are being built and people are moving in, will face a rising number of electors over the typical ten-year period of that Boundary Review's conclusions, whilst an MP in an older urban area would experience an outward migration of voters often taking him well below the average. Improvements in the Boundary Commission's proposals both to get constituencies nearer to the average size at the time of the review and to take into account demographic trends would improve the proportionality of the current system.

The present system is very good at discouraging fringe and extreme parties. The British system gave no encouragement to fascists or communists in the inter-war period when both those parties exploited the opportunities in proportional systems elsewhere to gain representation. Whilst elections in Britain give single-issue parties an opportunity to put their case, the electoral system is usually damning when it comes to judging their suitability to represent people on a broad front. There have been strong Eurosceptic and Green movements in this country. Each of these movements have chosen to field candidates in the name of the Referendum Party, the United Kingdom Independence Party and the Green Party at general elections to underline their point, but none of them have succeeded in getting anyone elected.

British people in elections distinguish between lobbying on behalf of single issues or strongly held convictions on a narrow front on the one hand and the offer to represent people across a broad front through a more general party programme on the other. In proportional systems people are more tempted to vote to express a strongly held single issue or principle, knowing that their minority will then get a voice or voices in the Parliament and may even have some impact on the coalition building of the Government. This changes the function of the Member of Parliament from representing the constituents' interests into representing the interests of a specific national lobby group or organisation.

Some people favour the Australian alternative-vote system. In this system a candidate has to receive more than half of the votes cast in order to be elected. If no candidate achieves this, the candidate with the fewest votes on the first count is eliminated. Each person has to express a second preference. The second preference on the ballot papers of those voting for the least popular candidate are then awarded to the other candidates in the race. If this produces a candidate with more than half the votes, then he wins. If there is still no winner, the second most unpopular candidate is eliminated and the second preferences of his voters are distributed. There are two big problems with this system. The first is that it is far from proportionate. An independent study by a democratic audit from the University of Essex in 1997 showed that the adoption of the Australian system of voting in the British general election of May 1997 would have increased rather than reduced the Labour majority, even though Labour had a minority of the votes. In that general election, with only 43 per cent of the votes Labour won 419 seats compared to 46 Liberal Democrats and 165 Conservatives. Essex University calculated that an alternative-voting system based on exit polls conducted at the time would have produced 436 Labour seats and only 110 Conservative seats, increasing the Labour majority over Conservatives from 179 to 213. Whilst many people wanted a change of government at the last general election, there are few who believe that Labour should have a bigger majority than they gained then, given that they only commanded a minority of the votes. Any proportionate system in May 1997 would have given the Conservatives more seats, not one-third fewer.

The second problem with the alternative-voting system is that it gives undue voting power to a small number of people who vote for the least popular candidate or candidates. In effect, people who vote for unpopular candidates vote twice whilst those who vote for the two or three most popular candidates only get to vote once. It is difficult to see the justice of this particular proposal. It is certainly an enticement for people to form more parties and to turn British politics more in the direction of single-subject campaigning away from traditional representation and party building. It would make a lot of sense for a whole range of single-issue parties to be established to make their point. They would be able to attract more support because they could tell their potential supporters that they would still get an opportunity through the alternative vote to decide the election anyway, even though they had not decided between the two most popular candidates in the first instance. The system is asymmetrical because it does not give strong supporters of the two main parties the opportunity at the same time to express their views on the single-subject issues, as a strong supporter of a main party would obviously want to vote on first preference for that party to try to obviate the need for the recasting of second preferences in the count.

Half of these difficulties are removed by the French system of the second ballot. In this a candidate must achieve an overall majority of the votes cast if he is to win. If no candidate receives more than half the votes, a further ballot is held at a later date with the removal of the least popular candidates from that ballot. This apparently overcomes the problem that only the supporters of the least popular parties vote twice but it is still far from proportionate and it is naturally more cumbersome and expensive than settling the whole matter in one single ballot. Both the French and the Australian systems tend to penalise the second most popular party, making it more difficult for an effective opposition to be mounted. Both systems therefore offer less voter choice than the present British first-past-the-post system. It is possible with alternative votes to preserve the link between the single member and the constituency.

Truly proportional systems depend upon lists. Voters are asked to vote for a particular party rather than a particular candidate. Seats are awarded to parties in relation to their overall share of the total vote. In Israel the list system entails awarding exactly the number of seats that are proportionate to the number of national votes cast for the party. This is the only way of getting a truly proportionate system. Adaptations to the list system are adopted in Germany. In Germany two different types of Member of Parliament are elected. One group are elected as in Britain by winning a simple majority of votes in a single member constituency. A second group come from using a list system awarded to each party so that its overall representation in the chamber reflects the overall share of the vote. The Jenkins Report concluded in favour of two types of MP for the UK – the Government is reluctant to tell us what it thinks of this proposal.

Creating two different types of member is very difficult. There would naturally be resentments between the two groups. Those that had been elected the hard way by securing an individual constituency nomination and voting endorsement would feel that they had to do much more work than those who were parachuted in from the list. The regular constituency MP would have to be prepared to take up the cases and issues that mattered to his constituents whilst the list MPs would be largely free to avoid those issues or problems that they didn't like or to free ride on the back of the constituency members. There would also be resentment if list MPs were more highly thought of by the party machinery that had chosen them, meaning that they were more likely to be selected for government or opposition frontbench office. The German system is, however, an improvement on the Israeli list system in that it does preserve the link between the member and the constituency in some cases and does give an individual constituent a route for his problem to be tackled.

The French system of two rounds of voting encourages tactical voting. A voter may vote in the first round for a candidate he does not wish to win in order to secure his chosen candidate's election in the second. This does seem to be a bizarre way of encouraging people to vote. If there are three candidates in a French-style election and you wish candidate one to be elected, it may make sense to vote for candidate three, rather than candidate one in the first round. You and other supporters of candidate one might decide it is easier for your candidate to beat candidate three than to beat candidate two in the second round. It is therefore in your interests to ensure that candidate two rather than candidate three is eliminated between the first and second rounds. Your best way of doing this is to vote for candidate three rather than candidate one. In the final round you can then reveal your true preference of candidate one.

In October 1996, New Zealand held its first elections under a form of proportional representation after years of using the first-past-the-post system successfully. Its mixed-member proportional system is similar to that in Germany. In order to implement such a system with a mixture of constituency MPs and list MPs, constituencies have to be made larger if you are to avoid increasing the numbers of the Members of Parliament and the costs of Parliament in total. This does to some extent weaken the representative function. More importantly, in New Zealand people had to wait for a few months before a government could be formed as no single party gained a majority. During the two months of negotiation, one political party switched its allegiance in a way that the electorate had not been expecting. In more recent opinion polls, 82 per cent of the electorate said they were unhappy with the coalition government which the new system had given them and 60 per cent said they wished to return to the first-past-the-post system. They have learnt the hard way that allegedly more fair systems can disrupt some of the representative functions of the constituency member and, more importantly, can lead to less stable rather than more stable government.

The Government has already introduced a hotchpotch of changes to our electoral system. The European parliamentary election system they have outlined replaces constituencies with much larger regions each electing a number of MEPs. In an attempt to introduce proportionality between the votes cast and the number of seats awarded the Government proposes the D'hondt method. This means that the first seat is given to the party or individual candidate with the greatest number of votes. The second and subsequent seats will be granted in the same way, except that the number of votes given to a party to which one or more seats have already been allocated shall be divided by the number of seats allocated plus one.

This is a complicated system which involves considerable mathematics on the night or day after the count to sort out how many seats are allocated to each party. Individual voters cannot express a preference between individual candidates. Although opinion surveys have shown that electors would prefer to influence both the name of the person and the party, the Government is insisting upon what is called a closed list. This means that the parties determine the order of preference in which their candidates will be elected. The voters can only cast a vote in favour of a particular party. The seat is then allocated to the individuals chosen by the party managements. The Conservative Party, disliking the lack of democracy in this system, is giving to every party member a vote not just on who should be Conservative candidates in the European elections but also to determine the order of merit on the list. In practice, in the Conservative Party the membership of the party will decide who are elected Members of the European Parliament whilst in the Labour Party the leadership will decide who will be elected. The electorate under the Government's proposals will only be invited to determine the broad proportions between Labour and Conservative MEPs: everything else will be decided by the parties themselves.

The results will not even be proportional nationally or Europe-wide, as the division of the United Kingdom into regions and the division of other parts of Europe into regions and countries will prevent the overall result being strictly proportional. The main consequence of the changes is to switch power over individual candidates from the electorate at large to either the party membership or the party leadership, depending on which party you are considering.

Not persuaded by its own method of election for the European Parliament, the Government has chosen different systems for Scotland and Wales. Seventy-three members of the Scottish Parliament will be elected on a first-past-the-post system on existing Westminster parliamentary constituencies except that Orkney and Shetland would each be entitled to a member. Similarly, 40 members of the Welsh Assembly will be elected on existing Westminster parliamentary boundaries using first-past-the-post. Top-up members will be given to the parties using current European constituency boundaries. The intention is that the total number of representatives the party had in either the Scottish Parliament or the Welsh Assembly in each current European constituency would reflect the proportions of the vote in that area. Seven members of the Scottish Parliament would be returned by each of the eight current Scottish Euro constituencies and four members of the Welsh Assembly from each of the five current Welsh Euro constituencies. The Government has decided to use the D'hondt system in this, as in the European elections, to choose these additional members. This hybrid is a particularly curious one. Choosing to use the current Euro constituencies at the very point where they are being abolished for the European Parliament is odd enough. It means that the proportionality is not as perfect as if the proportions were calculated throughout Scotland and throughout Wales respectively. Again the Government has chosen a closed-list system meaning that the electorate will have no part to play in choosing the individual candidates from within the party list.

It would be quite easy to have an open-list system instead. In an open-list system the electors can either vote for the party of their choice or vote for the individual candidate or candidates of their choice. Where they choose to vote for an individual candidate, this also counts as a vote for the party of that candidate and can be calculated accordingly when the computations are done to ensure a proportionate outcome in numbers of seats. This does give the electorate a direct say in the choice of candidates from within the party's list. This would be a real choice, as no party can look forward to winning every seat in any region of the country under this kind of voting system.

In its Green Paper on new and additional government for London, the Government was unable to conclude in favour of any particular voting system. They set out a range of options for the Mayor including first-past-the-post, the second-ballot system from France or the alternative-vote system. The paper did imply some criticism of the first-past-the-post system, whilst being neutral between the alternative-vote system and the two ballot rounds. When it came to the Assembly they left open a single-seat constituency model with either first-past-the-post or alternative-voting systems and multi-seat constituencies with anything from first past the post through additional members to lists or single transferable votes.

When the Government came to publish its White Paper it had decided upon the supplementary-vote system for electing the Mayor, a system which was not explicitly mentioned in its original Green Paper document. Under the supplementary-vote system voters mark their first and second choice of candidates on the ballot paper with the conventional 'X' rather than having to list the candidates in order of preference as they would under an alternative-vote system proper. Voters' first preferences are counted and if one counted gets 50 per cent of the vote or more he is elected. If no one gets 50 per cent of the vote, all the candidates except the two who received the highest number of votes are eliminated. The second preferences on the ballot papers of the eliminated candidates are examined and the votes cast from the two remaining candidates are given to those candidates. Whoever has the most votes at the end of that process is declared the winner.

The Government decided that for the Assembly they would use a similar system to the one they are proposing for the Scottish Parliament and the Welsh Assembly. Fourteen members of the 25-member Assembly will be elected from new constituencies still to be decided on a first-past-the-post system. Another 11 members will be chosen from party lists on the basis of the electorate's votes cast for the parties overall.

In these systems of election, including the London Assembly, where some members are elected proportionately, there will be no by-election if they resign or die in office. When a vacancy becomes available, the person next on the party list representing the party of the resigning or dead member will be automatically given the job.

The absence of by-elections in some of these systems is another anti-democratic feature of them. By-elections to councils and to Parliament give the electorate the chance to shift the balance a little if they are happy or unhappy with the governing party concerned. In cases where councils or even Parliament has been won by a small majority, a series of by-elections can actively change control, reflecting changed public preferences during the natural term of a council or Parliament. Under systems where people are automatically brought forward from a party list to replace the outgoing member, there is no such opportunity for reflecting changed electoral wishes during the full term of a council or Parliament.

In Northern Ireland, the Government is proposing something different again. It recommends a 108-member Assembly elected by proportional representation from existing Westminster constituencies. However, committee chairs and ministerships and committee membership have to be allocated strictly in proportion to party voting strength. Key decisions have to be taken on a cross-community basis with either parallel consent or a weighted majority (60 per cent) of members present and voting including at least 40 per cent of each of the Nationalist and Unionist designations. Ministerial posts have to be allocated to parties by reference to the number of seats each party has in the Assembly, whilst the Chairman and Deputy of the Assembly have to be elected on a cross-community basis. In Northern Ireland at the moment single transferable votes are used for both local and European elections already.

So what are we to make of all these different voting systems that are being proposed by this Labour Government? We can see from their constant experimentation with different styles of voting system that there is no fixed principle or clarity of view prevailing. We are committed to first-past-the-post for the time being at Westminster and for local councils; to regional lists for the European Parliament; to a German-style mixture of first-past-the-post and top-up lists for the Welsh Assembly and Scottish Parliament; for a similar system for the London Assembly; to a new system of calculating the winner for the mayoralty of London; and a different proportional system of voting in Northern Ireland. The electorate will get extremely confused about the different voting methods being used for different purposes. There will need to be rather more public education ahead of each election concerning the method of voting and the way of computing the result so that people can make more informed choices, including tactical choices, in each of the elections.

The choice of a wide range of systems by the Government implies that it does not believe there is a single satisfactory answer to the problem. The fact that it has left single-member constituencies based on first past the post for a preponderance of London Assembly members and for members of the Scottish Parliament and Welsh Assembly implies that even the radicals within the Government accept that the current system for Westminster elections has a lot to recommend it. The Government is clearly worried about breaking the single-member constituency principle completely in all elections save the European.

The Government's argument for the European Parliament assumes that there is already a rather weak constituency link because of the rather large sizes of the constituencies. Whilst it is true that the large size of constituency does limit the capacity of the member of the European Parliament to be fully acquainted with all the tides of local opinion and all of the local institutions in his area, the constituency link does ensure that there is just one named person responsible for dealing with any problems that the public wishes to take up at European parliamentary level. This will disappear with the new system of election to the European Parliament.

It remains to be seen how people elected under regional list systems will choose to carry out their job. It would be possible for the full team of regional MEPs, regardless of party, to nominate one amongst their number to cover each particular topic or responsibility. It would be possible to agree rough geographical divisions as if there were separate constituencies. It is more likely that arrangements will be made within parties rather than between parties. The most likely outcome is a range of spokesmanships over groups of related topics for MEPs of a given party in a given region. In some cases there may be no clear arrangements at all, leaving the public in a muddle as to who their Member of the European Parliament is and how they can get in touch with him.

The Labour/Liberal rhetoric in favour of more proportional systems of voting makes a virtue out of the need for coalitions. They claim that it will produce a new consensus type of politics. They believe that the British public is tired of confrontational politics with politicians of different parties arguing strongly against each other. They believe that there is too much unpleasantness, and that the public feels that some of the sound and fury of the disagreements is synthetic. The theory runs that if people have to build coalitions within a parliament or assembly across party lines they will agree on many more things and come to the right conclusion by having a more positive attitude.

This system misunderstands the nature of the British governing process and has tried to substitute for it one which has proved itself less capable of sorting out the issues of the day. The British governing process, embodied in the architecture of the House of Commons, is based on the proposition that you are either in favour of something or against it. The architecture and the structure of debate is based on the assumption that a government proposition is best tested by having people formally oppose it and probe the government to set out its thinking on why the proposal might be beneficial. Moving from this to 'less confrontational' styles of politics may just mean that there is less satisfactory debate or scrutiny, when the government wishes to bring forward a measure. No one will be charged with the formal task of opposing and no one may be bothered to point out the difficulties or problems or represent the disquiet of the public on the issue before it is adopted. The opposition in Parliament is under a moral duty to oppose most of what the government does. It is under a formal requirement to offer opinions on every major transaction the government brings before the House of Commons. A sensible opposition from time to time finds whole policies or elements of policies with which it agrees, but more often than not there are genuine disagreements in the community which it is the opposition's duty to expose.

Officials and government ministers need to be constantly tested when they are wielding the enormous powers they enjoy. It is fear of the telling parliamentary quotation, the probing parliamentary question or the revealing parliamentary statement that acts as the stimulus to less government or better government or forces the administration to think clearly about what it wishes to do before it attempts to do it. Were we to abandon the formal tradition of strong opposition, a large part of national opinion would be less well represented.

If a governing party wishes to propose a £1000 per family increase in taxation and the opposition party thinks there is no need for such an increase, it is best if the matter is put before the House of Commons in a budget, and during the course of a budget debate the pros and cons of higher taxes or more private spending can be argued through in front of the public. It is not always a good idea to take the Chancellor of the Exchequer and his opposition opponent to one side and make them sit in a room until they have decided that the tax rise should be somewhere between £400 and £600 depending upon their skill and strength of bargaining. The nation would not necessarily be better served. There may be some people who would take heart from the fact that Conservative and Labour had managed to get together and agree a more modest tax rise than Labour would have liked but a less satisfactory one than the Conservatives would have proposed. But, unless the negotiations and the arguments are conducted in public, the public is much less well served by its politicians because it will never know the arguments or considerations that made one group want an increase of £1000 and another group want no increase at all. Surely in this situation it is better to have the argument out in front of the public, for one team to be able to win the vote and then for the public to be able to judge the results.

If a compromise was struck over an issue like that, neither side would be happy and neither side would be properly to blame. When it came to the general election the Labour side could say, 'Well of course we were not able to do all we wanted to do for public services because we had to reach a consensus on tax levels and the Conservatives would not let us place as big a tax increase as we would like.' At the same election the Conservatives would be saying that the economy would have worked much better, more tax revenue would be collected from a growing economy and people would have been much happier if taxes had been lower, but unfortunately they had not been able to persuade the Labour team of the justice of keeping taxes down. It would be much more difficult for the public to judge who was to blame for the lack of economic success or the lack of improvement in public services.

British people are likely to react if we go further into alternative voting systems as the people of New Zealand have done. Initial acquiescence or even enthusiasm would rapidly give way to worry that something important had been lost. People do expect their politicians to debate the issues, to put the proposal and the alternative, to make a decision and then to defend it. People do want to have direct access to an individual representative who has a duty to take up their case or act as their voice. People do expect to be able to make a judgement from time to time on the success or failure of the government, the council, the body in authority over them.

One of the features of the new Labour Government is the reluctance to withstand a normal barrage of parliamentary debate and the wish to find as many ways as possible of softening the blows or removing the arguments altogether. It is now playing around with a series of different voting systems designed to produce more coalition and consensus and less debate and argument.

Argument is the very substance of democracy. An Englishman's liberty is his right to express his view and to find others to agree with him. We have a long tradition since the seventeenth century of settling things in the ballot box and in votes in the House of Commons. We have an equally long tradition of long and rowdy arguments in the pub, in the village hall, at a protest meeting, on radio and television and in the House of Commons itself. These are the healthy signs of a flourishing democracy. Take away some of them and the democracy is weakened.

The best way of keeping the link between elector and elected is by a single-member constituency of a manageable size. The best way of adjudging who is elected is to make sure that the person who gets more votes than any other candidate is duly returned. The best way to keep some proportionality in the system is to ensure that all constituencies are the same size. We do not want different types or values of MPs, members of the Scottish Parliament, or members of the London Assembly. We do not want complicated systems for calculating the results which take many hours after the votes have been cast. Above all, we do not wish to abolish the tradition of proposition and opposition, of being for or against and of having to argue one's corner accordingly. Sometimes it is better to keep the advantages of the system that you know, even with its imperfections, than to rush into substituting something different which others have tried and have found wanting. It is even rasher to replace the existing system with a whole multitude of different systems, betraying a lack of inner confidence in the case for change and a reticence to commit to any alternative system. If you wish to undermine Britain, undermine Parliament. Parliament is the political expression of the nation. Anything that weakens the links between government and the governed, between member and constituent, weakens the nation's right to be heard. Ultimately it weakens the nation. It is designed to further the European federal dream. It does not enhance the British reality.

8 Devolution

It has always been Europe's belief that it would be helpful if each member state had regional government along the lines of the German *Länder*. The absence of such regional government in Britain has been seen as a problem for the European Union. As part of the process of undermining the status and power of the nation state, the European Union has made a conscious effort to appeal over the heads of member states to the regions in each country. In the United Kingdom, in the absence of regional government the appeal has had to be made to the county councils, both rural and metropolitan. Europe has set up a committee of the regions and has paid special attention to promoting regional interests. Sometimes this builds on natural cultural and political affinities that already exist. In the case of Spain, people in Catalonia do feel very different from people in Castile who in turn are very separate from the Basques. In Italy, people in the Mezzogiorno feel very different from northern Italians.

It does prove more difficult in England. There are no huge regional differences or strong senses of individual regional identity. There are local and county differences that are reflected in government and in natural and contrived borders. If I travel west from my constituency I soon reach the border of the European regions of the South East and South West of England. Yet nothing perceptibly changes as you cross that tenuous border and there is nothing on either side to give a strong sense of identity or community that is distinctively South Eastern or South Western. Old loyalties to Wessex long since died. There has been considerable uncertainty in designing new regional borders that mean anything. In my own area we have different regional affiliations for the management of health, economic development, European parliamentary elections, policing and planning. Sometimes we are called the Thames Valley, sometimes the South East, sometimes the rest of the South East excluding London, sometimes simply the South. None of this matters very much to people, as they do not primarily see themselves as Thames Valley dwellers or South Easterners.

The new British Government has decided that it wants to move in the direction of a Europe of the regions but it does understand that England feels rather differently. As a result, under its usual cloak of modernising, the Government has proposed going back to ideas which it put forward as the then Labour government in the 1970s only to see them voted down by the electorates of Scotland and Wales. The Government has created a Welsh

Assembly and a Scottish Parliament. It has also decided to replace the Greater London Council abolished by the Conservative government of the 1980s and give London separate regional government as well. So far it has not come up with any proposals for granting elected regional government to the rest of England, understanding as it does the lack of regional feeling in many parts of England. It is complex, if not impossible, to draw boundaries that mean anything, even in those areas where there are strong local affiliations. Some people in North West England do feel that North West England is different from either South or North East England, but there are endless arguments about the boundaries. There is more disagreement between Liverpool and Manchester than there is agreement between those two pre-eminent cities of the North West.

As with voting systems, so with the newly elected governments for the regions: the Labour Government is unsure of how much power to entrust to them and has tailored individual solutions to the inherited circumstance and to its judgement of the times. By far the most powerful and wide-ranging of the regional governments it is proposing is that of the Scottish Parliament. All matters not specifically reserved for the United Kingdom Parliament are to be devolved to Scotland. The legislation reserves to the Parliament of the union constitutional matters, foreign affairs, civil service, defence, fiscal economic and monetary policy, currency, financial services, financial markets, regulating money laundering, data protection, controlling the misuse of drugs, immigration and nationality, emergency powers, general business and competition law, intellectual property, import and export control, energy, some transport matters, social security schemes, pensions and certain other detailed measures.

The list of devolved matters set out in the Government's White Paper is long and wide ranging. It includes health, education, science and research funding, careers advice, local government, social work, housing, planning, economic development and regeneration, financial assistance to industry, promotion of tourism, trade and exports, public transport, the criminal law, the civil law, judicial appointments in the criminal justice system, tribunals, legal aid, parole of prisons, police and fire services, civil defence and emergency planning, liquor licensing, the protection of animals, the environment, heritage, agriculture, food standards, forestry, fisheries, sport and the arts.

The responsibilities of the Welsh Assembly are considerably smaller. They include economic development, agriculture, forestry, fisheries and food, industry and training, education, local government, health and personal social services, housing, environment, planning, transport and roads, arts, culture and the Welsh language, heritage, sport and recreation. They are also differently drawn up. The Scottish Parliament is given powers to pass primary legislation in all the areas of its competence. Indeed, the Scottish Parliament is allowed to enact legislation on anything that is not deemed to be a reserved matter. In contrast, the Welsh Assembly can only fill out the details in secondary legislation underneath controlling Westminster primary enactments.

The difference can be seen in the field of education. Both the Parliament and the Assembly have responsibilities for education. Where the Scottish Parliament can pass laws reorganising schools and setting out detailed requirements of the schools, the Welsh Assembly is only empowered to make statutory instruments under existing English and Welsh educational legislation passed by the House of Commons. The Assembly in Wales can influence the Welsh curriculum but it cannot pass a law to expand or abolish the curriculum itself. In Scotland, the Scottish Parliament could decide to dispense with the requirement for a national curriculum altogether or expand it greatly through primary legislation.

The powers of the London Assembly are smaller again than those accruing to the Welsh Assembly. The London Assembly's prime role is to act as a body scrutinising the work of the Mayor. The Mayor himself is responsible for strategic planning, transport, the police and civil defence. He is not responsible for areas like education or health. As a result, the regional assembly for London is not responsible for these either. Its only executive power comes in circumstances where it is in disagreement with the Mayor about the budget for the items under the Mayor's control. After a long process of passing the budget backwards and forwards, the London Assembly could, as long as two-thirds of its members voted accordingly, put through a budget for the London mayoralty with which the Mayor himself was not happy. In these circumstances the London Assembly has executive power. In all other circumstances the Assembly is there to cross-examine and question the Mayor and to provide a forum for debate for the Mayor's plans.

The powers of the London Assembly are much more limited than either the Welsh or Scottish versions of devolved government for two main reasons. Firstly, the Assembly is an afterthought to an elected executive Mayor. There are no executive Mayors anywhere else in Britain. The Government had to leave the Mayor with some real authority, having claimed that he was going to be executive. Consequently it was important not to give the Assembly too much power to design its own policies, produce its own Cabinet or overturn the Mayor too often. Secondly, London regional government was seen as more of an adjunct to borough government. The London boroughs are left with most of the powers to spend most of the money in London on public services, being responsible for social services and education, the two largest spending areas by far. The Government decided against giving either the Mayor or the elected Assembly any direct powers over these areas. As a result, local government in London will continue to deal direct with Whitehall whereas local government in Wales and in Scotland will deal with the intermediary regional authority in each case.

The main reason for the difference in powers between Scotland and Wales is the different intensity of nationalist sentiment. Transfer of powers from Westminster and Whitehall to the Scottish and Welsh offices has continued apace in the post-war period. They gathered momentum under the Conservative administration of 1979–97. However, the big difference between Scotland and Wales resided in the preservation of a different form of criminal law and criminal justice system in Scotland from that of Wales. Since the amalgamation of England and Wales under the Tudors, the two have enjoyed a common law code. After the Act of Union with Scotland, it was decided to continue with a separate criminal justice system north of the border. As a result, the Westminster Parliament has regularly enacted two different kinds of legislation, often bearing a family resemblance one to the other, to suit the different circumstances in Scotland compared to England and Wales. The idea of the Scottish Parliament is to take over the Scottish criminal and civil law codes as well as the functions shared in common with the Welsh Office and transferred to the Welsh Assembly.

It has also been decided that the Scottish Parliament should have more power and should behave more like an independent government than the Welsh Assembly. This is based upon a Labour political judgement that enthusiasm for more home rule is much stronger in Scotland than in Wales and that this enthusiasm should be met by the offer of more genuine devolved authority. In a way it is a good thing that Labour respects the historical evolution of different parts of the Kingdom. In a way it is a bad thing that a party which pretends to be a party of the union of the United Kingdom should offer more devolved power to that part of the country where they are most worried about the strength of separatist as well as devolutionary tendencies. Usually, the granting of more and more powers for separate development and separate government within a once unified state leads inexorably to stronger nationalist movements and often to eventual separation.

Over the next few years, the new settlement of devolved government in three parts of the United Kingdom, and possibly in a fourth with a different structure in Northern Ireland, will sorely test the powers of cohesion of the union. The legislation setting out these new bodies contains within it plenty of scope for further disagreement. In the Scottish legislation the power is granted for the Scottish Parliament to set up solely Scottish bodies where currently there are UK or GB arrangements in place. Where it does not wish to do so immediately, it can require reports and oral evidence on the activities of the UK and GB bodies direct to itself. This is one of the areas where the tensions may become apparent. Those of a nationalist turn of mind in Scotland may make unreasonable demands upon GB or UK bodies and may press the Scottish executive to set up more and more independent Scottish bodies whatever the merits of the case.

A big opportunity for conflict arises in defining the Scottish Parliament's legislative powers. The Government states optimistically in its White Paper that 'given an open and constructive relationship between the UK government and the Scottish executive, problems will usually be resolved quickly and amicably'. The White Paper then goes on at considerable length to explain how disputes will be resolved, in a spirit of realism. There will indeed be such disputes. The Scottish Parliament and executive are requested to take legal advice before enacting any legislation, to make sure that it is within their powers. UK Government departments can make known to the Scottish Parliament any worry they may have about the scope of the enactment.

'Prior to a Scottish Bill being passed forward from the presiding office to receive royal assent, there will be a short delay period to ensure that the UK Government is content as to vires. In the event of a dispute between Scottish Executive and the UK Government about vires remaining unresolved, there will be provision for it to be referred to the judicial committee of the privy council.' The method envisaged is to ensure that there is a judicial committee with at least five law lords sitting on it who will then adjudicate as to whether the Scottish Parliament is entitled to pass the law it wishes or not.

There is also scope for disagreement over the United Kingdom's position in international activities. The British Government intends that the United Kingdom should speak with one voice. Realising that some in Scotland will want direct access in international bodies, certain sops are offered to the Scottish Parliament. The idea is offered that Scottish ministers serving on the Scottish executive in the Scottish Parliament would from time to time be able to represent the United Kingdom position in Council of Ministers meetings in Europe. The Scottish executive is invited to be involved in 'close liaison' with Whitehall departments concerned with international negotiations. In some cases direct representation will be offered to Scottish members on the UK delegation. Nonetheless, the White Paper leaves it clear that international foreign policy is a matter for the Parliament of the union and not for the Scottish Parliament. Where the Scottish Parliament disagrees with the line that the Parliament of the union is taking, there will undoubtedly be rows and tensions.

The flare-up is likely to be most acute in relationships with the European Union. The White Paper offers a rosy prospect. It suggests 'the role of Scottish ministers and officials will be to support and advance the single UK negotiating line which they have played a part in developing. The emphasis in negotiations has to be on working as a UK team.' The problem will arise if the Scottish Parliament has a different political balance from the Westminster one. It will then have an executive or government with a different political persuasion from Westminster. It could then have a very different view as to how Britain should handle a particular negotiation or its European relationship more generally. In these circumstances it is difficult to see how a Scottish executive would be happy to try to influence the United Kingdom general policy position in private before the meeting and then argue the United Kingdom case, whatever it may be, when it came to the Council of Ministers meeting itself. The United Kingdom Parliament also keeps a reserve power to legislate in any area where it needs to do so, to ensure compliance with European treaty obligations. The British Government is clearly not persuaded that it can rely upon the Scottish Parliament to fulfil all of the requirements of our European obligations and so it has kept the reserve power.

The next most obvious area of contention is money. The Government hopes that it can continue the current system of the Scottish block grant and take politics out of the settlement. Once there is a full-blooded Parliament in Edinburgh, it is most likely that the Parliament will constantly be demanding more money from the United Kingdom Parliament whilst the United Kingdom Parliament will be saying that Scotland has enough or more than enough. It is bound to politicise the settlement between Scotland and the United Kingdom, whereas in the past it has often not been a politically contentious matter as it has been settled between Cabinet members of the same ruling party. The annual running costs of the Scottish Parliament are estimated at £20–30 million. It will inherit a Scottish Office budget of £14,000 million.

The Welsh Assembly is similarly going to be financed by a continuation of the block-grant system currently running at £7000 million. The introduction of the Welsh Assembly is being used by the Government as an opportunity to streamline three of the economic development quangos in Wales. The intention is to amalgamate the Welsh Development Agency (WDA), the Development Board for Rural Wales (DBRW) and the Land Authority into one. Although sorting out and reducing the number of quangos is to be a devolved power for the Welsh Assembly, the Government has decided to do the work for them in one of the most important areas under their control, regardless of what their views might be. Where the Scottish Parliament is told it can decide to continue with council-tax capping or not as it sees fit, the Welsh Assembly is told that the Government will give it the answer on whether capping is going to be retained or not for England and Wales.

In the field of European relations, the Welsh Assembly is a very pale imitation of the Scottish Parliament. The prime responsibility for the relationship will continue to rest with the Secretary of State for Wales. There is no suggestion that members of the Welsh Assembly can attend Council of Ministers meetings on behalf of the United Kingdom. The Assembly is offered the opportunity to discuss and debate European initiatives. Their views are to be taken into account through the Secretary of State when the United Kingdom forms its view. Despite the reduced workload, considerably less power than the Scottish Parliament and the fact that Wales has a much smaller population, the Assembly in Wales is still expected to cost £15–20 million a year to run.

People in Wales who want independence or proper devolution naturally feel upset that they have so much less on offer than Scotland. The Assembly is largely a talking shop. Many of the important structural decisions about quangos and local government have been taken, or are about to be taken, by the British Government before the Assembly can express its view.

Nationalist movements in both Scotland and Wales will now have an easy time creating campaigns against the power of the centre. In Wales, Plaid Cymru is likely to run campaigns based on the theme of an 'insult to Wales'. It will present the more modest Welsh settlement as unsatisfactory. It will claim that Wales should have at least the same powers as Scotland to make its own decisions. It will want to gradually detach Welsh law from English law and gain more control over decisions in Wales. It will want to move its Assembly from an advisory body and talking shop to a more powerful executive modelled on Scottish lines. It will wish to exert more and more control and pressure over the Secretary of State for Wales, who under this settlement retains many of the former powers of the office despite the existence of the Assembly. Indeed, the whole Welsh devolution document is written in a different and rather dismissive tone from the Scottish one. Crucial decisions which should be the Authority's to settle, are settled already or will be settled for it, in due course, by the British Government.

In Scotland, the Scottish Nationalist movement will now attempt to foment a series of crises, creating conflicts between the Scottish Parliament and the Westminster one. They will argue incessantly that only if the Scottish

Parliament digs in, countermands the Westminster one and battles for the rights of Scotland, can it be said to be a success and a proper Parliament in its own right. Only if the Scottish Parliament succeeds in getting more powers under its control will they say it is doing its job properly. There are three areas in particular where the Scottish Nationalist movement could hope to create havoc for Westminster and the Labour Government. The first is money. The Scottish Parliament is very likely to say that Scotland needs more money than it is permitted under the block-grant formula, more than it can raise with the 3p additional income tax power. The Parliament may well set about increasing local taxation more dramatically than in England. It may invent a series of charges or prices to develop a form of surrogate taxation. We could see the Scottish Parliament behaving rather like the Stuart monarchy before the Civil War. It will find a number of ploys for raising money which in the end the Westminster Parliament may have to challenge as being outside its powers.

The second area is likely to be the limits of devolved law. Scottish nationalists could propose legislation in areas on the edge of the stated powers of the Scottish Parliament. They will argue passionately that it would be absurd for Scottish people to be unable to express a different view and have a different law in those areas given that they are allowed a different view in many other areas. They will probably try to find an important test case which pushes the limits of devolved law considerably further in the direction of Scottish authority.

The third area likely to cause difficulties is European policy and European representation itself. The nationalists are unlikely to be happy with the current state of play. They do not really wish to have a common United Kingdom position on anything. They would prefer a Scottish position with direct Scottish representation or even membership of the Community. It will be quite easy to identify policy areas where nationalists believe that Scottish or Welsh interests differ from those of the rest of the United Kingdom. They may well be encouraged in this belief by the European Community itself.

In the long-running arguments over beef, the Community introduced the principle of differentiating between different parts of the United Kingdom. It succeeded in splitting Scottish and Northern Irish farmers away from English ones by hinting or confirming that the ban could be lifted at different times in different parts of the United Kingdom and that the problem was less acute in Northern Ireland than it was in England. With devolved assemblies it would be more and more difficult to keep a common United Kingdom line on issues like this, where both nationalist opinion is seeking to make differences within the United Kingdom and the European Union itself is encouraging the development of such differences by its own policy stance. One of the main unresolved issues in the devolution proposals is what has become known as the West Lothian question. The question first formulated by the MP for that part of Scotland has two forms. Why can a Scottish Member of the Westminster Parliament, once devolution has taken place, vote on matters like education and health for England but not on such matters for Scotland? The English variant of the question is, why can a Scottish Member of Parliament vote on health and education in England when an English Member of Parliament cannot return the compliment and vote on such matters for Scotland?

There is a partial answer to the question of why a Scottish Member of the Westminster Parliament should vote on English issues that are the province in Scotland for the devolved Parliament. It would be possible for the Westminster Parliament to form itself into an English grand committee to debate and vote on the English issues and exclude Scottish members from such a grand committee. It is not possible to solve the other problem. Once devolution is in place, there will always be two different types of MP at Westminster. The English Member of Parliament will have a full range of powers covering all the current government functions whilst the Scottish Member of Parliament will only have a limited number of functions relating to union matters. If the United Kingdom does form an English grand committee to deal with English matters, then the Scottish Member of Parliament has very little to do indeed. If the Parliament continues to allow Scottish members to participate in English matters within the United Kingdom Parliament, then the Scottish MP is in the ridiculous position of having to explain to his electors why he can have opinions and influence on health and education in England but not in Scotland.

It is surprising that the Government has come forward with these proposals which already look 30 years out of date, being so similar to the proposals which the Scottish and Welsh people rejected in the 1970s. It is true that the Scottish proposals received enthusiastic support in the referendum. The Welsh proposals only just scraped home with a bare majority on a low turn-out. Only one-quarter of the people of Wales thought the Assembly a sufficiently good idea to go and vote for it. This is not surprising given how limited its powers are and how irrelevant extra government is to the problems of the United Kingdom.

The Government's document on the Mayor and Assembly for London looks dated already, set as it is in 1970s thinking. At the beginning of the chapter on functions in the Government's White Paper, it makes clear that the Mayor will have an important part to play in creating sustainable development. Great emphasis is laid upon a new duty to be imposed on the Mayor to promote sustainable strategies. The document asserts that the quality of London as an environment has deteriorated in many respects in recent years. There is no understanding of the great impact that later twentieth-century legislation has had upon air and water quality. There has been a massive clean-up in London in the twentieth century. The rivers are now far cleaner, as demonstrated by the presence of salmon and other fish in them, and the air is much cleaner than in the age of the great London smogs. This has been achieved by national legislation and national and international targets reducing the amount of airborne and water-borne pollution dramatically.

The Mayor is also required to set out an integrated transport strategy in London. This is a curious requirement to place on the Mayor given that he is to be directly elected. It would be perfectly reasonable for a candidate for the mayoralty to say that a government-led integrated transport strategy is the opposite of what London needs. London's transport problems in part stem from having a nationalised monopoly Underground railway system, a commuter overland railway system that was until recently a monopoly nationalised business, and a vigorously controlled bus system with little competition or choice. A mayoralty candidate could argue that what London needs is more choice and competition rather than more integration and planning. Years of planning and integration of tube and bus travel through common ownership of the businesses failed to deliver the better transport system that the Government now seeks.

The Government does not have full confidence in a democratic system in London. It states that it will be taking powers to limit the amount of spending the new Mayor can undertake. Although the Mayor is meant to have power to switch money from development to planning to transport to fire within his overall block grant, the Government also tends to lay down minimum amounts of money that have to go to the main functions.

The early skirmishes in the mayoralty campaigns of leading candidates have already shown how much scope there is in regional government for rows to develop between different parts of the United Kingdom. A constant refrain of potential candidates for the mayoralty is that Scotland receives too much money from the Government at the expense of London. At the very time when the Government is reassuring Scotland that it can have its own Parliament and maintain its current block formula to receive the same amount of money as it has been receiving in the past, those who are running for the most powerful elected office beneath the government in the country, seeking the position of Mayor of London, are immediately plunging into controversy by saying that the current distribution of moneys between the different parts of the United Kingdom is unfair. On their side they have the evidence that the people in Scotland receive substantially more per head in terms of total public spending and government grant than people in London. They can also now point to a similarity in income levels, unemployment rates and the like between the Scottish average and the London average. They can point to areas of London which show every bit as much deprivation and unemployment, if not more, than the worst parts of Glasgow.

It also tells us something about the way in which regional government will develop. It is to be expected that people in charge of regional governments will rather blame the central government for not giving them enough money than accept any responsibility themselves for the adequacies and inadequacies of the services that they are providing. It is a much easier way of proceeding to blame someone else, than to accept that there is sufficient money and it is a question of how well it is spent and what priorities are chosen.

The more government there is, the more the public will lose out. Every one of these new governing authorities comes with a bill attached. Every one is likely to prove more expensive to set up than the original Government estimates. In each case there have been difficulties finding suitable accommodation for the new bodies. The worst problems have arisen in Wales. It had been assumed that the Welsh Assembly would be able to use the old Cardiff City Hall by agreement with Cardiff City. A row ensued, Cardiff City held out for too much money and as a result the Secretary of State is now proposing to build an entirely new property somewhere in Cardiff. The costs of this project are likely to escalate and get the Assembly off to a very bad start in terms of providing value for money. In Scotland, many had thought that the old Royal High School on Carlton Hill would be chosen. However, the Government now regards the access as poor and thinks that there is insufficient suitable space in the main building for Members of Parliament to meet their constituents and that there would be a need for substantial additional office accommodation. As a result, in Scotland, as in Wales, they are now erecting a completely new building with all the associated costs.

In London, the old headquarters of the Greater London Council has been sold and adapted for new purposes. The Mayor and the Greater London Assembly will be looking for purpose-built office accommodation in an expensive central London market. Decisions still have to be taken about salaries, but it seems likely that these regional government members are going to be treated as full-time politicians with salaries rather than as councillors doing it as a part-time job for expenses and attendance allowances. Doubtless too, there will be substantial back-up staffs for the

Scottish executive, for the mayoralty in London and even for the Assembly in Cardiff.

Once an elected layer of government is established and an officialdom built around it, it usually wishes to do more and more things to demonstrate its worth and to expand its empire. These new regional governments will be competing in a very crowded government market place. Beneath them are the boroughs and the unitary authorities of Scottish and Welsh local government. Above them are not just the departments of Whitehall and the powers of Parliament but also the ever-increasing powers of the European Commission, the European Community and the European Parliament. Whilst there will be plenty of scope for liaising, co-ordinating, networking and responding to each other's consultation documents, there will also be considerable scope for rows over jurisdiction and for over-government, as more than one layer of government comes to be involved in the same problem.

The rows between the different types of regional government in the United Kingdom will be useful to those seeking to create a European superstate by whipping up those very regional differences. At some point the current British Government will want to tackle the anomaly that, where London, Wales and Scotland have varying types of elected body, the rest of England has regional government offices that are mere branches of Whitehall with no elected assembly above. There are half-hearted attempts to provide some indirectly elected cover for regional government in England. There are bodies bringing together representatives of councillors in different parts of the country for planning and other purposes. There is a strong wish to give more work to the regional government offices to conduct. They have become an unnecessary intermediary or buffer between local government in the regions of England and Whitehall, which controls, guides and finances them.

In my own part of the country, in the Thames Valley, we are part of the government office of the South East in Guildford. This covers a very wide-ranging area of the South East but excludes London. It means that we are treated in common with places like Kent and Essex but not in common with the capital city some 35 miles down the road. Few of my constituents ever travel to Kent and few of them work there, whereas a large number of my constituents have daily or weekly links with London, using it as a place of employment, entertainment and leisure or as a source of contracts and a place for business meetings. When my local council now wishes to influence government opinion on planning matters, financial matters or legislative matters, it is encouraged to put its representations through the government of the South East office rather than direct to ministers in Whitehall. It is difficult to see what advantage this brings to anyone other than those enjoying the sorrows in the government office. Ultimately, if there is a serious problem between my local authority and the government, it will fall to myself and councillors to go and see the minister in an effort to sort it out. If there are problems that can be resolved at official level, this used to be done by direct negotiation between council offices and staff in the Department of the Environment in Whitehall. Now those officers have to deal with intermediary staff in the government of the South East office, who then have to take their case separately to those same officials in Whitehall that the officers used to deal with direct. There is more chance of the message becoming garbled or the argument being less well put; less chance of a satisfactory outcome; and considerably more danger of more people being involved and more money spent on trying to resolve these disputes.

The thrust of the Government's argument is that this regional government level is desirable, necessary and inevitable and that in due course the regional governments for England will have to be made democratic in the way in which Wales, Scotland and London are being made democratic – or at least in one of these ways, as they are all different. It is already quite difficult persuading people that being a councillor responsible for the substantial budgets of a unitary authority or a county council in England is a worthwhile job. This is a great pity. Properly done, it is a very worthwhile job. My own local unitary authority has a budget in excess of £100 million and has wide-ranging powers to do good or ill in the provision of schools, social service facilities, the environment and planning. Yet, because for many years the press and some councillors have conspired to tell us that all power has drained from local authorities to the centre, many are now put off the idea of undertaking community service by becoming a councillor. They do not see that it is relevant to their daily lives or fear that they will not have much power to do good if elected.

Far from making this problem easier, the election of regional governments will undoubtedly make it worse. Regional governments will in part take their power by removing power or influence from the level of government beneath them. A council leader in an important local authority who can appear in the local paper alongside a Member of Parliament will suddenly have to take a back seat beneath the stories covering the debates in the regional assembly on the self-same matters that his council is trying to solve.

It is argued that there are strategic issues which go wider than a typical local authority area but are not sufficiently large to warrant national government attention. We can see in the document on London the Government desperately trying to find such issues in the capital city. The case of roads is an important one. There are at the moment systems of trunk roads which fall to the central government to plan. All the trunk roads in London are the commencement of routes which extend tens or hundreds of miles beyond the boundaries of London to the opposite ends of these islands. It is difficult to see why the A2 trunk road, starting from central London and running down to Dover, should be the province of a London authority in its London area, when the rest of it is properly controlled by national government authority. It is difficult to see why the A1, running north from London, should be under the control of the London Mayor for a few miles and then under the control of the national Government as it heads north to Scotland. It is even more curious that the Government has left out the M1, M11 and M4 spurs which go into the capital city, and kept these as national matters, when it is transferring the other trunk roads to the London Authority. The Government also accepts that some roads will have to be transferred from current borough responsibility to the London mayoralty. This implies that the Government has the wrong classifications at the moment regarding trunk and local roads. The document is cautious about the extent of this transfer because it realises that boroughs will resent losing control over roads that they have for many years maintained and developed in the way they saw fit.

The main island of Great Britain is relatively compact. It is quite possible to design a road system from the centre. Of course, it has to be thought through and fought through in each locality. That is why we have elaborate planning enquiry processes for any new road proposal and why we bend over backwards to be extremely democratic in hearing out local communities on road issues. It is difficult to see how a set of regional governments would plan a suitable nationwide trunk road network. They would be subject to exactly the same kind of border and boundary disputes on trunk road development that the Government complains about in local road development between boroughs, districts, counties and unitary authorities. It would be unhelpful to northern regions if London decided that it was going to place traffic humps or too many traffic signals on the southern end of the M1 or the A1M. Similarly it would be unhelpful to the London region if its chosen route for main trunk roads north of the capital ushered traffic into newly designed traffic traps, if the regional authority to the north of London did not agree that those roads should be major haul routes. This surely is a matter better left to national government.

Similarly, the Government is trying to give the London mayoralty entrée into the matter of the national railway system. The compromise position it has arrived at is to give the Mayor more direct powers over that bit of the rail network that is actually within his territory and fewer powers for the commuter network when it goes beyond the London boundaries. This, like trunk roads, makes little sense. In order to plan proper commuter routes into and out of London, you need to plan the complete route, not just to influence or control one part of it. This is surely something better done by an authority with a bigger remit than that of just London. Indeed, might it not be better done by a national authority?

One of the big growth areas will be regional development. The Government has an old-fashioned view of economic development. Whilst it claims to have accepted some of the lessons of market place economics of the last 20 years, its language and its institutional creations make clear that it believes that governments could, should and will intervene to encourage economic development in the less favoured areas between and within regions. In each of the Scottish, Welsh and London cases, development agencies are being beefed up or created. London is to have a big development agency of its own capable of subsidising, clearing land, encouraging inward investment and helping generate jobs. In Wales, the WDA, the DBRW and the Land Authority are being put into one super development agency under the general democratic guidance of the Assembly.

There is little evidence from recent years of development agencies that they have accelerated the rate of growth in the areas where they are deployed. There remains a strong correlation between the areas that have development agencies and relative lack of success in economic development. Their supporters would say that they were created because the areas lacked economic success and it is not surprising if those areas are still trailing behind somewhat. They would hope to prove that there has been some relative improvement thanks to the development agency.

There is a danger that development agencies, if they are too powerful and conducted in the wrong way, will do damage rather than help the development of their regional economies. In the case of Wales the intervention of the WDA and the Land Authority in the land market meant that there was no vital competitive land market for those wishing to build industrial or commercial property when coming to Wales. This put off some people who would have preferred competition and choice rather than having to deal with a government-inspired body before they could find land to develop in the way they saw fit. There is also a danger that these bodies sell the idea of failure rather than success. Some of those on the road recommending Scotland, Wales, Northern Ireland or parts of England as suitable places for inward investment will say openly that they are recommending these areas because they have been less successful and because they therefore attract substantial grants. Any inward investor worth his salt would immediately realise that he can, with diplomatic skill and arm twisting, extract a considerable price for bringing his investment to a particular part of the United Kingdom even though he had always intended to bring it to the UK one way or another. Development agencies should be told that they should not be selling grants and creating a bad impression over an area in desperate need of inward investment. They should be selling success and setting out why the United Kingdom in general, and their part of it in particular, is vibrant, lively and exciting enough to be a good place to spend money.

Countries promote jobs and investment by having the right general policies rather than through specific incentives to specific regions. It is far better to have low corporate tax rates throughout the United Kingdom than to have high subsidies in parts of it. It is far better to have less law and regulation than competitive countries, than to have government involvement in the land market and planning developments in certain parts of the country. The Government has not yet worked out how to prevent competitive auctions of grant between different parts of the United Kingdom. Indeed this very issue has shown how flimsy is its belief in devolution as a whole.

When the Government came to office it recognised that there were already dangers in the inherited practice of one region bidding against another for the same inward investment. The inward investor could sit back and enjoy the competition as he saw the British taxpayer competing with himself, offering first £10 million in Wales and then £15 million in the North East and so on until the sums were very considerable. The Government decided that there had to be national co-ordination through the Board of Trade and there had to be limits placed upon this kind of process.

Immediately, the Welsh Secretary let it be known that that was taking away an important devolved power from the Welsh office to vary the grant and make the kind of offer it saw fit to attract the investment to Wales. Even within a collective and fairly secretive Cabinet it has so far proved impossible to resolve this tension. Imagine how much more difficult it is going to be when a Scottish Parliament is egging on its development agency, an elected Mayor in London is egging on his development agency and the Welsh Development Agency is being encouraged by the Welsh Assembly. It is difficult to see how the centre will reassert control and prevent damaging competitive auctions of grant occurring. The beneficiaries will be the overseas investors. The losers will be the British taxpayers.

True devolution comes by giving people, companies and families more choices in their own lives. It comes by giving them more freedom rather than by imposing on them more layers of government. People's frustrations with government have not come about because there is insufficient of it. The frustrations have come about either because there is too much of it impeding their normal progress and limiting the choices they can make in their daily lives, or because the government they do have is unresponsive to their requirements. True devolution can be driven forward by identifying those areas of life that have been under government control where more freedom can be introduced. True devolution comes by encouraging rival senses of power in communities outside the Government altogether. A free society thrives upon a mixture of government and non-government institutions and arrangements. People can and should look to the Church as well as to the State for guidance on what is right and what is wrong. It is valuable to have independent charities and institutions concerned about the environment as well as a programme of public action designed by the government. A successful transport policy requires more than a government policy. It requires bus and train companies, airlines and shipping companies capable of actually carrying people and freight to where they wish to go.

The government undertakes three important distinct roles. The first is to set a framework of law and regulation under which everything else takes place. Free markets need some regulation. There needs to be a law of contract and a law of property for them to succeed. Too much regulation can start to stifle them, preventing legitimate activities taking place.

The second task, which has developed mightily in the twentieth century, is to transfer money from richer areas, richer people and richer companies to poorer areas, poorer people and poorer companies. This is now done on a huge scale through the mechanisms of the welfare state, through regional and social policies and through the complex arrangements for taxation and tax breaks and subsidies to the corporate sector.

The third task some recommend is for government to run services and make goods. In a free society this should be limited to those areas where only the State can make the provision. Most people agree that it makes sense for the State to provide the defence forces of the realm. Individuals would be unwilling to club together to provide these services on a free-market basis. It does make sense to levy a charge on everyone to provide them centrally. There is much less evidence that allowing the government to run normal trading corporations in markets that are or could be competitive is a good idea. Government has not proved adept at running businesses in most parts of the world. The large privatisation movement which commenced in the 1980s in Britain has now been transferred to most countries around the globe. All have come to the same perception at about the same time that it is better to take government out of the business of running business.

If the government believes that customers are not getting a sufficiently good deal or a group of businesses are not encouraging safety, it can always regulate to achieve the desired effect. It does not need to take the businesses over and run them itself. If the government believes that poorer consumers are not being looked after, the most obvious thing the government can do is to boost the incomes of the poorer customers so that they have more power in the market place. If it wishes to target its help more specifically, it can invent schemes to buy the goods and services on behalf of poor people from a competitive private market. These are less damaging means of intervening in a free market than taking over the whole business as well.

The danger of introducing new tiers of government at the European and the regional level is that in each of the three areas of government activity we are likely to see more government rather than less, reducing people's freedoms. Every subsidy paid to a company a regional government wishes to attract or help has to be levied in tax from a successful company, which will then be less able to invest in the future and develop its success. Every additional layer of government panicking about health and safety or the environment is likely to produce a bigger regulatory response. The more layers of government, the more likelihood there is of competing rules and regulations and of too much law in total. The more layers of government there are, the more likelihood there is of self-cancelling schemes routing money from those thought to have too much to those thought to be in need and back again. There is a lot to be said for concentration of government effort in these fields rather than for spreading it ever more widely through different layers of government.

The rise of regulation is one of the biggest threats to freedom in the modern Western world. We can all agree that we would rather live in a low-risk or a risk-free world than in a risky one. We all know in our hearts that we will never be able to remove all the risks or threats to life in a complex world. If you ask people if they would like the government to make sure that there is never any danger of their food poisoning them, people say yes they do want the government to do that. There are several ways in which the government can fulfil this requirement. The legislature can pass a law saying that it is a criminal offence to manufacture and sell food which poisons people. Enforcement can be left to the normal processes and people in business will know that breaking this law could lead to a prison sentence. The government could decide that it would never be good business practice to try to sell people food that poisons them. You would only do it once and then you would be driven out of business very rapidly. On this basis, the government could say that, whilst we the government clearly condemn the supply of poisoned food to people, we believe that the market will take care of the problem as no one in their right mind would try to make a business out of supplying poisoned food. The third possibility is for the government to set up an agency, to hire an army of inspectors and to go round trying to satisfy itself that no one is in danger of poisoning the food they are selling.

Usually governments intensify their regulation after something has gone wrong. Regulation regularly fails. The Bank of England fails to spot the impending bankruptcy of a bank. People do not conclude from this that banking regulation is ineffective or wrong. They conclude that there needs to be more of it and immediately set about intensifying financial regulation. Similarly, each time there is a food scare the cry goes up for more law, more inspectors, bigger and better agencies to enforce the very simple proposition that food should be healthy and edible.

Adopting too heavy-handed a regulatory system produces its own problems. It makes the government more to blame than it would be were it simply to establish a framework of law and tell free agents to get on with it. It makes the government to blame in an area where, however tight the regulation, there will inevitably be errors or mistakes from time to time. No financial regulatory system in the world has ever had a period of years free from bankruptcies, frauds or scandals. The regulators would claim that their very existence has reduced the numbers and instances of this. There is little in the historical record to prove that this is true either. Given that before the intensification of regulation in the later part of the twentieth century there were other civil and criminal sanctions against people who misbehaved in business, the pressures are not very different between the two systems.

Intensification of regulation serves to raise business costs. It often drives out of the market place the small, more entrepreneurial, more competitive firms who are unable to cope with the bureaucracy and the extra cost entailed. If regulation gets too tight, the market can be gravely damaged, reducing the number of new challenges, raising prices and even reducing service standards.

A third, related problem of heavy-handed regulation is a reduction in the pace of innovation and service improvement. Regulators want to standardise, harmonise and specify in considerable detail. They make it their business to set up training courses, write manuals and explain to people exactly how they should do their job. The innovator can then become the rule breaker, or even the criminal. Where, in a dynamic market, innovation, new ideas, improved services and products are welcomed, in a heavily regulated market they have to be delayed or stopped altogether. The regulators fear that the new way of doing something may have risks they had not thought through. They therefore conclude that it is better not to allow the new device or the new service to appear on stage at all.

The move to devolution is part of this much bigger picture of an intensi-fication of government effort in the belief that inequalities of income can be levelled by government action and in the belief that more and more risks can be removed from normal daily life. In both areas the advocates for devolution are likely to be disappointed. There is nothing in the current devolution proposals for Scotland or Wales which suggests that they have a new solution to the problems of relatively high unemployment and low economic success in some parts of those regions. Nor is there anything in the regional governments approach to regulation which implies that they have learnt the lesson that excessive regulation can damage jobs and stifle new ways of doing things.

True devolution, the granting of rights and opportunities to individuals under the law, is more manifest in policies like council house sales and privatisation than in the establishment of new layers of government. At the beginning of the twentieth century it was fashionable to believe that most people had to live in rented accommodation. The argument ran that they would not be able to afford the money to buy their own house and to maintain it to a decent standard. There was a strong feeling that they would not rise to the responsibility of ownership. They were told that they needed landlords to make sure that the house was properly maintained and controlled. The twentieth century has proved that way of thinking wrong. In towns and villages today, the housing stock that is in worst repair is that which is rented, particularly under the ownership of a public body. Most people have now acquired their own home, some by being able to purchase houses from councils and the government. They have risen magnificently to the challenge. By and large, the homes in private ownership are better maintained, they are stronger expressions of the individuality of the family living in them and they bring more pleasure than the rented housing stock around them.

When people move from renting to owning they gain several freedoms. They gain the freedom to decide on the decoration, extension and embellishment of their property. They gain the freedom from paying rent in old age once they have paid off the mortgage. Given a similar style of house, it is cheaper over a normal lifetime to buy a house on a mortgage and live there for the rest of your life than to pay even subsidised rents to the council throughout your adult years.

Similarly, freedoms have been enhanced by the privatisation movement. Taking state monopolies and introducing competition has given people real choice and has improved the prices, the range of service and the quality on offer. In the early 1980s people could only rent a telephone, they could not buy one. There was little choice of equipment and they might have to wait up to six months to get connected to the network at all. In the 1990s there is now an enormous choice of service ranging from radio and mobile through competing fixed-link systems to satellite systems. There is a whole range of equipment that can be added onto the network and connections can be made within a matter of hours or within a few days. Prices have come down and customers are much better served.

At the same time, the privatisation movement has given managers and employees the opportunity to own a share in their business and to have more say in how their business is conducted. Nationalised monopolies have bad records not only for the service they offered customers but also for the way they treated their employees. Many people lost their jobs as the nationalised monopolies proved unable to adjust to the market requirements. They were unable to build global businesses, confining practically all their activities to the relatively small domestic market. There was no scope for owning shares or participating in the profits of a nationalised concern.

In order to give people more choices and control in their daily lives, these movements need to be taken further. What could be done in telephones could also be done in the water industry. The water pipe system could become a common carrier. Competing companies could be invited to collect water and send it through the pipes. Customers could then make a choice about which water company they wished to deal with. There would be price and service quality competition.

Government paranoia comes into this argument. Before telephones were privatised the government itself argued that the telephone was too sensitive and important a piece of equipment to be left to a private market place to supply. It was even argued in government that people in business would sell individuals phones that would damage the network. This was a preposterous idea. It implied that you could make a business out of selling phones that did not work. Not only would they not work, according to the theory, but they would be so bad that they would prevent the network working in the interests of others as well. It is difficult to see how anybody could have persuaded people to buy such implements. Yet by such arguments the monopoly was preserved.

Exactly the same type of argument is being used to defend the monopoly provision of water. It is argued that different types of water would not mix in the pipes. Competing companies would then end up supplying water that could be damaging to people's health. If the water industry was opened up to competition, it would still be a criminal offence to supply water that was dangerous. Again, it would not be good business practice to try to supply people with water that was poisonous. What competition would do is ensure that people could buy water whenever they wanted it. It takes a special kind of genius, in rain-swept islands like the United Kingdom, for people to end up, in the few hot, dry summer months we get, being short of water and told that watering their plants and keeping them alive is against the public interest. This would all change if we had a competitive water industry.

In education, the answer to devolution is to give more power to the schools and to parents. It is unlikely that there will be better decisions taken about education in Wales because they have a devolved Assembly. It is an intermediary between Whitehall, which votes most of the money, and local government, which manages the system closer to the schools. What is the Welsh Assembly going to say or do that would make a big difference to the conduct of education in Wales? The success of Welsh education rests now and in the future, as it has always done, on the success of head teachers and their teaching teams, school by school. What matters is how good those teachers are, what they teach and how successful they are at motivating the children. This is not immediately going to change as the result of the creation of the Welsh Assembly.

The best way of encouraging good changes in our schools is to give more power to the parents. The parents, by and large, are concerned for their children and do distinguish quite readily between schools with good records and strong academic achievement and those with poor records. In my own constituency parents usually research which school they would like their child to go to and are keen to give the child the best opportunity to go to the school in their area which meets their expectations on discipline, academic achievement and extracurricular activities. Where there are schools that are falling well below the required standard, parents are naturally reluctant to see their children sent there.

Strengthening parental choice and encouraging successful schools to grow is the most obvious way of encouraging success. We have had years of planning, of ordering people which school they are to go to, coupled with a system of inspection and advice from the education authority. The inspectors have often done a reasonable job revealing unsatisfactory teaching and poor standards. The education authorities have rarely followed up and taken the difficult but necessary decisions to sort out the problems of underachievement in many schools. This is not going to change as the result of another layer of devolved government. The only way change can be brought about is to give more parents the right to send their child to a school of their choice. As more parents vote with their feet, so the poor-performing schools will have to do something if they wish to attract a reasonable number of pupils.

It is better for parents to be able to make a choice which affects the way schools behave than to give them another set of politicians to go to. It is better if parents are encouraged to sit on governing bodies of schools so that they can make real decisions about the school itself, around the governing body table, than that they are given new politicians to lobby in some remote centre. True devolution of power means shifting as many decisions as possible governing the school from Whitehall and from the education authority, and now from the devolved government in the regions, to the schools themselves. Some schools are reluctant to accept these responsibilities. They say they wish to be told what to do by education advisors from the education authority. We need to find or encourage greater independence of spirit within the schooling system and recruit that generation of school leaders as head teachers who wish to make more of their own decisions and will accept responsibility for the consequences and the results.

True devolution in planning will not be brought about by devolved regional government either. People are passionate about planning matters in their local area. In hard-pressed parts of the country, especially in the South East of England, people feel that too many houses have already been built. They know that their own quality of life will be damaged if more houses are built, more cars put on the road, more urbanisation permitted. They find it very difficult to get this message across to their governing authority. It is unlikely that regional governments will be any more responsive than Whitehall to this very strong feeling of people in the countryside and former country areas beyond our big cities. Regional government will take over the regional planning teams that have done most of the damage and have been most hostile to the public mood. In the South East of England planning is conducted through the South East Regional Plan. It is this plan which has insisted upon more houses being built in many counties of the South East than local people wish to see. If the Government was serious about devolution, it would give powers to local communities to say no to more housing, regardless of what regional or national planners believed. This could be done by accepting the structure plan or unitary plan targets that the local authorities have constructed, rather than overturning them or increasing them in the interests of regional or national planning.

The Government will object that if you add up the numbers of homes that the counties in Southern England are prepared to see built, the answer will be too small. How does the Government know this? It is relying on some shaky forecasts of future housing demand. These forecasts assume a continuing high rate of marriage break-up. Maybe they do not allow enough for the possibility that many people whose first marriages broke up create a second marriage which brings the housing requirement back to the numbers before the first marriage broke up. If fewer houses are supplied in the rural areas of the South East, business opportunities will occur to supply more houses in other parts of the country where local opinion and planning opinion are more relaxed. The market would balance, even with tighter planning restrictions in those areas where it is a strongly held view that they should be tighter.

There is no point in setting up a devolved government if the central government is not prepared to trust the judgement of local people on issues of great importance like this. If the Government is adamant in saying that local people are wrong in their views of how many houses should be built, the Government should not at the same time say that it wishes to give more power to local people to settle matters of importance to them. In my area, there is no matter of more importance to my constituents than the issue of planning. My post bag is dominated by the issue and has been for many years. We will not believe that we have any true devolution of power until we are given the right to make exactly that kind of decision upon the basis of our best judgement of what our local area will stand.

The language of the Government is a strange mixture. It is in the main hectoring. The Government stands in its own mind as the embodiment of modernisation. Every constitutional change it wishes to put through is a necessary and desirable modernisation which will in the Government's view meet the spirit of the times. It says it wishes to carry government closer to the people, yet its plans reveal the strong belief of the centre that the centre still knows better than the regions in many important respects. The centre reckons it is a better judge of how much local authorities in Scotland should be allowed to spend than the Scottish Parliament will be. As a result it has kept reserved powers just in case. The Government believes it is a better judge of Scotland's interest in Europe than the Scottish people would be, so it has kept reserve powers. The Government has been dismissive of any real ambition in Wales for self-government. It has created a talking-shop Assembly and left most of the important powers with the Secretary of State and the Westminster Parliament. It has never really explained satisfactorily why Wales is offered such a different system of devolution to Scotland. The Prime Minister insists on his own candidate as First Minister despite the popularity of an alternative in Wales. In London, it prides itself in setting up a powerful executive Mayor, but he is given no powers over health, perhaps the most important public service of all to people in the capital. The powerful executive Mayor is not even given control over the budget. Twenty-five Assembly men and women can set a budget they prefer instead if there is a row between the Assembly and the Mayor.

Undoubtedly, the Government's devolution plans will create more tension and conflict rather than less. We already see London complaining that Scotland is getting too much money. We will soon see Wales complaining that it is not being treated seriously and Scotland complaining that the powers it has received are not enough. The only thing that will unite the devolved assemblies is a common cry that there is not enough money in total, between their bouts of infighting over who got more and who got less. It is all playing into the Commission's hands beautifully. It is creating a Europe of the regions in the way the Commission wants. It is helping to fuel nationalist movements in Scotland and Wales. London is useful to begin the process of regionalising England and balkanising Britain.

The end result will be a more divided, more factious, more overgoverned, more overregulated United Kingdom. Far from producing less or better government, it will produce more and worse. Far from solving problems, it will just create more armies of bureaucrats and politicians wringing their hands, complaining that they do not have enough power, and levying money from people to keep themselves in a lifestyle to which they wish to become accustomed. It will not reconnect the people with the politicians. It will confirm the public in their view that politicians by and large do not solve problems, do cost too much and are good at misleading the public in their own interests.

PART III

Britain's Future?

9 British Business – Euro Champions or Global Players?

At the same time as Western European politicians and officials are pulling their countries ever closer together, creating a single government for the larger area, companies in Western Europe are caught up in the rapid progress of globalisation. Some argue that, because business is going to be conducted more and more by multinationals operating on a worldwide basis, there is a need for government at the European level. Such government, they argue, would be big enough to stand up to these large corporations, where a single European country government at the moment is not powerful enough. This may all be wishful thinking. The multinationals are so powerful it may need world action, through the efforts of a range of governments coming together, to defend the customer interest. It also assumes an innocent explanation for greater European government, when the intention may be somewhat different. In Western Europe there is a strong strand of thinking which believes that European government should shield and foster European champion companies. Where they cannot compete worldwide they should be protected. There will be a long and important struggle between the free traders and the protectionists in Europe. We will have to learn all over again the truth that protection leads to higher prices, worse service, less innovation, and eventually to an economy that falls further and further behind.

Big businesses like to get bigger. In many businessmen's minds there is a vision of being the Chairman or Chief Executive of one of the world's truly great corporations. Size brings a sense of power and importance. It can also bring some protection from the vagaries of the market place and the damage that competitors can otherwise do. Many a businessman will tell you that he favours competition, but his views of his competitors are often unprintable. Competition is good for others but not necessarily good for him.

As the twentieth century draws to a close, there are heated arguments about how far the process of globalisation can and should go, and what should be the response of individual companies, countries and continents to this process. You can see the development of the global market place in all sorts of business areas. It is coming about in manufacturing, in services, in telecommunications, in pharmaceuticals. Everywhere business services are traded, there are pressures for more things to be carried out by huge companies operating across frontiers.

Progress for all this has been superimposed upon the political changes towards more European integration. Sometimes the two are confused, sometimes they are related. One of the arguments for the single-market programme in Western Europe was the argument that, as business operated across frontiers more and more frequently, so government needed to respond by becoming bigger in its turn. Proponents of this school of thought pointed out that an individual government might be heavily outgunned by the ability of a large multinational to switch profits, invoices, product and activity across frontiers according to where the regulation and taxation was lightest. The competition authority might find it difficult to sustain a case in a single country when the real burden of the case related to the dominance of the company in many national markets together.

The rapid pace of change in the last 40 years has been breathtaking. In an area like telecommunications we have moved rapidly from having a set of discrete national systems, with relatively little international traffic beyond national frontiers, to large global corporations creating global networks where international business is the fastest growing area of all. The advent of new technologies providing mobile and cellular telephony have driven the industry to accept new standards and systems which can operate on a continent-wide or a global scale. The nationally based systems rapidly became obsolete, unable to respond to fast changes in design and to the growing demand for telecommunications without frontiers. Telecommunications are the paradigm of national markets turning global, driven by the power of consumer choice and by the speed of technological development.

The motor industry, a more traditional manufacturing area, has shown a similar trend. In the 1960s there was a series of separate national motor industries. The United States industry produced very large cars capable of travelling long distances on the freeways of the United States but not geared to difficult urban driving conditions, or to the more tortuous and narrow streets and roads of Europe or parts of Asia. In Western Europe, a series of national car companies emerged country by country.

The Volkswagen Beetle was very different in style and appearance from the Mini, which was very different from the Citroën 2CV or the Fiat 500. Each of the major countries, Italy, France, Germany and the United Kingdom, had their own substantial motor industries serving primarily a national market. They exported to countries in the world with whom they had strong links and combined together to service the smaller national markets of Western Europe where there were no such indigenous motor industries. In the 1980s there was a coming together of European styles. For a brief period it could be said that there were Europe-wide models which were still different from the models of those of the United States of America. Some or all of the national differences between the British, French, Italian and German motor industries of the 1960s and early 1970s were removed. Ford of Europe started producing a common car for the whole of Western Europe where a decade earlier it had produced different styles for the German and British requirements.

By the 1990s the industry had moved on from its continental flirtation to developing the global model. The Japanese had always had ambitions to achieve such a development. Japan produced the most spectacularly successful motor industry in the 1960s to the early 1990s. It grew from being small and heavily dependent upon Western technology to being the market leader in many areas. The Japanese took the 4x4 off-road vehicle concept and made a huge industry out of it. They developed and improved the style of their family saloons until they were market leaders in many of those. They even entered the luxury end of the market with the Lexus product. Japan proved that it was possible to sell the same or similar models in Britain, Germany, the United States of America and the Asian countries. Where they went, the ever-larger conglomerates soon followed.

By the 1990s Ford was capable of designing a world car. Some in the United States of America wanted a smaller, lighter, more manoeuvrable product than the traditional American gas-guzzler. Asian and European tastes started to come together under the relentless drive of global design and global branding.

The Europeans decided to use this as an opportunity to expand and to remove some of the domestic competition within the wider European market. The stunning success of the Japanese in design and productivity, followed by aggressive competition emerging in countries like Korea and Malaysia, led many to conclude that the European motor industry was too big, with too many companies involved. Instead of the new competition encouraging a more competitive response with more designs, more experiments and a wider range of products and companies, the European motor industry decided on a series of defensive mergers and alliances, leading to the closure of capacity, the removal of models and the concentration of power in fewer and fewer hands.

The British motor industry had moved from being one of the important industries in the 1960s to being one of the weakest in the 1980s. Although it greatly improved and was greatly strengthened, partly through the advent of Japanese investment and technology in the later 1980s, it was still less strong financially and in corporate terms than the German industry by the

1990s. One by one, British companies were either removed from the production map or were taken over by foreign competitors.

Jaguar had a brief flourishing as an independent British company following denationalisation, only to be acquired at considerable expense by Ford of America. The Rover Group had a long courtship with Honda, who assisted it with engine and gearbox technology for a number of years, only to sell itself out to BMW. The German company acquired Rover at the very point when it was beginning to offer serious competition, with its new saloons, to the BMW model range. The Austin and Morris names disappeared altogether. MG, acquired as part of the domestic agglomeration of the 1960s, disappeared without trace only to be successfully revived in the final years of an independent British Rover Group. Vauxhall is firmly in American ownership, producing a range of General Motors vehicles. The Rootes Group of companies, including Hillman, Singer and Triumph, are no more.

In 1998, the final denouement came with the sale of Rolls-Royce Motors to a German buyer. The collapse of confidence in the British corporate sector at the ability of Britain to own, develop and run a successful motor company was summed up by the negotiations over the sale of two of the most famous car marques the world has ever seen. Both Rolls-Royce and Bentley cars were owned by Rolls-Royce Motors, which had in turn fallen into public ownership when the Rolls-Royce aerospace company got into financial difficulties in the early 1970s. They were privatised with the aero-engine company, sold on to the British engineering conglomerate Vickers and were finally sold on to German owners just in time for the millennium.

The sad neglect of these two great brands and images in the British corporate sector was palpable. Rolls-Royce and Bentley sales trickled along at around two thousand cars a year. Whilst they are internationally famous brands, the British market still accounted for a disproportionate share of the pitiful total sales. Of course, in order to maintain the prestige of a brand the numbers should be limited and the prices high. But no one seriously believed that selling only around two thousand instead of ten thousand, was essential to the maintenance of the brand value. Everybody could see that selling such a small number meant great difficulty in generating the cash necessary to design the next generation of products.

I telephoned several people in the City of London when it was announced that Rolls-Royce and Bentley were to be sold, to see if anybody would help organise a consortium of serious British bidders that could take on the management and future development of the marques. I reckoned the City would need to raise about £1000 million to buy the company and then to plough in sufficient money to develop the new models they would require.

The answer everywhere was the same. It was disbelief that Britain could mount such a bid and an assumption that either BMW or Volkswagen would coast home in the competition, so there was no need to contest it. There was a strong industrial lobby already within Britain in favour of BMW ownership and the threat of legal action from the owners of the brand names that they would block the sale to any group other than BMW. The amazing twist in the story came when Volkswagen was forced to give up the Rolls-Royce name to BMW, even though VW had paid good money for the factory to make both Rolls-Royce and Bentley cars.

A group of Rolls-Royce and Bentley enthusiasts clubbed together to see if they could save their company. They met with a uniformly hostile response from those in the City, who could have turned it into a serious bid, and from the vendor who did not seem to wish them to appear as a possible rival to BMW. For many weeks they were thwarted in their wish even to see the doc-umentation concerning the sale, making it that much more difficult for them to get together a serious bidding consortium.

It should be one of Britain's great strengths that its industry can be allied to one of the large financial markets of the world, one of the top three. The City of London is flexible, shrewd and capable. It does have access to prodigious sums of money. And yet, when it came to something as relatively straightforward as rescuing Rolls-Royce for a relatively modest sum of money, the answer was no. The City was very happy to act as corporate advisor to foreign rivals but not prepared to put in the ground work necessary to put together a serious British consortium. Did the City really believe that there is no British management left capable of developing fine brands like Rolls-Royce and Bentley? Did the City really believe that it is now impossible for a company, even backed by several hundred million pounds of new equity, to do what is needed to develop and sell a very exclusive specialist vehicle to a limited number of customers? The City decided before the competition began that there could be and should be no British answer.

The advent of the global car has led to the advent of the global conglomerate. Any company operating from a strong position in a national or even a continent-wide market can use the argument with the competition authorities that, now there is a global industry, companies need to get bigger. They claim that there is no threat to competition because there are global competitiors, but argue that they need a stronger position in their local or national market to be able to survive. The competition authorities would be wise to be sceptical about these arguments. Whilst it is undoubtedly the case that markets are becoming more global, there is still danger in allowing a company with disproportionate power in a particular country or region to merge with its biggest rival. Such a merger may help them compete in a far away market in which they have a much less substantial involvement at the price of giving them too much power at home.

Some in the European Union believe that we now need to have Euro champions in order to survive in these fiercely competitive markets. They have in mind allowing the principal European companies in a given industry to develop joint alliances or even to merge with one another with a view to creating a strong company that can withstand the international pressures. On such an analysis there is nothing wrong with Rover being swallowed by BMW. Indeed, should they wish to do so, there would be nothing wrong with Mercedes and BMW or BMW and Renault linking hands to go out and fight the good fight against the Japanese and American competition.

There is little evidence that such mega-mergers do produce good results for customers and shareholders. Very often, the defensive nature of the alliance generates exactly the wrong kind of thinking in the businessman running the enlarged organisation. Because they think they are buying protection from competitive pressures when they purchase each other's assets, they can then become complacent or negative in their approach to the dynamic global market place. They usually set up large departments to lobby national, European and international governmental organisations to try to turn the legal and trade regulatory framework in their favour. Instead of concentrating all their efforts upon innovation, customer research and improvement of their product, they see themselves as surrogate politicians trying to create legal and governmental conditions which will guarantee their future security.

The Japanese industry, the most successful in the world in the last 30 years, did not achieve its success by creating just one or two national Japanese car companies and protecting them in the home market. Toyota faces Honda, Nissan and several others, fighting it out in a very competitive home market for Japanese companies. Europe should learn from this, and not try to limit competition.

This is most obvious when the industry has access to public money or is nationalised. The British motor industry was at its least successful when most of it was publicly owned through the government shareholding in British Leyland. Huge sums of taxpayers' money were routed in to design new ranges of cars. Each design range proved less successful and less popular than the one it replaced. The senior executives of British Leyland became much more expert at putting their case to Parliament, lobbying the government for more money and developing excuses for the permanent decline in their market share, than they were at finding the cars that people wanted to buy.

There is a danger that the European industry is going in a similar direction if too much credence is given to the idea of creating Euro champions. The globalisation of the economy means that the national or continental origins of the brand name or the ownership matter less than where the research, design, production and marketing are concentrated. Is BMW a more European company, by virtue of its original German national origins, than Ford of Europe, which has made a substantial investment commitment to several companies in Western Europe over many years and sees itself as a European corporation, ultimately owned by an American parent? If Rolls-Royce and Bentley had been acquired by a Japanese owner who had decided to put in British management and continue with the British traditions and British production, would that have become a foreign company or could it still be truly said to be a traditional British company which just happens to have a different share ownership structure? If BMW appointed an American chief executive, would that in any way dilute its German or its European origins? If BMW sets up large production facilities in Asia, eventually reaching the point where Asian output is larger than European, does it then cease to be the European company that people now think it is?

There are no easy answers to these questions in a global market. What matters from the point of view of the individual country, region or continent is where the production facilities are located and where the important jobs are based. You could make out an argument to say that Nissan of Britain, designing, engineering, manufacturing and marketing its cars in Britain, is a more British company than some British textile companies, where British shareholders may be in the preponderance and where they still have their original British brands but now make the cloth and manufacture the garments in Asian countries. The global market place is rapidly breaking down not just the national but also the continental barriers that once existed.

Many consumers are global in their attitudes: not many people look at the country or continent of origin before deciding on a purchase. Britain's growing links with the economies of continental Western Europe have taken place at a time when British wine consumers have become relatively much more interested in buying American, Australian and New Zealand wine, moving away from their traditional dependence upon the French and German industry. At a time when the European motor industry is trying to build European champions, the British motoring public has developed quite a strong love affair with Japanese vehicles, favouring them on many occasions for their engineering excellence and their reliability. In the supermarket, shelf-loads of produce are available from around the world every day of the trading week. Customers rarely pause to consider whether they should back the heavily subsidised and not very competitive European farm industry or whether they should enjoy products from a range of other continents.

The services have erected more barriers to cross-border trading than manufacturers. Where manufacturers were encouraged by progressive tariff reductions on a worldwide basis through the General Agreement on Tariffs and Trade (GATT), service de-regulation internationally has been slower to arrive. Services are also more restricted to national markets by language and by the institutional framework.

In the 1960s, an accountancy firm or a legal firm primarily specialised in providing a good legal or accountancy service to a company or individual based in their national market place. If a British company wished to undertake a legal transaction in a foreign country, the British legal firm was more likely to recommend that they went direct to a lawyer in the country of their transaction. Few legal firms in the 1960s were equipped to provide a global legal service. In the 1990s there has been a rapid development of the global legal services firm. Despite the many different law codes and systems around the world, despite the different languages in use, firms now are able to offer the global service through a series of alliances or take-overs of foreign firms. It has been easiest in the Anglo-Saxon world. There is considerable commonality of legal practice in the common law systems of these countries and the common language makes the task so much easier.

A similar pattern has developed in accountancy. Large London- and New York-based accountancy firms now have very good data banks of the different tax and legal requirements country by country around the world. They have adapted to providing advice on an international basis. They have accepted, especially in the Anglo-Saxon countries, that there is a strong move towards common accounting requirements, an acceptance of US reporting standards in many countries and a need to provide accounting in many different countries as business goes global.

The defence and aerospace industries provide a very sensitive test of whether we are going global or European. Defence and aerospace is an area where the United States of America has come to have substantial market dominance in the post-war period. It has based this upon the large demand of its own armed forces and upon a highly competitive domestic market where a large number of different companies with rival technologies jostle for supremacy. Gaining a contract from the Pentagon is often crucial to the survival and development of these businesses. The contracts are awarded following extensive competition.

The success of United States aero-defence industries has been mirrored by the success of Boeing, Lockheed and Macdonald-Douglas in the civil aircraft business. The United Kingdom kept going in this business in the immediate post-war period. It launched the first jet airliner, the Comet, and had a competitive range of other products. The VC10 did battle with Boeing for a number of years. As time passed, the United Kingdom companies found it more and more difficult to keep up with the prodigious sums of capital and the degree of innovation required to keep in the business.

The European Community decided that it would take on the task of subsidising and encouraging a mainstream rival to the Boeing corporation. Airbus Industrie was set up between a series of Western European company and country partners with each country and company specialising in a different part of the aircraft and a different type of technology. The United Kingdom specialised in wing technology, through British Aerospace. In the early years the business absorbed substantial sums of money and it was difficult getting the market share they sought. Being a very cyclical industry, Airbus discovered it was easiest to sell aeroplanes towards the top of a business cycle. There has been considerable political involvement and a great deal of disagreement between the US and the European authorities. The United States claims that Airbus had unreasonable access to public subsidy and has traded unfairly as a result. Europeans counter by saying that the American civil aerospace industry has an effective cross-subsidy from the weapons research contracts given to the US companies. It is one of several large trade issues which dominate dogged exchanges when the United States and the European Community get together.

The arms trade brings out the stark questions about modern loyalties and governmental intentions. Is the United Kingdom right to think that it can no longer have an independent weapons capability given the scale of modern military contracts and the costs of developing certain technologies? Would it be best advised to go into direct partnership with the United States of America given the technological lead that the United States enjoys? Or should it do in weapons what it has been doing in civil aerospace, and go into partnership with other European companies? Even the civil aerospace model itself gives no clear answer to this question. Whilst British Aerospace put a great deal into Airbus Industrie, Rolls-Royce has developed a successful partnership with Boeing, supplying Rolls-Royce engines to many Boeing planes sold around the world.

Advocates of European union believe that the remaining defence companies of Western Europe should be rationalised into one or two large players capable of competing, in their view, against the might of similarly placed US corporations. Others in Britain fear that putting all of our technology and industrial development into a European project could cut us off from the more successful strands of US technological development and could prejudice our defences in certain circumstances. They point out that when Britain wished to use weapons to recover the Falkland Islands from Argentina, some continental countries with close links to Argentina were very unhappy and even thought of applying pressure through the mechanism of common arms supply. Common defence procurement would be a further big step on the way to a common European army and foreign policy. What a European multinational company can grant to a government or to given armed forces, they can also withhold in certain circumstances. It could soon become a weapon of policy limiting or preventing independent British action.

Some United States contracts also come with some limitations upon the use to which the weapons can be put. The United States, through its Helms-Burton legislation, attempts to prevent European and other companies from around the world selling specified goods to Cuba, Libya and Iraq. The United States understandably feels threatened by Cuba in the long aftermath of the Cuban missile crisis, whilst it fears terrorist intervention from Libya and Iraq. European companies and some European countries object to America's assertion of extraterritorial jurisdiction, seeking to trade freely with these countries that the United States thinks are beyond the pale.

The European position has always been equivocal over American might and American protection. The truth is that Western Europe would not have been protected and could not have guaranteed its freedoms without the American military presence and the American nuclear trip-wire in place during the long period of the Cold War. Despite this, many on the continent, especially in a country like France, resent the strength of the American position and are constantly seeking to undermine it. Their plans for European union are designed to create a superpower which they believe could withstand the American giant or could act as a counter-magnet around the world. Part of the dream behind the Euro is to create an economy and a currency that rivals the dollar. Part of the idea behind mega-mergers in the aerospace and defence industry area is to create an aircraft and defence manufacturing capability that can rival that of some of the large American corporations. What they have failed to realise is that, even if all this came true, Europe could still be a minnow compared with the United States when looking at its defence capability. The European peoples have not been prepared to spend as much energy, technology and money on defending themselves as the United States. As a result, even adding together the weapons capability and armed forces of France, Germany, Italy and Britain would leave a European power very weak compared with the United States.

It is also strange that a group of countries should wish to create a strong counter-magnet to their principal ally and defender. There could come a point where the European scheme could be sufficiently provocative to the United

States that it could prove to be damaging to Europe's interests. Many have been reluctant to accept the fact that the American presence has on the whole been benign in Western Europe. The United States since the war has been a force for peace and for democracy. It has been a bulwark for the democratic values that finally triumphed in 1945 over the tyranny of Nazism on the continent.

In other walks of economic life, the process of muddling and mixing the ownership and management of companies and industries continues apace. The United Kingdom has been one of the world leaders in pharmaceuticals alongside the United States and Switzerland. In recent years there have been large tie-ups between the British industry and the US industry. Again, these have been argued in terms of the creation of a global market and the imperative for ever bigger, internationally based research and development, marketing and sales organisations. The merger of Beecham with SmithKline began the process. It was followed by the merger of Glaxo and Wellcome. Pharmaceuticals are pre-eminently globally traded products. They are relatively small and lightweight and easy to transport. They have a very high value, permitting all the extra costs of research, sales, marketing and transport to be added on without too much difficulty given the structure of the market. The United Kingdom has been an attractive haven, given its relative freedom from undesirable overregulation and the relative surplus of talented scientists who wish to seek research appointments in well based companies. There have not been the same tie-ups with companies from member countries of the European Union owing to the relative backwardness of the European Union industry and the common culture shared across the Atlantic between US and UK companies.

The picture has been rather different in the City of London. Although there are clear links across the Atlantic and now most of the big US houses have a strong presence in the London market place itself, the most interesting developments have been the acquisition of a large number of British-based companies by continental rivals. The whole process began with the Big Bang at the end of the 1980s. Up to that point the British stock market was a nationally based institution. A whole host of small jobbing and stockbroking firms made the market and introduced clients to the market. It was regulated as a gentlemen's club under the aegis of the London Stock Exchange authorities.

Clustered around the stock market were a number of important domestic investment houses and merchant banks. Whilst many of the merchant banks had central and Eastern European origins, they became quintessentially British institutions and thrived in the relatively unregulated and relatively stable atmosphere of London. The Rothschilds came to London at the end

of the eighteenth century from central Europe. The Warburgs fled to London
to escape Nazi persecution in the twentieth century. Flemings grew up in
Scotland through strong transatlantic investment links. Hambros specialised
in the Scandinavian trade. Hill Samuel and Schroder Wagg developed good
domestic-based businesses. Alongside them were large insurance companies,
led by the Prudential, and newer investment houses like Save & Prosper and
M&G, specialising in unit trusts.

The Big Bang was designed to modernise and change the trading system
of the London Stock Exchange. It enabled many more participants in the
market to make a market. The large institutions which had considerable client
capital and money of their own were allowed at last to job in their own right,
to run positions in stocks and shares and to offer them in the market place
direct. Computer-based and telephone-based trading came to replace
physical trading on the floor where broker and jobber eyeballed each other
before completing their transaction. The original idea was to strengthen the
capital base of the London market, permitting others than the small jobbing
firms to own stocks and shares and supply them to the market when the
market needed them. It soon became transformed into a merger mania with
companies from all round the world realising that London was opening up.
They saw an opportunity to obtain a place at the table.

Many partners in stockbroking firms decided it was time to sell out. The
market was at a high level and foreign companies were offering very large
prices to all those who were prepared to sell. The old City, based on broking
names like Hoare Govett, Strauss Turnbull, Laurie Millbank, Wood
Mackenzie and Kemp-Gee, was soon replaced by the new City based on
Deutsche Morgan Grenfell, Société General, Swiss Bank and Crédit
Lyonnais. The Americans also became a much bigger presence through the
direct representation in London of the big names like Merrill Lynch, Morgan
Stanley, Paine Webber and other famous Wall Street houses.

The progress of Morgan Grenfell, taken over by Deutsche Bank, is
instructive. When the merger first occurred, Deutsche Bank made it clear that
they wished Morgan Grenfell to continue trading as Morgan Grenfell, run
by British people who were expert in the London system. That, after all, was
what they were paying for – London expertise and the flexibility of London's
markets. Within a few years they found the results of Morgan Grenfell very
disappointing. Morgan Grenfell came under increasing German direction
from the holding company. Finally it was decided to remove the trading name
of Morgan Grenfell, for which they had paid good money, and to complete
their long-term aim of having a London-based activity fully under the control
and under the trading name of the parent company.

With the coming of the Euro the question is, will London maintain its lead as Europe's pre-eminent financial centre? Most people are optimistic that London will maintain its premier position. They point out that nothing of any importance will change with the advent of the Euro. London should still be more flexible and larger, offering finer prices and quicker dealing than many other European centres. However, there is a new factor in the equation. Given that French, German and other continental firms have acquired a substantial share of London's capital structure, it is always open to the holding companies to switch some or all of that business back to their domestic centres in Paris, Frankfurt and the other leading continental financial cities. It will be important to watch how things develop with the coming of the Euro from 1 January 1999 onwards.

The corporate world is very jumpy. An enormous amount of well paid brain power is now concentrated in advisory firms on the edges of the productive sector proper. A huge amount of effort goes into advising companies on bids and deals, on accountancy and legal matters and on lobbying governments. Very often a senior businessman thinks the answer to a business problem is a new settlement from a government or a new bid or deal in the market place rather than working away at the tried and tested methods of innovating, testing out new products, streamlining production activities and making a better mouse trap. As a result, no one can be sure at any time which company or country is stealing the edge. The new uncertainties in the world make it a very interdependent place where supremacy can be temporary. No company, however large, is proof from bid, deal or shareholder revolt. Certainly no company, however large, is immune from legal action or possible governmental or international regulatory retaliation. Even Microsoft, the world's most successful software company by a long way, which has grown entirely organically and not by acquisition, is now subject to legal actions from the United States government on behalf of others who feel that Microsoft has excluded them from the market in ways they find unacceptable.

It is definitely the case that the old idea of British industry has gone out of the window. In most industries now there is no single British market leader or group of British companies that are British owned, British managed and important players in the British market. We have seen how in pharmaceuticals British successes have formed alliances across the Atlantic. We have seen how in the motor industry British industry in its traditional sense has been almost eliminated but a new British-based industry has sprung up with the best companies and names from around the world congregating to make certain cars in these islands. Even in telecoms, where a few years ago there was a single dominant monopoly owned and financed by British people, the market is now being opened up to all comers with an influx of American capital and talent coming in through the cable television companies.

The chemical industry is still the nearest to the old-fashioned paradigm. ICI remains a well known British company with an important presence in some sections of the chemical market. Even here, however, there has been substantial erosion of ICI's once strong position. The textile industry has been broken open by new technologies and by global competition. The petrochemical industry is now more concentrated in the hands of the large oil companies, like Shell and Esso, bringing international ideas and capital to bear, than it is in the plants of ICI. ICI itself has a strategy of becoming a specialist or niche chemical manufacturer, fearing that it is no longer big enough to span most branches of the industry and maintain an important presence in each.

Whilst America remains the dominant economic nation of the world, it no longer enjoys the dominance it once held. In the immediate post-war period, the American economy was bigger than all the other economies in the world put together. We have since seen the reconstruction of several European economies, the rise of Japan to world status and the rise of several other Asian economies to become important international players even allowing for the recent financial catastrophe in some of these places. As the supreme power of America has relatively declined, so it has become more obvious that more things have to be settled by international negotiation and agreement. Parallel to the movement towards European government has been a movement to settle more things globally through international conferences and treaty agreements.

The early pioneer was the GATT. A progressively wider area of trade came to be regulated by the GATT, a liberal-inclining set of decisions designed to promote more cross-border trade. More recently, the world community has come together to hammer out green and environmental targets which have a substantial bearing on business conduct. In the post-war period, the International Monetary Fund and the World Bank have been instrumental in channelling and redirecting economic policy in economies that are struggling and need access to international funds to keep going. They work to a fashionable agenda of the day, but in recent years this agenda has included freeing markets, opening themselves up to more foreign trade and foreign inward investment and trusting markets more at home to settle prices and to make decisions on priorities.

Within the European Union a struggle is going on for the soul of the proto-government. The northern free-traders believe that all Europe needs to do is to apply the GATT international agreements and to press to liberalise ever more things. This group has succeeded in getting into the founding treaties a hatred of industrial subsidy and a strong competition ethos. On the other hand, there remain substantial pressures in the European Union to build European champions by encouraging and permitting mergers between large national companies in the same area and to give a panoply of subsidies, regulatory encouragements and other inducements to these fledgling Euro champions to go about their task. This type of thinking will lead to greater trade conflict with the United States of America and will at the same time serve to impoverish the European people. The more the governments interfere, the more they deliberately limit domestic competition, the more they think they know the answer to building a successful industry, the more likely it is that they will cut Western Europe off from the main technological breakthroughs going on around the world.

He who has the money usually has the management. The collapse of British industry as we know it has been characterised by the willingness of the British people to sell out controlling stakes in a wide range of industries and companies coupled with a more understandable and sensible policy on the part of government to open up ever more areas of life to domestic and foreign competitive challenge. It was British industry itself which made a mess of the motor industry and sold out its controlling interest to the Americans and the Germans. It was the British Government which opened up telecoms to international competition, leading to a surge of inward investment into Britain and to a technological leap forward. Judged by the new criteria of where the industry is based, where the research takes place and where the manufacturing takes place, Britain is faring rather better. During the 1980s and 1990s, the solution to Britain's labour relations problems through new trade union law, coupled with the freeing of many markets permitting greater entrepreneurship, has led to a greater amount of industry being based in the United Kingdom. The presence of so much foreign ownership also leaves British industry even more vulnerable should at some point in the future government, or others, worsen the terms for industrial trade in this country. It is a relatively easy task now for foreign owners to route the business out of Britain to other centres when costs and legislation require them to do so.

In classical economic theory businessmen are always motivated by the wish to maximise their profits. In such a theory, the transfer of ownership from British entrepreneurs to foreign entrepreneurs will make no difference. If Britain maintains its position as a relatively low-taxed, relatively lightly regulated economy, it will continue to encourage a lot of manufacturers to make things here and keep their production here. Should that change, they will move. However, it is an oversimplification to pretend that every entrepreneur is a profit maximiser in the classical sense. Traditional British business owners and entrepreneurs were unlikely to uproot their production and their general business activity from Britain and base it in Germany or France just because the terms of trade had temporarily moved in favour of doing so. They did have ties of loyalty and familiarity to the British landscape. Whilst they were only too ready to sell out their interests when a suitable buyer came along, all the time the business remained in their ownership or control they were likely to remain fixed in a region or location that suited them for a range of reasons. Wedgwood has remained based in the potteries where Josiah Wedgwood first established it. Jaguar remain based in Coventry under successive British owners. These feelings are not so strong, if present at all, in the new global corporations that are taking over. It would be inconceivable that British owners of Rolls-Royce or Bentley would have wished to make their cars in Stuttgart. It is not inconceivable that that could happen now that they are being taken over by new owners. As soon as the world downturn began in 1998, a whole series of British factories were closed by foreign multinationals. Britain was no longer so competitive, thanks to high interest rates, high sterling and higher corporate taxes imposed by the new Labour Government. With no traditonal ties or loyalties Siemens, Rover-BMW, Fujitsu and others pulled out of British manufacturing plants.

All of these changes are serving to erode local and national loyalties and are serving to make people feel even more uncertain about their futures. The relentless, footloose, hectoring, insecure behaviours of modern managements are making it more and more difficult for modern employees. People are now resigned to the fact that there are no longer jobs for life in Western Europe. They accept that their jobs come from the market place, that they need to adapt to the market place to survive. They are still, nonetheless, finding it extremely difficult to keep up with the endless bids, deals, reorganisations and management shake-ups that characterise the modern global corporation. The fears become the greater, the bigger the corporation. People know that what was once an important job in British line management is now a very unimportant job in the general scheme of things. The decision may be made in Detroit or Tokyo or Berlin, by someone they have never met, which could mean the end of the line for their particular section, division or job. They have to become corporate survivors learning the new corporate jargon and playing the new corporate games.

British politicians have begun to adapt to the changed climate by seeing that they have a duty to stand up for Britain and British competitiveness and to put on a good face for Britain when it comes to promoting it as a place in which people should do business and invest. A big transformation occurred in the early 1990s when the Labour Party turned from opposing inward investment to helping woo it. They had come to see what many had already understood, that the global market required at least a business-friendly face if jobs were to be created and sustained in any given country. What they have not yet realised is that the incursions of European government and European merger strategies may not be in the long-term interest of basing more business activity here in the United Kingdom.

Conflicts lie ahead between the protectionist Euro champion school and the free-trade school. To the extent that the protectionists win, they may succeed in congregating ever more ownership in a limited number of hands on the continent. This in due course may be used against Britain, as the continent comes to see job creation as a zero-sum game where jobs may have to be removed from Britain in order to create more in France or Germany.

In 1998, the high level of sterling began to make life very difficult for British-based manufacturers. The loss of the Siemens plant in Newcastle was a symbol of the problem. A brand new plant, representing an investment of many hundreds of millions of pounds, was to close. The company's plants elsewhere, many of them less recently constructed, were to stay open. It showed how sensitive to interest rates and currency rates modern business has become, and how large companies now take a global view of their capacity. Britain may have had the dearest and the most modern plant, but it was no protection when domestic economic policy hit manufacturers, and when a multinational had to make the decision about what to close.

Free-traders see the development of a level of European government as at best an irrelevance and at worst an encumbrance for the companies based in Western Europe. Given the pace of global change, what we need is more reliance upon international agreements that span the world. The creation of a mezzanine floor of regulation and law-making at the European level is both unhelpful and outdated. If it is allied with a protectionist impulse, it may merely mean that Europe is bypassed by the most exciting, vibrant and dynamic companies and technologies that the world will develop. People do not have to come to Europe. They will only do so if Europe is sensitive to the global ambitions and the pace of global change.

10   The Single Currency – Why Britain Must Stay Out

The European Union seriously thinks it can tame the global market by creating a single currency. It sees the important symbolism of having its own notes and coins with pictures of Europe on. It sees the economic power it will bring over companies and national economies, once fixing the interest rates, currency rates and bank lending is in its own hands. It believes that then it can have a single voice on bodies like the old G7, the IMF and the World Bank. It hopes to achieve parity with the US and pre-eminence over everyone else. It may find instead that it has laid the foundations for the long break-up of the Union they are so desperate to create.

There have been three unsuccessful attempts so far by the European Community to create a single currency, since the early 1970s. The first was to establish a single currency by 1980. Its early construction depended on each member currency joining a system known as the Snake. The Snake was constricted within its skin to limit the fluctuations of each individual currency. The aim was to bring the currencies under the discipline of the Snake, so volatility would subside. It was a relatively easy step in the eyes of the designers to move from that to a single currency.

The United Kingdom joined the Snake under the Heath government but found it could only survive within it for one month. Other currencies also experienced the strains. The Snake was abandoned and the idea of monetary union put on hold.

In the 1980s, schemes of currency union were revived with the development of the Exchange Rate Mechanism. The architects of the ERM decided that the Snake should be tried again. They recognised that the economies of Western Europe need to be brought into closer alignment for the currencies to behave in a more restrained way, one against the other. They talked a great deal about bringing the economies together, but they decided to lead their new scheme for a single currency with another version of the Snake. This time every currency was given a central rate against the others and against a basket of European currencies called the European Currency Unit or ECU. The theory behind this scheme was that the permitted fluctuation should be progressively narrowed until, as with the Snake, the stable currencies could be easily replaced with one currency.

The scheme developed both broad and narrow bands. Apprentice currencies had to keep within 6 per cent of their central rates, permitting them considerable deviation. Serious members were limited to 2.25 per cent deviaitions either side of their mid-rates. The intention was for each currency to move from the broad to the narrow bands, and then to narrow the bands even further.

In the early days of the system, countries had to resort to realignments of the rates. At the time of the negotiation of the Maastricht part of the Treaty of the European Union, the founders of the scheme were optimistic that many currencies could survive within the narrow bands. Exchange rate conformity was one of the requirements set out in the treaty for member currencies to meet before the country concerned could join the single currency. The treaty always envisaged a replacement of the member states' currencies by the ECU.

This scheme was destroyed in a similar way to the Snake. In 1992, the markets decided that the Deutschmark was much stronger than the permitted mid-points and bands of the ERM allowed. Remorseless pressure day by day in the markets threw several currencies out of the ERM altogether and forced others into devaluations against the German mark. As the member states and the Commission surveyed the damage towards the end of the year, they effectively decided that the Maastricht scheme had been scuppered. Out went the narrow bands. In their place they allowed 15 per cent variation on either side of the central rate, an enormous latitude for currencies even in volatile markets. They accepted that countries like Italy and the United Kingdom would not be in the ERM, at least for the foreseeable future, and they decided that they could no longer persevere with substituting the ECU for the national currencies in their single-currency scheme.

The third scheme, a less formal one than the Snake and the ERM, was based on a British idea developed in the 1980s as an alternative to the Maastricht route. Called by the British government the 'Hard ECU Scheme', it entailed promoting and developing the ECU as an alternative currency for business and for investors. Although this scheme was never formally adopted as the official scheme of the European Union, the Commission worked closely with Britain and took the scheme over, developing it as a parallel or transitional stage in the run-up to what it saw as full monetary union based upon the Maastricht model.

The Commission was energetic in demanding the use of the ECU in transactions with institutions of the European Union. Many companies and individuals obtaining contracts with the Commission or the European

Parliament or other European bodies were forced to accept payment in ECUs and had to render their accounts in ECUs. The Commission actively promoted an ECU market by issuing debt instruments in the basket currency. The British government and other member states were also enthusiastic, issuing ECU bonds and encouraging trading in ECU securities on the back of it. Banks were brought into the scheme and offered ECU banking facilities to any company that wished to take them up. The ECU existed as a business currency. It could be used through bank accounts to settle invoices for clearing cheques, it could be deposited, it could be saved, it could be invested in bonds, it could be traded in the currency markets. The only thing you could not do with the ECU was draw the money out of your bank account in the form of notes and coin.

This scheme too perished as the result of the combination of disbelief and an unwillingness on the part of Europe's businesses to adopt it as their currency. I have regularly surveyed British business audiences asking them, particularly those who are enthusiastic about a single currency, whether they have been using the ECU for their own transactions. With the exception of those businesses who have to invoice in ECUs where they have contracts with European institutions, I have to this day never encountered a British business that has willingly established an ECU bank account and has carried out transactions in ECUs with its customers or suppliers. It puts into perspective the demands of businesses that a single or common currency would be a benefit to them. It shows that it is not a sufficient benefit for them to volunteer to use such a scheme when it is available as a choice amongst many. Many more businesses in Britain use the dollar as a common currency for their transactions than use any individual European currency. None have replaced the dollar with the ECU.

We are now embarking on the fourth scheme in the last 30 years for currency union. Although the scheme is still based on the requirements of the Maastricht Treaty, it is a rather different scheme from that envisaged by the creators or from that recorded still in the unamended treaty. The Community has decided that it is too difficult to amend the treaty to bring it into line with the modern reality. They have instead tried to amend the treaty by means of secondary legislation or regulation, or merely by means of statements and conclusions from meetings that have no treaty or statutory force. It is a curious way of proceeding when so many millions of contracts and so many billions of Deutschmarks and French francs worth of activity will have to be compulsorily changed by June 2002 at the latest, from national currencies into the new Euro.

One of the revealing things about the single-currency scheme is the demonstration of how a Community which normally proceeds by strict legalism, based upon treaty and interpretation of the treaty and a series of court judgments enlarging the power of the Community, has decided to embark upon the single-currency scheme relying rather more on negotiation, political deals and political judgements overriding the strict terms of the agreements. We saw this on full display in the meeting of 1–2 May 1998 to settle the membership of the participating currencies in the single-currency scheme. Article 121 of the treaty – the former Article 109J – sets out four important tests which any country must meet before it is adjudged suitable as an entrant into the single currency. These are:

1) 'The achievement of a higher degree of price stability; this will be apparent from a rate of inflation which is close to that of, at most, the three best performing member states in terms of price stability.'
2) 'The sustainability of the Government financial stability; this will be apparent from having achieved a government budgetary position without a deficit that is excessive as determined in accordance with article 104(C).'
3) 'The observance of the normal fluctuation margins provided for by the ERM of the European monetary system, for at least two years, without devaluing against the currency of any other Member State.'
4) 'The durability of convergence achieved by the member state and of its participation in the ERM of the European monetary system being reflected in the long-term interest rate levels.'

The Commission convergence report in March 1998 makes clear that the member states with the exception of Luxemburg have found it difficult to meet all these economic requirements. The maximum inflation rate permitted under the terms of the treaty is 2.7 per cent – the average of Austria's 1.1 per cent and France's 1.2 per cent and Ireland's 1.2 per cent plus the 1.5 per cent points permitted deviation from the best three. This leaves Greece, at 5.2 per cent, well outside the new requirement. Although the British retail price index is above the average permitted reference level, on the Community's method of calculating figures the UK is also beneath the permitted ceiling.

The two requirements on the government budgetary position are a running deficit for the government of less than 3 per cent of national income in 1997 and a total stock of debt of less than 60 per cent of GDP. The Commission, in its report, claims that only Greece breaks the deficit requirement in 1997, with a deficit of 4 per cent of GDP. However, a number of countries including Germany, France and Italy have to indulge in some creative accounting to get down to a figure at or just below the 3 per cent. The stock figure has caused much more trouble. The Commission concludes that only

France, Luxemburg, Finland and the United Kingdom meet the treaty requirement by being below the 60 per cent reference value. Even Germany, which is only just above the 60 per cent reference value, has the added humiliation that its debt ratio has been rising, preventing the Commission from arguing that at least Germany has a relatively low value and it is falling. Some of the countries have exceeded the requirement by a huge margin. In Belgium the debt ratio was 122.2 per cent of GDP, more than twice the permitted ceiling, and in Italy a similarly ignominious result shows the debt stock standing at 121.6 per cent of GDP. Greece at 108.7 per cent of GDP, the Netherlands at 72.1 per cent and Sweden at 76.6 per cent also exceeded the ceiling by a large measure.

The Commission draws attention to the impact of creative accounting on the running deficits, quantifying the impact of between 0.1 and 1.0 percentage point of GDP depending on the country concerned. By inference, it criticises the use of privatisation proceeds to reduce debt ratios through temporary or one-off provisions. It might also have added the one-year Euro tax in Italy and the revaluation of gold reserves. The Commission remains very critical of the progress in many member states to comply with the requirements over debt and borrowing in the treaty. It states in its report:

> Further substantial consolidation is warranted in most Member States in order to achieve lasting compliance with the fiscal criteria and the medium-term objective for having a budgetary position that is close to balance or in surplus, as required by the stability and growth pact, effective from 1999 onwards. This applies in particular to Belgium, Germany, Greece, Spain, France, Italy, the Netherlands, Austria and Portugal where deficits in 1998 were forecast to be between 1.6 and 2.9% of GDP. For most of these countries, these consolidation requirements also apply when comparing the fiscal deficit ratios as projected in the convergence programmes for 1999–2000 with the medium term objective of the stability and growth pact.

This says in Commission prose that nine countries, including four of the five biggest in the Community, have failed to meet the deficit requirements in the treaty and need to take further strong budgetary action in order to meet them in the future. The Commission is keen to stress that meeting the requirements in 1997 was only the first part of a continuing programme. The idea was not that countries should temporarily meet the requirements and then go back to their old ways of borrowing too much and building up too big a stock of debt. The intention was that once they had met the requirements they should then keep beneath them by applying the same strict measures in perpetuity. The Commission called on countries to undertake substantial changes in their fiscal policies in order to make more rapid progress to cut their stock of debt and to get their annual borrowing down to a sensible level. The Commission does expect a country to spend two years in the ERM before qualifying. It points out that only nine currencies, given that the Belgium and Luxemburg currency are combined, have been in the ERM for the statutory two years before the Commission report. The Finnish marka and the Italian lira rejoined the ERM in October 1996 and November 1996 respectively. Three currencies remained outside the ERM, the drachma, the Swedish krona and the pound sterling. The Commission is satisfied that out of the nine currencies in the ERM only the Irish pound was too volatile to meet the requirement. It states, 'The Irish pound has normally traded significantly above its unchanged central rates against other ERM currencies; at the end of the reference period the Irish pound stood just over 3 per cent above its central rates.' From 16 March 1998, as a result, the Irish pound was revalued by 3 per cent against the other ERM currencies. Only Greece is found to be outside the long-term interest rate requirement of the unweighted arithmetic average of the long-term interest rates in the three countries with the lowest rates of the inflation plus the permitted 2 per cent tolerance. The Commission reports its disappointment that the ECU market contracted in 1997, reflecting declines in bank assets and liabilities and a reduction in the number of international bonds outstanding. This is not surprising given both the unpopularity of the ECU during its formative years and the decision of the Community to switch from the ECU to the Euro.

The individual comments on countries underline the basic message that most countries have failed to meet the requirements of the treaty. For example, in the case of Belgium the Commission reports:

> There is an evident ongoing concern as to whether the ratio of government debt to GDP 'will be sufficiently diminishing and approaching the reference value at a satisfactory pace' and whether sustainability of the fiscal position has been achieved; addressing this issue will have to remain a key priority for the Belgium authorities. The maintenance of a primary surplus of at least 6% of GDP per year and the achievement of growing in sizeable overall fiscal surpluses are needed in order to be able to forcibly reduce the debt ratio to 60 per cent within an appropriate period of time.

Ireland is reprimanded not only for its exchange rate volatility but also for two imperfections in its legal framework for creating independence of its central bank. Luxemburg too, after reporting the only clear round in the Maastricht hurdles, has to deal with two imperfections in its statute for the central bank in order to qualify.

On the Commission's own analysis, no country meets all requirements of the treaty. It appeared for some time that Luxemburg and Finland would qualify comfortably, as they were the only two countries wishing to join the single currency that had kept their stock of debt down and had good control of their public finances. Unfortunately, the Finnish currency has been outside the ERM and has been too volatile for part of the period to meet all of the requirements, whilst even Luxemburg has let herself down by failing to legislate in all the necessary ways to make her central bank truly independent.

None of this worried the member states at their meeting in May 1998. The German central bank fulminated in even stronger terms against the member states who failed to meet the requirements than did the Commission. The Bank of England did not bother to produce its own report but has issued general warnings about the dangers of proceeding with the single currency if countries and economies have not converged. There is general agreement across Western Europe that a single currency proceeding without proper economic convergence could cause terrible stresses and strains to build up in the system. Why then are the countries so breathless in their purpose to create a single currency when the economic, monetary and statutory under-pinnings are so insecure?

It demonstrates that the main purpose behind the single-currency scheme is political and not economic. No independent group of economists studying the position would recommend the early abolition of 11 member states' currencies on the basis of the current figures. At the time of the negotiation of the Maastricht Treaty, the requirements placed into that treaty in protocols and annexes underpinning clear statements in the treaty itself were thought to be the minimum necessary to ensure reasonable convergence. There were countries and politicians who felt that, in addition to requiring interest rate, exchange rate, deficit and inflation convergence, there should also be stipulations about social security budgets, unemployment levels, growth rates and other real activity variables. It is extremely difficult combining two rather differing economies if one has an unemployment rate of 3–4 per cent and another has an unemployment rate of 20 per cent. In most single currency areas around the world there would have to be transfer payments from the high-employment to the low-employment areas. The Community has not developed its thinking far enough about the extent of the obligations one territory will hold to another in the world of early union.

One of the reasons why the Community has been so blasé about the failure of so many states to meet the requirements, is that at the time of Maastricht, when France and Germany were decisive in driving forward the scheme, neither country felt that they would have difficulties in meeting the requirements themselves. The phenomenal impact of East German unification with West Germany upon the German budgetary position has unfolded in recent years. It has driven German debt up much higher than expected and has given the German state a persistent problem of running annual deficits as well as a problem with the stock of debt. The French had not envisaged such a long period of recessionary conditions, in part created by tying French francs so strongly and dramatically to the German mark at a time of strains in the German economy. As a result, French state debt and the French deficit have been higher and more persistent than the French government was expecting at the time of Maastricht.

When the two most important states in the Union, who have been most influential in constructing the terms of the Union, are themselves having difficulties in meeting the requirements, it becomes complicated, if not impossible, for them to insist on other states meeting the requirements as well. An additional rogue card was the very high level of Belgian state debt. Although there is no good reason why Belgium should be granted entry to the single currency whatever her economic figures, many people on the continent have felt that of course Belgium must join, given her geographical position sandwiched between France and Germany and given the geographical location of many Community institutions in Brussels, the joint capital of the European Union and of Belgium.

These two random developments, which few foresaw at the time of Maastricht, have led to a more generous interpretation of the requirements for other states. Greece has been a sacrificial lamb. Everyone has been forced to accept that, although the Greek economy has made rapid strides in the construction of much better numbers to meet the requirements of the treaty, Greece has remained well outside the reference levels in every respect, making it impossible to argue her case for early entry. Even Greece, however, is told that she can join quite soon after the first wave and is given every encouragement to continue moving her numbers in the right direction so that she too could benefit from a liberal interpretation of the range of requirements under the treaty.

A single currency is a dramatic step on the way to a United States of Europe. A single currency of course implies a single economy. It automatically creates a single exchange rate for all the participating countries, a single interest rate for them all and a single set of rules governing conduct of government economic policy and fiscal deficits. EMU stands for Economic and Monetary Union. The intention is to create a single economy as well as a single currency.

There are those in Britain who have seen the single currency as a mere technical matter, a convenience for those travelling abroad, a convenience for business, which deals at the moment in a multiplicity of currencies when conducting trade on the continent of Europe. Nothing could be further from the truth. The single currency is not a convenient form of traveller's cheque or a way of avoiding foreign exchange transaction costs with no other political or economic implications. It is the cement that binds a single economy. It is the way of building a single country. In the continental mind it leads to a single Finance Minister, a single economic policy and single taxation.

Those who argue that it is possible to have a single economic policy and a monetary union without a single group of politicians in charge, and without common taxation, are misleading people. One of the instabilities in the current single-currency scheme is the division of opinion between France and Germany over how much political control shall be exercised over the common economic policy. Under the treaty, interest rates and monetary policy are very clearly in the hands of independent bankers in Frankfurt. The intention is that the politicians should not be able to interfere with the interest rate nor influence the monetary policy in any direction other than the creation of zero inflation. The independent Central Bank of Europe and its satellite banks, the newly independent national central banks who form part of the system and become the agents of the European Central Bank in the fullness of time, are all charged with a single task. They have to create price stability. There is no latitude given in the treaty. It does not say that they can choose to have mild inflation if they felt that was better for jobs or growth. They are not invited to consider the general health of the European economy or the circumstances that might aid more business formation. Their single, undivided purpose under statute and treaty is to create zero inflation.

The French political establishment are not very happy with this proposal. Whilst they favour low rather than high inflation, they know there are trade-offs, they know that there are limits to the amount of unemployment that the Western European peoples will stand. They do envisage circumstances in which the politicians might want to influence the bank in the direction of lower interest rates, and possibly higher inflation, in order to get the economy moving again.

The treaty gives politicians a bigger role when it comes to other aspects of the Common Economic Policy. Although the treaty lays down fiscal requirements to control budget deficits and the stock of debt, politicians arguably need a bigger say in how quickly these are met and how the policies should be constructed to encourage fiscal probity. Politicians are also given some role when it comes to influencing the value of the currency in external markets, to the extent that this is possible and to the extent that it does not conflict with the primary duty of the bank to preserve price stability.

All these indecisions will give rise to rows in the months and years ahead. The battle has not been finally won between the German view of an independent system driven by the pursuit of zero inflation, and the French idea of a more politically orientated system accepting conflicting objectives and having to make decisions about trade-offs between them. At some point the Western European peoples may also be involved in the argument. There may be levels of unemployment or economic mismanagement which give rise to popular protest movements or to electoral changes which in their turn trigger new departures in economic policy. A firm institutional framework laid down in the treaty may turn out to be nothing more than shifting sands. If the member states and the Commission between them have already decided to ditch the ECU and create the Euro and have already decided that 11 countries can join the scheme which none of them is technically qualified to join under the treaty, anything is possible when it comes to the implementation of the Economic and Monetary Policy.

People in the City have been trying to gauge what might happen. A lot of attention centres upon Ireland. Ireland is a country with very strong trading links with sterling and with other non Euro-land currencies. Having lost the ability to raise domestic interest rates or to push the currency higher, the Irish authorities could quickly find themselves with an overinflated economy. In the run-up to the introduction to the single currency, property prices are ablaze in the Irish Republic, reflecting the much easier money conditions required in Ireland to prepare for single-currency convergence. Ireland will have to cut her interest rates when she needs them higher to control inflation. Her only course of action will be to raise taxes, to try to take some steam out of the economy, once she has lost control of her own interest and exchange rates.

Similar problems could occur for Finland, if the Euro in its early days depreciated rapidly against the other Scandinavian currencies that stay outside the system. This could produce a similar inflationary build-up in the Finnish economy to that currently being created in the Irish economy by preparation for the Euro. City commentators are also worried that one or two countries might decide to misbehave within the currency union. It takes up to three years before a country can be heavily fined to bring its budget deficit into line with the requirements of the treaty. In the intervening period, one or more countries might decide it is a good idea to have lower taxes than they should or to have higher public spending than they should, in order to gain some advantage and to provide some stimulus to their economy. The adverse consequences in higher interest rates and less investor enthusiasm from outside Euro-land would be felt by all of the countries in the bloc, meaning that it could be advantageous to an individual country to take this illegal action under the treaty. Daiwa, in one of its recent reports, concluded, 'There is little to deter individual EMU states from persistent fiscal expansion. Indeed, one could argue that the shared interest cost effect of EMU actively encourages states to free ride on the fiscal frugality of their partner nations.'

Even *The Economist*, a long-time exponent of a single currency, is worried by the lack of proper economic convergence in order to create the right conditions for a single currency. In its April survey of EMU, it identified three necessities for a successful currency union. The first is mobility of labour. The second is the flexibility of wages and prices enabling a country or region in the single-currency area to adjust quickly if there are shocks to the system. The third is some automatic mechanism for transferring money from the richer to the poorer parts of the union or to the parts of the union suffering from an individual shock.

There have been a number of shocks to the European economy in recent years. It is quite possible that there could be similar shocks in the future. For example, the merger of the two Germanys created totally new economic conditions in the centre of Euro-land and put enormous pressure on the ERM and the other member states of the Union. The loss of Finland's trade with the Soviet Union put great pressures on the Finnish economy and disrupted the relationships within Scandinavia. The immediate and most likely disruptive prospect is the currency movement between sterling and the Deutschmark which is putting unreasonable strains on the Irish economy, locked into the ERM.

Many of us have argued long and hard that you cannot have a single-currency area without a common labour market. It is difficult to see how Western Europe can produce one when so many people speak only one language, which differs from the other languages in other parts of the Union. The ossification of the European labour market is reinforced by both European and national legislation. There have been no serious attempts to reduce these artificial barriers to the movement and employment of people. A combination of Maastricht and ERM economics, producing high interest rates and deflationary conditions for most of the time, along with the labour laws of Western Europe have conspired to keep unemployment at very high levels in recent years in all of the major economies on the continent. Unless this problem can be tackled before a single currency is introduced, it will mean that different parts of the single currency area will experience very difficult conditions.

As long ago as 1977, Macdougall reported on the expansion of the European Community budget to 7 per cent of GDP, more than a five-fold increase in its current level, in order to transfer money around the Union from the poorer to the richer areas. Such a level of transfer payments would be normal in a single-currency area. The level of transfer payments within the United Kingdom sterling area is much greater than the current level of transfer payments between the nations for Western Europe. Similarly, in the United States of America's dollar-currency union, there are large transfers state to state.

If a country or region in Euro-land finds it is encountering persistently high unemployment and is unable to become competitive at the exchange rate at which it is locked into the Euro, its options are distinctly limited. With a national currency the domestic authorities can vary both interest rates and, through their influence, the exchange rate, to make that part of the world more competitive again. Both these options are removed by the transfer of powers to the European Central Bank to settle interest rates and the abolition of the national currency unit. If prices and wages do not fall to make that part of Euro-land more competitive, high unemployment will develop and persist. The normal way of handling this in a single-currency, single country is to transfer payments. This can take the form of benefit payments to the unemployed, regional aid and other social transfers. In addition, sometimes differential tax regimes are set in either local or national taxation to provide some stimulus or help.

None of this has been developed properly before creating the single European currency. Doubtless, when the scheme is up and running there will be many within Euro-land who argue the case for developing such structures as the natural component of the single currency.

Why is it that none of this has been worked out in advance? It comes back to the fatal combination in the scheme of a political purpose masquerading as a mere technical matter. The politicians keenest on creating a federal state are acutely aware that there is not enough consent amongst the Western European peoples to be completely open in their aims and to set out the full extent of the scheme at the beginning. They are trying to reassure those sceptical of the scheme by claiming that each step is but a small step and represents the complete journey. Some of them may even have been convinced by their own rhetoric that the single currency is a technical banking matter of no great moment.

If, as some of us fear, some parts of Western Europe overheat, experiencing labour and skill shortages and rising wages and prices, and other parts of Euro-land experience difficult conditions with rising unemployment, lack of activity and the movement of investment money away from them, the politicians will be forced into new actions. They will doubtless conclude that there is not enough power at the centre of Euro-land to enforce the necessary transfers of money from the richer to the poorer areas. They will conclude that, as those countries or areas no longer have powers over interest rates and currencies, the centre needs to take other powers which could make the necessary arrangements. They will find that their flexibility is distinctly limited. There is no immediate answer to the problem of inflexible labour markets. People unemployed in Sicily, speaking only Italian and Sicilian dialects, are not readily employable in fast-growing Ireland. A few might migrate there and get jobs in Italian restaurants but most would find it too difficult to learn the language and establish themselves in an English-speaking culture. It would even be difficult for former industrial workers made redundant in north-east France to make their way to Kent to find jobs, although in current conditions there are many more jobs on offer in Kent than there are in north-east France. The language barriers will be insuperable for the foreseeable future.

The politicians will also be reluctant to remove their own legislative barriers to jobs. There is a strong strand of thinking on the continent that it is better to protect the jobs of those who already have them than to open up the market to create jobs for those who do not. There is no obvious sign of this general judgement shifting. It is based upon the underlying political realisation that more people have jobs than do not have them and that they will welcome measures which they think might buttress their position even if it is at the expense of those seeking work.

It is safe to predict that the single currency will go ahead and that its bumpy ride will be used as a reason by the federal-inclining politicians of Western Europe to increase the number of powers held at the centre. There is no chance of the single currency working smoothly and well, promoting more prosperity and more jobs without adverse incident. The exponents of the scheme claim that its great benefit is to save as much as 1 per cent of GDP in reduced transaction costs when the new system is up and running. This is an extremely unlikely development.

The Commission has designed a very expensive way of introducing a new currency. Between 1 January 1999 and 1 January 2002, the Euro will exist as a business currency. It will be possible to have a bank account denominated in Euros. It will be possible to buy Euro-denominated bonds, to invoice in Euros, to write cheques in Euros and transmit money through the banking system in Euros. It will not be possible to draw the money out in the form of notes and coins. From 1 January 2002 until 30 June in the same year, notes and coins will be gradually issued in parallel with the national currencies still circulating in each country. Retailers and others handling cash from the public for that six-month period will have to accept as legal tender either their national currency or the Euro.

This means that the cost of introduction will be enormous. Every shop in a Euro-land country will need to have double its current amount of till space. This probably means that it will need double the number of tills. Early trials have shown it is extremely difficult handling two currencies continuously in the same till. The easiest solution is to segregate the currencies by having a Euro till and a national currency till. The problem is even greater for those collecting cash from the public in slot machines. Leisure arcades and machine-vending concerns will need to have new coin registers added for the Euro alongside the existing coin registers for the national currencies. At the end of the six-month period, the national currency tills and slot machines will have to be removed.

Various estimates have been made of the likely cost of setting up such a scheme throughout Western Europe. My estimate of the minimum costs to set up the scheme in the United Kingdom, were we to go ahead with it, amounts to £10,000 million for the business community. The main brunt of the cost would be borne by retailers, those with cash dispensers and cash-collecting machinery and the banking sector. For every company in the country, they would need to rewrite their computer programmes for accounting, convert their share capital, convert all their contracts with customers and suppliers and prepare to handle two different coinages during the transitional period.

The Commission has made the task especially difficult by its recommended method of undertaking the calculations. It has insisted upon six places of decimals where British businesses usually have a maximum of two places of decimals for their calculations. It has also proposed using the triangulation method during the transitional period. This means that businesses wishing to calculate the value of marks in francs, or pesetas in lira, have to carry out two calculations not one. Firstly they calculate the value of the marks in Euros and then they calculate the number of French francs you would get for that value of Euro. Different answers would be reached if a business insisted on using the more normal method of taking the cross-rate between the mark and the franc, owing to rounding differences.

The idea that the banking sector of Western Europe would be prepared to spend the huge sums of money required to change from the national currencies to the new currency without trying to recoup any of that investment is difficult to credit. Given that banks will spend huge sums of money on re-equipping with new tools, new cash machines and new accounting systems, they will be looking for a way to remunerate this investment capital. At the same time, they will be losing a portion of their foreign exchange business, losing all of the transactions between the par-ticipating currencies going into the Euro. This means that they will need additional revenue to compensate for that loss. The most likely way that banks will proceed will be to increase the charges for switching money around the Community. We should expect money transmission charges to increase, probably under cover of the banks arguing that the level of service has improved with the advent of the new currency. This will offset some of the gains that business is making resulting from the absence of foreign exchange transaction charges. In a typical transaction where a company in France settles the bill with a company in Germany, the current costs of moving the money are greater than the costs of exchanging the francs for the marks already, and in the world of the Euro it is likely that these money transmission charges will rise.

If they stay the same or fall, it will mean that the banks become much less profitable and have made a large commitment of capital to setting up the Euro which actually serves to undermine their profit and loss account. This will only happen in conditions of great competition, where the banks discover that they are all price followers and unable to make price increases stick in the market. Looking at the range of commissions and charges around European banks at the moment, this is unlikely.

In 1998, worries grew that the single-currency scheme would not be able to withstand big external shocks. In April, the French Interior Minister warned that the lack of flexibility and the lack of political control over the Central Bank meant it was heading for disaster. He likened the whole project to sailing on the *Titanic*. He said that the ship was majestic, the orchestra was playing well, the food and wine were good but the ship was heading straight for the iceberg. He warned that unemployment was likely to become a problem in parts of the European Union and that there was no means for the Bank to do anything about this under the statute, given the way the German government and others were interpreting the treaty. In this he was echoing a wide range of professional opinion in the business community.

These worries were repeated by the opinion of the Economic and Social Committee of the European Community itself. It stated:

> In the light of the Commission's analysis, a scenario could be imagined in which the Euro exchange rate is initially fixed at a level quite different from that suggested by the fundamentals of the European economy in all its diversity. The European Central Bank could in fact be obliged to impose an excessively tight monetary policy and to raise interest rates in response to financial market scepticism as to the objective of price stability arising as the result of policies pursued by certain countries.

It was particularly significant that a group of people working within the European Community framework and on advice from the Commission felt it necessary to warn against particular countries pursuing policies that started to pull the single currency apart, rather than putting it together.

The Economic and Social Committee also drew attention to the possibility of foreign exchange market turbulence. It and other commentators became increasingly alarmed at the prospect of trying to keep the exchange rates fixed from 3 May 1998 right through until the abolition of the national currencies on 30 June 2002. Many have experience of the impact of the markets on previous currency schemes and were naturally becoming alarmed at the lack of measures being taken to ensure that the fixed exchange rates from 3 May 1998 were to stick and succeed.

The British debate has been the most active of any in the European Community, but it has still lacked depth and breadth. It is conventionally seen as two separate but interrelated debates. Firstly, there is the debate about whether the scheme would bring economic benefits to Britain or not. This is often narrowed to the question, would the Euro be good for business and does the business community wish us to enter? The second question is, what impact would the Euro have on our constitutional settlement and would this be an acceptable price to pay?

One of the curious features of the British debates is the unwillingness of any mainstream politician or political party to argue the case for a federal Europe. Although some of the words of the Liberal Party manifesto and the statements of Liberal spokesmen imply that Liberals would be happy to see Britain as a region in a federal Europe, whenever it comes to elections, Liberal candidates back off this proposition very rapidly and claim that they are seeking a more friendly and co-operative kind of Europe but not a federal superstate. The two main parties, Labour and Conservative, are always adamant that they have no intention of taking Britain into a federal Europe. Those who argue the case for the single currency, if they wish to stay in the mainstream, never put forward the proposition that the single currency would be good as an important stepping stone on the way to a single country. If they are put under pressure, they nearly always suggest that this is not a necessary consequence.

In this respect the British debate is out of line with the debate on the continent. Continental politicians are much keener to set out their enthusiasm for a federal Europe. The Germans wish to create a new kind of Europe based on the German federal model. They believe the powers that the German state has left to *Länder*, like Bavaria or Brandenburg, are sufficient and should also suffice for the *Länder* of the proto-European state, whether those *Länder* be Bavaria and Brandenburg or Yorkshire and London. The French view too favours political as well as economic and monetary union. Although they began by wishing to control the mighty Deutschmark, they have come to see the need for political institutions and political power to be exercised over the emerging bodies of the European Community.

Taking the argument to the business community has been an interesting experience. Small businesses share the general scepticism of the British public about the desirability of the single currency. They readily understand the point that for them a single currency is all cost and no benefit. Most businesses in Britain are small. Some three million people are self-employed and several hundred thousand businesses employ just a few people. In practically every case these businesses serve only a local, regional or national market in the United Kingdom. There is little point in trying to win customers in Germany from a business based in Leeds if you have still not tackled Birmingham. By definition, businesses serving only the UK market will get no savings at all from the single currency scheme. They do not deal in French francs and Deutschmarks. They do not have to combat currency variability or pay foreign exchange commission costs. They will, should we join a single currency, have to spend considerable sums of money on re-equipping in order to handle the new notes and coins. Many small businesses take money direct from the public. They need to change their tills and cash machines in order to handle the new arrangements. Every small business needs to change its banking arrangements and alter its accounts from sterling to the Euro, should we go in.

Some of these small companies believe that a single currency is inevitable. They are worried that they will be forced into adopting it where they do have counter parties abroad. Some even fear that they will be forced into using the Euro where their customers are multinational businesses operating in Britain but with their headquarters somewhere on the continent. If Britain is outside the single currency but other countries are in it, there will still be a currency risk for those forced to use the Euro for invoicing but still accounting to themselves and their shareholders in sterling.

A business will not have to switch from dealing in sterling to dealing in Euros unless its customers insist on the switch and have the necessary market power to enforce it. Again, most small businesses dealing only in the British market will not face any such problem, as their customers will be as keen to persevere in sterling. In some other cases, where small businesses do supply multinationals in Britain or companies abroad, they may well be sufficiently price competitive or have a special service or product that means they can resist any demand from their customers that they should invoice in Euros. Only in a limited number of cases will the small company be in a position where it has to go along with the requirement to invoice in Euros. This will usually be where it already has to invoice in Deustchmarks or

French francs anyway. To the extent that it is merely replacing the mark with the Euro, there is no added currency risk.

The bigger business community is more divided in its attitude towards the Euro in Britain. There are many businesses who believe the Euro is 'inevitable'. If this means that the 11 countries in Western Europe on the continent intend to go ahead with it, that is clearly true. It is difficult to see why the political will of the continent means that the Euro is inevitable in Britain. Some argue that, because a lot of trade on the continent will be conducted in Euros, it becomes inevitable that we have to adopt it as our currency. This is a particularly strange argument given the current dominance of the dollar in world trade. At the moment, half of all world trade is conducted in dollars. Half of all foreign-held bank deposits are denominated in dollars. Half of all foreign exchange transactions around the world include the dollar as one of the two currencies in the transaction and two-thirds of the official foreign currency reserves of the world are held in the form of dollar balances. Despite this overwhelming dominance of the dollar, no one suggests that it is inevitable that we must join the dollar bloc and surrender the pound in favour of the American currency. Businesses are quite used to dealing in dollars on a regular basis. I have run an international business which invoiced in dollars and then converted the dollars into sterling when we thought it sensible to do so. There was no complication in this. Any business not wishing to run the currency risk could cover the currencies forward or switch them as soon as the dollars were earned, obviating any real foreign exchange risk in the transactions.

It has always been possible to conduct business in a currency other than the domestic currency of the country in which the business is based. The same could be true when some countries in Europe have adopted the Euro. We do not have to go along with them. British businesses would have the freedom to decide whether to invoice and deposit in Euros or whether to continue in pounds or dollars or some other currency.

Bigger businesses are also conscious that some of their counterparts on the continent may force them to take the currency risk by demanding Euro invoices. This is again similar to what happens at the moment. Some companies already have to take the foreign exchange risk by invoicing in Deutschmarks or French francs. Many more have to take the foreign exchange risk of the US dollar, accepting that their international market place is dollar-denominated. If they wish to compete, they have to invoice in dollars like the rest. Some large businesses believe that the Euro could be beneficial to them. Given this belief, it is surprising that none of these businesses have volunteered to use the ECU in recent years when it was available to give them all the benefits of the common currency that they could desire. Nor do any of them volunteer that they will automatically use the Euro even if Britain does not join the scheme. This should put into perspective business claims that the Euro or the ECU, or some other single European currency, offers them a great advantage.

There has always been a British business feeling amongst some companies and individuals that the attitude of successive British governments to the European Union has been damaging to business. Because the Labour government of the 1970s argued in public over whether to withdraw from the Community or not and only finally resolved the matter through a referendum, there was a strong feeling in the 1970s that the British government was not fully committed to the European project. In the 1980s some in the business community were upset by Margaret Thatcher's firm handling of Community matters, especially her attempts at what they regarded as handbag diplomacy to get our budget rebate. In the 1990s John Major's successful negotiation of an opt-out from the Maastricht Treaty was taken as another sign that Britain was not fully engaged. Now the business community is discovering that exactly the same is true of the Blair-led Government. Mr Blair, despite protestations of being a good European, will not name a date to sign up for the single currency. Mr Blair, whilst signing a federal Amsterdam Treaty, made it clear that Britain could not join in the arrangements for common frontiers. Mr Blair and his colleagues made it clear that they do not agree with the Agricultural Policy in many respects, especially in its handling of the British beef crisis.

Some businessmen worry that the successive disagreements between the United Kingdom, under any government, and the rest of the Community makes it more difficult for them to win orders. There is no evidence, looking at the figures, that British businesses have encountered this difficulty in the market place. It would be a surprising development in foreign trade if free societies started refusing to deal with other free societies because of statements or actions of domestic governments. There are many occasions when I do not like what the German or the United States governments are doing. It does not alter my attitude towards products in the market place. When I am buying something, I judge it on price, quality, reliability, design and all the other things that matter when making a purchasing decision. As there is no government of a major country in the world at the moment with which I agree, it could make it rather difficult for me when going to the shops if I allowed this to influence my trading patterns.

British business, through its formal representation, speaks with a forked tongue on matters European. Whilst claiming that we should be friendlier and more engaged in the centre of events, British business is also very critical of much of the European Commission and Community agenda.

British business does not wish to see taxes harmonised at higher levels. It is not in favour of the Social Chapter and employment agenda unfolding from Brussels. It does not favour all of the detailed and often pettifogging regulations put through in the name of the single-market programme. Business has to decide how far it wishes any British government to go in resisting these measures or in speaking out against them. Given that the Community activity takes place usually by consensus behind closed doors under the strong influence of the Commission, the only way to try to change the direction is to combine use of the veto with strong language. Business should beware that the next task of the Community, if they conclude their single currency, will be tax harmonisation. A recent communication from the Commission to the Council entitled 'Towards tax co-ordination in the European Union' sets out 'a package to tackle harmful tax competition'.

This document states that, once the single market and EMU have been completed, 'Taxation is increasingly identifiable as a key factor influencing economic decisions. And as the introduction of the single currency eliminates exchange rate risks and reduces transaction costs, the differences between national tax systems will become more visible and will have an even greater influence on decisions.' The Community proposes a common withholding tax on interest payments made to residents of other member states, higher minimum levels of taxation established at Community level for energy products and a new code of conduct designed to inform government authorities in the Community.

The drift of policy is quite clear. The first step was to create the single market legal framework. The second step is full economic and monetary union. The third step is common taxation. As the Commission recognises, if you move to a single economy eliminating many of the other differences between the member states, those who favour federal direction will clearly wish to eliminate the differences caused by different levels of national taxation. What is worrying about the Commission document is the proposal that taxes should be harmonised in an upwards rather than a downwards direction. Tax breaks are seen as unhelpful rather than high taxes being seen as unhelpful. Business should beware that the next stage in the scheme is to impose a minimum withholding tax on savings and investment flows and higher indirect taxes. The Commission will do this under cover of suggesting that as a result taxes on employment can be reduced. More likely, the extra tax revenue will be swallowed up both to control the otherwise burgeoning deficits of Western European governments and to finance the higher spending which the Community as well as the member states are likely to undertake.

Some in the European Union favour the creation of the Euro as the world's second reserve currency. They resent the importance and influence of the dollar. They believe that by pooling the currencies of the major continental countries they could create a large enough unit of account with sufficient backing for it to become a regular form of settlement for companies and countries outside the European Union. It is not quite clear why they think this is an advantage. It could only come about if the European Union as a whole ran a large balance of payments deficit with the rest of the world for a concerted period of time. The large dollar overhang has been created by large US balance of payments deficits. These have been matched and financed by Asian and European investors buying American shares, bonds and treasury bills. Not every American citizen would regard this as a helpful or desirable development. The one advantage for the US authorities is the money they make on seignorage on the currency. The price they pay has been much greater volatility in US markets dependent upon the whims of overseas investors. The European Union spends quite a lot of its time sounding off against the actions of so-called speculators around the world. If the serious intention is to create the Euro as a reserve currency, it will mean that the European economy is much more subject to the attitudes and actions of such investors of large amounts of mobile capital.

The main purpose behind the drive to create the Euro as the world's second reserve currency is political. People see it as another way of projecting the power and influence of the new country of Europe onto the world stage. It is linked in the minds of many with the wish to have European rather than German or French or British representation on the main economic and monetary councils of the world. At the moment, Britain, France, Germany and Italy are all members of the G7 group of the richest countries of the world, which meet regularly to review world economic problems. Those who favour European integration would like to see this as a G4 group with Britain, Germany, France and Italy represented by a single European representative speaking on behalf of the Euro bloc. Similarly, there is a wish to see Europe represented at the IMF and World Bank as a single entity rather than as a group of individual countries with their own representation. This has already happened in world trade fora, where the EC commissioner for international trade matters takes the place of the representatives of the individual Western European countries, as this is an area where authority has already clearly passed from the member states to the European Union.

All this is more evidence, if evidence were needed, that the serious intent behind the single-currency scheme is to create a new country called the United States of Europe. There is a lot of sense in saying that members of a single-currency scheme should be represented by one plenipotentiary at international, economic and monetary gatherings, rather than by individual ministers or officials from member state governments. No one believes that the Mayor of London or the leader of the Scottish Parliament should appear at meetings of the IMF or the G7. Everyone accepts that London and Scotland should be represented by the British Government with a spokesman at a senior level representing the British sterling currency union. In a few years time, it will seem equally obvious if there is a completed single currency on the continent that representation in world bodies should come from the European Central Bank or from the European Council of Ministers rather than from the member states direct.

No one should doubt that if Britain joined a single-currency scheme it would have a fundamental impact on political, economic and social life in our country. It would make a huge difference to our traditional democracy. Most British general elections in the twentieth century have been fought about the issues of jobs, mortgages and prosperity. Rival parties present rival ways of influencing or managing the economy. The electorate give their judgement on whether the outgoing government have made them better off and whether they deserve another period in office to continue the good work, or not. None of this would be possible if we joined a single currency. There would be no point in politicians in general elections debating mortgages, interest rates, the availability of bank credit for business, the fate of our foreign exchange reserves or how much money should be in circulation. All of these things would clearly become the sole province of the European Central Bank. There would be little point in discussing how much the State can borrow, how much indirect or withholding tax should be imposed or how the economy might grow, as these matters would have largely or wholly passed out of the grasp of British politicians into the hands of the European institutions.

General elections would be about more local and parochial matters and may well go on the slippery slope that has been followed by local elections. The more the councillors see their role as providing criticism or ineffectual opposition to the government of the day, the fewer are the number of voters who turn out to vote in such local elections. Many local councillors see their position as without influence, able only to condemn the government. There is a reluctance to take responsibility even for those things which remain within their power, as they are always looking upwards to the superior authority. When there is a problem, local councillors often want the government to do something about it, Parliament to legislate or more money to be made available from the centre. Rarely do councillors say, here is a problem which is within our power to tackle, there is plenty of legislation giving us the authority, we have a large budget, we will sort it out from within our own means.

It would not be long before the same sort of thing happened to British national politics, if we went into the single currency. It would be much easier for national politicians to complain that they could not solve a particularly intractable problem because the Community would not allow the country to borrow more or because the state of the economy was malfunctioning under the exchange rate and interest regime coming from the central bank. The Chancellor of the Exchequer would have little to do and his authority would have been severely diminished by relinquishing most of the powers of his office to others.

We can see the beginnings of this process in the rows currently under way over the so-called independence of the Bank of England. The Chancellor has given the Bank of England the power to settle the interest rates and decide how much money should be in circulation. He wants people to believe that he can have no influence over it. He remains responsible for deciding how much the State should borrow, how much to raise in taxation, and how much to spend on different programmes. The resulting tensions, given the split of responsibilities, have become manifest. At a time when sterling was very high and manufacturing industry finding it very difficult to compete, the Chancellor claimed privately that this was the fault of the Bank of England and the Bank of England complained privately that it was the fault of the Chancellor's policies. The country is not particularly grateful for having a war between the respective spin-doctors of two institutions, the Government and the Bank, with no sign of an early resolution of the underlying difficulty.

It would be far worse if the independent body were the European Central Bank. Everyone knows that the Chancellor of the Exchequer in Britain can still take the powers back from the Bank of England if he wishes, or if the pressures on him become too great. That way out would not be available to a Chancellor who had joined a single currency. Everyone knows that the Chancellor of the Exchequer can still borrow more than the Maastricht ceiling if he wishes. That would not be the way out, even in extreme circumstances, for a Chancellor who joined a single currency. A Chancellor who had gone into the Euro would have burned practically all his boats. If he then found he was on a desert island, there would be no way back to a green and prosperous Britain.

The role of the individual Member of Parliament would also be greatly changed. Many people do write to Members of Parliament about their own job prospects, their family income, their general economic circumstances. They do so because they know that at the moment a Member of Parliament can write to the Chancellor, put pressure on the Chancellor, ask questions in the House or form a movement with other Members of Parliament or with the British press to try to get a change of policy in the direction his constituents wish. Just as the Chancellor's freedom of manoeuvre would be greatly restricted in a single currency, so would the Member of Parliament's. What would be the point of writing to an MP if your mortgage rate was unacceptably high, if neither he nor the Chancellor of the Exchequer could have any influence over it? What would be the point of telling your MP that you were unhappy with the high level of unemployment in your country or region and that you wanted a job, if the European Central Bank and the Council of Ministers held most of the powers needed to do anything about the problem?

A Member of Parliament's postbag is very sensitive to the question of how much influence he has. The postbag is always swelled enormously on a free-vote issue. This is not just because free-vote issues are particularly sensitive issues like capital punishment, the homosexual age of consent or fox-hunting. It is also because the British public understands full well that in a whipped party system a Member of Parliament is much more important in a free-vote matter than when he is responding to a government proposal. The public is also beginning to discern that a Member of Parliament is propor-tionately more influential even on whipped government business than on business which falls under the influence of the European authorities. This would be reflected should we go further into a federal Europe.

British democracy has always been noisy, boisterous, often angry and argumentative. Although many people have a low estimation of Members of Parliament and of politicians and although many claim to dislike the scenes from Prime Minister's Question Time on television each week, there is a strong feeling in Britain that the system is needed, that it is there for the redress of grievance and the representation of the public's view. It is difficult to know what would come to replace this if we joined Britain to Euro-land. How would the public give vent to its anger if unemployment was too high? What could be done about mortgage rates if they went through the roof? What action should be taken if parts of Britain overheated as the result of a monetary policy that did not suit us? None of these questions have been properly resolved by the architects of the new Europe. Because they are so optimistic that their currency will work smoothly and well, they have not thought about how to replace the broken democratic input that they are destroying by their new idea.

Before a single-currency scheme is introduced it is important to make sure that the people living under it feel that they are one people. They have to believe that they can move to any part of the Union to get a job should the need arise. They have to wish to give money from the richer to the poorer parts of the Union as a matter of course. They need to feel that there is a way that their voices will be heard should things go wrong. In summary, they need to feel that they belong to the same country.

A single currency can only work for those countries which wish to destroy their primary and national identity and replace it with a new identity, a European identity, membership of the United States of Europe. It took the United States of America many years to get to a single federal banking system. It was part of a plan in the United States to build one country. The dollar bill became as strong a symbol of American prosperity and the unity of American identity as the Stars and Stripes itself.

There was some difficulty in designing the right Euro notes and coins. It showed the crisis of identity that still characterises the Western European countries and peoples. Until that crisis of identity is resolved decisively in a European direction, a single European currency is a very hazardous adventure. It is more than a new banking arrangement. It is far more than a mere technical economic matter. As its true architects understand full well, it is a vital set of building blocks in the creation of a new country. Those who sell it dishonestly to people are doing most to endanger its slender chances of success.

The more countries, currencies and economies that are brought in, the bigger the risks and the greater the dangers. It is certainly not right for Britain today. Britain remains an outward-looking global economy with strong transatlantic links. It would be more sensible to recommend joining the dollar than the Euro, but best of all is to stay with the pound and to remain British. The opposition says that the UK should stay out of the Euro for at least two parliaments. We need to see it work in good times and bad. We need to see if we are right that it entails too big a sacrifice of our sovereignty. There has been enough crisis in British identity already. Taking on a new European identity in place of that hard-won feeling that the United Kingdom is one country is a risk too far.

11 Conclusions

If you travel the 28 miles from Land's End to the Isles of Scilly, you make a journey back in time to a world we are losing. The close, small island communities on each of the five inhabited islands of the group have many of the characteristics of communal life that English villages and small market towns enjoyed 30 or 40 years ago.

There is no visible police presence, yet people leave the money for the milkman by their gate and no one steals it. Locals leave vegetables, seeds, bulbs and other items for sale along with the jar to put the coins in, trusting the customers. Many leave their doors unlocked and unbolted when they are out. Tractors and boats are left lying around with no obvious security.

The council of the islands sorts out what little issues need to be settled by local government without the big party posturing that you see in councils on the mainland. Locals are at one with their past and their environment. They tell you of the time Sir Cloudesley Shovell wrecked some naval ships on the rocks. The year was 1707 but it might as well have been yesterday. They know and love their islands, talking you through each rock, each long barrow and cairn, each shipwreck and each new building. They are at peace with their past.

Many locals also are good naturalists and countrymen. They can tell their great black-backed gull from their lesser one; they can tell their tern from their petrel. They can identify the different types of wild flower and know the medicinal uses to which they can be put.

There is something about island life which sets itself off and makes things possible which are no longer possible in a metropolis. The global market does intrude in several ways. From time to time container ships beach on the rocks in a storm or in fog, spilling their wares. The islands will take advantage, as they have over the centuries. Daily, the *Scillonian III* makes the crossing from Penzance with the supplies from the choice of the world market. Daily, she plies back with the orders to keep the islands going.

What is interesting about the Scilly community is that it shows in microcosm how, even in a global market place with access to the best in the world, it is possible to keep something unique, distinctive, special which everyone there values. Visitors who go there return time and again, appreciating the quiet, the happy balance between man and nature, the beauty and the tranquillity of the islands.

Some will say that believing that an island community can keep something special is out of date, a clouded romance of times past or even an imperfect understanding of the strain and struggle that such island existence can represent. I am not so sure. At a time when a whirlwind of economic change has been unleashed on people, there is even more of an instinct to go back to something firm, stable, of lasting value. The endless search for greater prosperity through the market place needs to be supplemented by some act of piety, an act of beauty, a belief in tradition, an understanding of what makes a community greater than a market place.

Left-wing critics of Mr Blair's Government dislike the way that he is accepting some of the Conservative economic inheritance, turning instead to constitutional change and social authoritarianism to provide some difference. They would like to see a radical, separate economic programme based on large-scale Government intervention and regulation of the enterprise economy. They are grateful for those areas where Mr Blair is moving away from his Conservative inheritance. They admire the minimum wage but want it to be higher. They are pleased with the incorporation of the European Social Chapter into British law but would like it to go further. They wish to see trade union power restored in full and would like to see a packet of measures to divorce the British economy from the power of the international financial market place.

They are not amused by Mr Blair's constitutional radicalism. They are against the independent monetary committee of the Bank of England, taking away the opportunity for them or others to influence monetary policy in the direction they wish. They do not like the passage of more and more powers to quangos away from parliamentary accountability and influence. There is little in Mr Blair's health or education changes for them to welcome.

Many of them are even more depressed by what they see as his social authoritarianism. It was a Labour government rather than a Conservative one that introduced the idea of curfews on young people. It is Mr Blair and Mr Straw, the Home Secretary, who have gone further than the Conservatives in lengthening prison sentences and in toughening the regime. There is no sign of Mr Blair wishing to liberalise drugs or relax the police presence on our streets: the Left look in vain for any such genuflection in their direction.

This means that there is some common cause between Left and Right against the many changes that this Labour Government is driving through. The one thing that does unite Right and Left is the belief that British democracy still has an important role to play and must be preserved. Whilst Left and Right wish to use their British democracy to further different policies, we are at one in saying that the best system to sort out our differences is a democratically elected Parliament in Britain with the sovereign power to make choices on behalf of the voters. Both Left and Right are becoming worried by the enormity of the changes the Government is putting through and by the apparent ease so far with which it has been able to affect them. The more it does, the more easily the Government is able to do it, the more likely the permanent damage in the medium and longer term.

The Government claims to have found a middle way between socialism and free-market capitalism. In this it is no different from any of its predecessors, Conservative or Labour. Britain has long had regulated markets, and has long accepted substantial taxation for the State to spend as it sees fit. The Government's exaggerated claim for its constitutional revolution is that they have found a Third Way. This is untrue. They have decided to press hard down the European road, accepting a European-inspired constitutional revolution. As a result, they are threatening great damage to tradtional British democracy without placing anything better in its stead. Fettering the monarchy and abolishing hereditary peers is partly very Old Labour, but is also European modernisation. Proportional representation is being copied from the continent. Splitting the kingdom by devolution is best European practice, and is often urged upon us to bring us into line with the continent. Our competition policy, and approach to many industrial issues, is part of a concerted plan to make Europe the area of government rather than Britain.

The Government's analysis is flawed and the analysis of many commentators is partial or obscured by the rhetoric. Mr Blair's analysis is that the Conservative inheritance was not bad. It needs meddling with and changing in minor ways: a bit more social intervention here, a strengthened quango there, to toughen food safety standards or pursue an independent money policy. He also believes that, because he does not have a major new economic agenda to match privatisation or trade union reform of the Thatcher years, he will turn instead to the Charter 88 programme of constitutional devastation.

In the name of democracy, they aim to take more and more decisions away from democratically elected representatives. In the name of democracy, they take more and more things away from the House of Commons and give them to the European Community, to regional government or to unelected quangos. In the name of democracy, Mr Blair decides to modernise the constitution, overthrowing some of the checks, balances and traditions that make it special.

It is never easy to define what makes or constitutes a nation. New Labour say that the Conservative view of the British nation is out of date. They have been trying desperately to get away from the image of beefeaters at the Tower, of the State Opening of Parliament, of Big Ben and pomp and circumstance music. Not for them a land of castles and lords, of ancient institutions and well established ceremonies. The Blair image is of a 1960s modernism. He is looking back to gain the future. He sees Britain as a land of Carnaby Street and the Beatles, of rock bands and fashion icons, of out-of-doors *nouvelle cuisine* restaurants by the Tower of London and singles by Elton John. What he has to understand is that both sets of images and traditions are part of Britain and being British. You do not have to annihilate the one to establish the other. The sense of national consciousness is diffuse, all-embracing, wide-ranging and complex. There are many people who feel unhappy in Mr Blair's back-to-the-sixties Britain, just as there are people who felt unhappy with John Major's warm beer and cricket on the village green, with its images of a cosy 1950s, before the new liberalism arrived.

Perhaps you can best define a nation by people's sense of belonging. All the time that most people going abroad from Great Britain say they are British, when asked the question, there is that clear strong feeling of identity. An Englishman abroad would rarely say he was English rather than British. The growing sense of Scottish nationhood is visible in the large numbers of people now from Scotland who might well reply that they are Scottish rather than British. Very few Scottish, British or English people would claim to be European before anything else.

When I speak in schools I often ask, before I speak, how pupils identify themselves. I have been told that we are plunging into Europe for the young, that we are building an exciting new state because it is what young people want. I invariably find that English schoolchildren reply almost without exception that they are primarily British.

A sense of identity does not always exclude some other sense of identity as well. If someone asks me where I come from, I consider the answer based on how much they know about my part of the world. If someone in London asks me where I come from, I don't say I am British or from the United Kingdom. If I think their geography is good, I will tell them I come from Wokingham. If I think their geography is a little rusty, I will tell them I live 35 miles west of London. Although Reading is the nearest big town to Wokingham, I would never say I come from Reading, because people from Wokingham have a very different sense of belonging from people from Reading. They have made a conscious choice not to live in Reading and are proud of their separate Wokingham existence. If talking to a foreigner, I would be much more likely to say I was from Britain, or I might use a phrase about proximity to London, the one city I could be sure they knew about.

I, like many of my constituents, have a sense of identity and loyalty to Wokingham, the town and district, to Berkshire, our geographical and spiritual county, and to the United Kingdom, the centre of our government and the origin of much else.

It is not just the sense of place that defines the nation. The United Kingdom is my nation, rather than England or the Wokingham district. That is a fact of history, a belief that I have and a proposition centred around a long period of stable government of the United Kingdom as a whole through the Westminster Parliament. Governments are important in helping to define nations, but it is possible for a nation to be smaller than the government area in which it finds itself, or for a new larger nation to emerge out of groupings of smaller countries. The United States nation emerged despite the strong and fierce loyalties to the separate states of the union, as many people decided that loyalty to the greater whole made more sense for all sorts of reasons. It also took a brutal civil war to complete the unification. Scottish nationalists will claim that their sense of nationhood is, if anything, strengthened by their present plight within the United Kingdom. It gives them something to rebel against, a cause around which they can fashion their sense of Scottish purpose. The same feelings predominate in the Catalan areas of Spain, in parts of northern Italy, in Belgium and in other regions and provinces around the proto-United States of Europe.

As we have seen, a strong case can be made out to say that unleashing too many challenges to the feeling of identity and of the past that people enjoy at this juncture doubly destabilises an insecure world. If the plan is completed and the regions, nations, provinces and areas of Europe are forced under a single government from Brussels and Frankfurt, the tensions may become insupportable. The single currency is the most dramatic part of the project currently on the table. No one has thought through how individual regions and former countries can or will respond when they discover that the one interest rate and one monetary policy does not suit all. What will they do and say when it does not work for them? No one has yet decided how much money will need to be sent to the poorer regions of Europe suffering under the impact of the single interest rate and the single exchange rate. No one has worked out whether the richer regions of Europe will be prepared to make those payments. The strains of uniting the two Germanys were very great. People in West Germany became very reluctant to pay the necessary taxation to salvage something amidst the redundancies and the unemployed of East Germany. How much more difficult will it be to get people to take on the burden within the European Union when there is no common language or common sense of national purpose that undoubtedly existed when the two Germanys were put together.

Similar strains will tell as the European Court of Justice and the European Human Rights declaration become more and more onerous, overwhelming the nationally and locally agreed law codes around the Community. For every litigant who succeeds in a European court, there will be another who fails. For every person who thinks the legal changes are for the better, there could be one or two who think they are for the worse. At some point, those who feel that they are losing out from the evolution of European law may begin to doubt its authority, or to seek to undermine its wisdom.

It is the unemployed who are likely to represent the biggest stumbling block for the European state. They will resent the two-tier world into which they have been thrust. They will see that the legislative protection for those in work is doing nothing to help them find work. They will see that the politicians of Western Europe are trying to create a club-class world for themselves and the large corporations but have not necessarily remembered the conditions at the back of the aircraft.

We have seen that there are very few examples of federal states worldwide that work. Federalism is usually a stepping stone on the way to a centralised empire or a temporary resting place on the way to the break-up of a larger state. Too much devolution encourages separatist and nationalist movements. Too little means that the central state has arrived. The European Union is a group of disparate states on a route march to unity. They are attempting the very difficult if not the impossible. There are very few examples in world history of states coming together by agreement when they represent such a wide range of cultures, languages, religions and experiences as are represented by the countries of Western Europe. It is a deeply dangerous experiment. If it fails, it will spawn more separate states than went into the mix in the first place. It might well see the break-up of countries like Spain and Italy, as the individual nationalists movements within them struggle to get out both of the current states and of the European superstate in the making, when it too is seen to be oppressive by those in the nationalist movement.

It is now the historic task of the Conservative Party to offer the people a choice, to remind them of our inheritance, and to propose that we keep more of it than we dismiss. We must do so in a modern way. A more educated people want more individual control over their own lives. That means lower taxes, more self-reliance, less government. People want to relate more strongly to their local areas and communities. That means more devolved power to the school board, the hospital trust, the local council. People want access to the best in the world, as well as respect for the best of our traditions. That means looking across the Atlantic as well as across the Channel. It means building links with the North American Free Trade Area, as well as with the single market of Europe. It means being energetic in pursuing worldwide agreement on technology, intellectual property, free trade and the environment. It means recognising that Europe is too small to solve many of the problems.

This book has been primarily concerned about the United Kingdom. The United Kingdom is being destroyed from within and without. This New Labour Government is besotted by the constitution. It is determined to transfer massive powers from an elected Parliament to Brussels. It is determined to transfer other massive powers from an elected Parliament to quangos and intermediary bodies. It is resolved to begin the process of creating devolved parliaments and assemblies in different parts of the United Kingdom. It wrongly believed that a Scottish Parliament would cement the Union, only to see an enormous flowering of Scottish nationalism on the back of the decision. It wrongly believes that it could keep the Ulster Unionists on its side in its efforts to find peace, only to shatter the Ulster Unionist movement too, by its decisions. It wrongly believed that an independent central bank would run the economy well, failing to understand that the democratic politicians still governed a substantial part of the economic policy which turned out to be pulling in the opposite direction to the way the bank wished to go. The Government has signed up to joining a single currency in principle but failed to check the small print about the entry rate and the terms and conditions that will apply. The Government pretends that Britain could join a single currency without us having to adopt common taxation. Meanwhile, on the continent plans are developing apace for that very common taxation which the British Government says is impossible.

The United Kingdom has been a most successful country. Following English and Welsh union in 1485 and the full Scottish union in 1707, there has been a great flourishing of technical, cultural and economic achievement by the British peoples. British armies and navies have been respected worldwide. They have been a force for good in the world, intervening in favour of democracy and the freedom of peoples. Britain pioneered the campaign to abolish slavery, stood alone to keep Europe free in the twentieth century, offered advice and help to many countries around the world in establishing their own Westminster-style democracies. It is a crowning irony that, following decades or centuries of success with the Westminster model and our belief in freedom, this Government and this European Union should now be uniting to destroy much of what is best in the Mother of Parliaments.

What is the point of Parliament if a common foreign policy for Britain is hammered out by our partners on the continent? What is the point of a Parliament if the most important decisions about economic policy are taken by an independent central bank in Frankfurt? What is the point of Parliament if many of the important issues of health and education and local government are determined in regional assemblies and not at Westminster? How much democracy will there be if crucial decisions are taken behind closed doors in Brussels meetings or around a board table of the Central Bank? What is the point in putting through a Freedom of Information Act if most of the information people might want to see has passed to other more secretive bodies? What is the point of having a more formal, written convention of human rights if at the very same time British politicians are wriggling away from accountability and proper debate?

The British people are sleep-walking into this disaster. People do not want to believe that their Parliament is being taken away from them. It is fashionable in bars and pubs to joke that Guy Fawkes was right, that Parliament is too raucous and noisy, that we can get on without so many of these politicians. One day, however, the British people will collectively wake up to realise that Parliament, the fountain of so many of their liberties, no longer has much water in it. They will wake up to see that, where once they could create a noise, get redress or turf the malefactors out, they are no longer able to do so. They will discover that their power to hold a government to account is worth very little when so many things the government used to do are done elsewhere.

They will discover that there is no direct way of protesting effectively against the Common Agricultural Policy or the Common Economic Policy from Brussels and Frankfurt. They will discover that there are so many layers of politicians and bureaucrats from town hall through district council through county council through regional assembly through Westminster to Brussels, that they very rarely get a straight answer to anything and find it extremely difficult to work out who, if anyone, is to blame. They will become disenchanted with elections where the link between the individual member and the constituency has been lost, and where there is no clarity over what, if anything, the elected politician will be able to do once elected to the body in question. The Scots will get restless for more independence. The Irish problem will continue. Londoners will be pitched against North Westerners in an unseemly scrabble for more money. Politicians, already held in scant regard, will be despised the more.

Labour's constitutional blueprint is nothing more than a plan for the destruction of United Kingdom democracy. It threatens splits within the kingdom. It threatens transferring far too much out of democratic control. It gives far too much ground to the federal plan on the continent. It dares to do all of these things in the name of more democracy, when the result will be less.

The British people always take time to wake up to these threats to their freedom. They have always in the past woken up. This book is meant as an alarm call. The time is ticking by when people can still do anything about it. Many of the bricks of the new structure are now in place. House of Lords reform is under way, devolution has been unleashed, the Treaty of

Amsterdam is a very federal treaty and the Government still says that in principle it wishes to destroy the pound.

The Commons has been marginalised and the spin-doctors given too much free rein. British ailments do not need major constitutional surgery or more spin-doctoring. They need a good old-fashioned dose of honest debate and some respect for our tradition of liberty and outspoken argument.

The fight to save the pound will be one of the most important battles in the war to save a British democracy. This battle is about to be joined. It is most important that all those who believe in British democracy win.

Select Bibliography

Treaties Establishing the European Communities (HMSO) 1998.

Treaty of Amsterdam (HMSO) 1997.

European Monetary Institute, *Convergence Reports* (Frankfurt).

Treasury Committee, *The Prognosis for Stage III of Economic and Monetary Union* HC 283-I 1996.

Treasury Committee, *The UK and Preparations for Stage III of Economic and Monetary Union* HC503-I 1998.

Action Plan for the Single Market, Communication of the Commission, June 1997.

European Commission, *Preparing Financial Information Systems for the Euro* 1997.

European Parliamentary Elections Act 1999.

The Referendum (Scotland and Wales) Act 1997.

Scotland Act 1998.

Government of Wales Act 1998.

Scotland's Parliament (Scottish Office) 1997.

A Voice for Wales: the government's proposals for a Welsh Assembly (Welsh Office/HMSO) 1997.

The Belfast Agreement (HMSO) April 1998.

Northern Ireland Act 1998.

New Leadership for London (Stationery Office).

A Mayor and Assembly for London (Stationery Office).

The Greater London Authority Act 1999.

A Prohibition Approach to Anti-competitive Agreements and Abuse of Dominant Position: draft bill (HMSO) 1997.

Competition Bill 1998.

The American Constitution

W. Bagehot, The English Constitution 1872.

A. Barnett and P. Carty, *The Athenian Option: Radical Reform for the House of Lords* 1998.

V. Bogdanor, *Of Power and the People: A Guide to Constitutional Reform* 1997.

D. Butler, *The Electoral System in Britain Since 1918* 1963.

Commission for Local Democracy *Taking Charge: the Rebirth of Local Democracy* 1995.

The Constitution Unit, *Rebalancing the Lords: the Numbers* 1998.

The Constitution Unit, *Reforming the Lords: a Step by Step Guide* 1998.

R. Cranbourne, *The Individual, the Constitution and the Tory Party* 1996.

D. Currie, *The Constitution of the Federal Republic of Germany* 1994.

D. Elazar, *Federal Systems of the World* 1994.

D. Farrell, *Comparing Electoral Systems* 1997.

W. Hague, *Change and Tradition: Thinking Creatively About the Constitution* (Centre for Policy Studies) 1998.

C. Johnson, *Out with the Pound, in with the Euro* 1996.

H. Jones, *Liberalism and the House of Lords: the Story of the Veto Battle 1832–1911* 1912.

Parliament Bill 1947 Agreed statement on Conclusion of Conference of Party Leaders February–April 1948 (HMSO) 1948.

M. Pugh, *The Evolution of the British Electoral System 1837–1987* 1989.

J. Redwood, *Our Currency, Our Country* 1997.

A. Tyrie, *Reforming the Lords: a Conservative Approach* 1998.

Index